PARIS
TO THE
PYRENEES

PARIS TO THE PYRENEES

A SKEPTIC PILGRIM WALKS THE WAY OF SAINT JAMES

DAVID DOWNIE

PHOTOGRAPHS BY ALISON HARRIS

PEGASUS BOOKS
NEW YORK LONDON

PARIS TO THE PYRENEES

Pegasus Books Ltd
148 West 37th Street, 13th Floor
New York, NY 10018

Copyright © 2013 by David Downie

Copyright © 2013 all photographs by Alison Harris

Map copyright © 2013 by Rick Britton

First Pegasus Books hardcover edition 2013
First Pegasus Books trade paperback edition 2014

Interior design by Maria Fernandez

Library of Congress Cataloging-in-Publication Data is available.

ISBN: 978-1-60598-556-5

Printed in the United States of America
Distributed by W. W. Norton & Company

For Alison:
Another one from the heart.

ACKNOWLEDGMENTS AND THANKS

Special thanks go to our friend and colleague G. Y. Dryansky for his strategic assistance, to our wonderful agent Alice Martell, and to my inquisitive editor Jessica Case and distinguished publisher Claiborne Hancock, for their enthusiasm and generosity.

A warm merci to our many friends who cheered us on, and the countless helpful and inspiring people we met before leaving or encountered on the road, including Joel Avirom and Jason Snyder, Michael Balter, Steven Barclay and Garth Bixler, Jane Beirn, Martine Bouchet, Huub Broxterman, Françoise Cabanne, Kimberley Cameron and David Brody, Henri Clerc, Jacques Clouteau, Bertrand Devillard, Robert and Solange Ducreux, Marie-Pierre Emery, Mark Eversman, Eva Fage, John Flinn, Frère Jean-Régis of Sainte-Foy Abbey, Sandra Gilbert, Anton Gill, Karine Gribenski, the late Canon Denis Grivot of Autun Cathedral, Jean-Claude Jacquinot, Dominique

Jacquot, Jean Kahn, Barrie Kerper, Peter Jan Leeman and Aad van der Krogt, Margaret Mahan, David Malone, Sarah McNally of McNally-Jackson books, Mia Monasterli, Ghislain Moureaux, Anthony Oldcorn, Elaine and Bill Petrocelli at Book Passage, the late Polly Platt, Priscilla Pointer and the late Bob Symonds, Georges and Bernie Risoud, Harriet Welty Rochefort, Russ Schleipmann, Paul Taylor, Robert Tolmach, The Tortoise, Rob Urie, Jacques Vaud, Claudio Volpetti, Steven Voss, and Karen West at Book Passage.

KEY PEOPLE, PLACES AND EVENTS

Aedui: A Gallic tribe whose territory corresponds to the Saône-et-Loire and Nièvre administrative *départements* of central-southern Burgundy. Their capital was Bibracte. The Aedui were "friends of Rome" and, according to Julius Caesar, called upon the Romans to help them resist invasion by rival Celtic and Germanic tribes. The Roman response set in motion the Gallic Wars.

Alésia: Gallic fortified town where Vercingétorix (see below) and other Gallic chieftains took refuge from Julius Caesar during the final battle in the Conquest of Gaul. After a siege, the Gauls surrendered. Vercingétorix was taken prisoner, led to Rome, and murdered some years later. Alésia became a Roman city but fell into ruin in the Middle Ages. It has been excavated and transformed into a historical theme park.

Astérix: Fictional Gallic hero, living beyond Roman-conquered Gaul in Armorica (Brittany, western France) circa 50 BC. The name merges "asterisk" and "Vercingétorix" (see below). Originally humorous and subversive, Astérix has been adopted by the French mainstream (movies, Parc Astérix amusement park) and elements of the nationalist fringe. To some he is a symbol of resistance against foreign influence, from Caesar to immigrants and American-led globalization.

Autun: see Bibracte.

Bibracte: Important Gallic fortified city or *Oppidum*, capital of the Aedui, founded circa 200 BC and abandoned or destroyed in the 1st century AD. It crowned Mont Beuvray, a mountain in the Morvan region of Burgundy. Vercingétorix was declared leader of the Gallic resistance at Bibracte. Caesar dictated part of his chronicle, *The Conquest of Gaul*, in Bibracte. During the lifetime of Augustus Caesar (63 BC–14 AD), the city's inhabitants were resettled in nearby Autun, originally "Augusto Dunum" (city of Augustus). Bibracte is a national park, comprising archeological excavations and the Celtic Civilization Museum.

Burgundy: Region of central-eastern France, divided into four administrative départements: Yonne, Nièvre, Côte d'Or and Saône-et-Loire. Celebrated for wine, it is also the heartland of ancient Gaul, where decisive battles were fought between Gallic tribes and Julius Caesar's legions.

Julius Caesar: Roman military and political leader, 100 BC–44 BC. Caesar led the legions into Gaul in 58 BC in a campaign lasting nearly a decade. Victory over Vercingétorix came in 52 BC.

Celts: Ancient peoples speaking Celtic languages, of uncertain origin, thought to have migrated into Western Europe from the Balkans starting circa 1200 BC. They settled an area occupying much of eastern-central and western Europe and came into conflict with rival Germanic tribes and the Romans. Their homeland, Gaul, is today's France. The terms "Celt" and "Gaul" are interchangeable. The Gauls gave rise to the Gallo-Roman civilization.

Charlemagne: King of the Franks, 742-814 AD, declared Emperor in Rome in 800 AD. In 778 he led an army across the Pyrenees into Spain at the behest of Moorish rulers in conflict with the Emir of Cordoba. Charlemagne's army antagonized the Basques, who decimated its rear guard at Roncevalles. Among the dead was Roland, Duke of the Marches of Brittany. The episode inspired the epic poem, *The Song of Roland*.

Cluny: Town of 5,000 inhabitants in the southern Saône-et-Loire département of Burgundy, site of a ruined medieval abbey, formerly the largest church outside the Vatican.

Dumnorix: Chief of the Aedui tribe during Julius Caesar's invasion of Gaul.

Franco-Prussian War: Fought between France and Prussia (a German state), 1870–71.

Franks: Germanic tribe of northwestern France, Belgium, Holland, and western Germany. The Franks originated the Merovingian Dynasty of France, starting circa 450 AD, and rose to prominence as leaders of western Europe under Charlemagne.

Gaul, Gauls: see Celts.

François Mitterrand: 1916–96, a former socialist president of France (1981–95). Controversial and enigmatic, his World War Two record remains the object of scrutiny.

Morvan: Mountainous region of Burgundy, extending from Vézelay south to Autun.

Reconquista: The Christian "re-conquest" of the Moorish-occupied Iberian Peninsula, 792–1492.

Résistance: The French armed resistance to the Nazi Occupation and collaborationist Vichy government.

Roncesvalles: Roncevaux in French, a Romanesque abbey in the Pyrenees, site of the ambush of Charlemagne's rear guard, and an important stopover or starting point on the Camino de Santiago de Compostela pilgrimage route.

Berthe and Girart de Roussillon: Founders of Vézelay Abbey, circa 855.

Saint James the Greater: Known as Matamoro or Moorslayer, died in 44 AD in Judea. According to legend, his remains were discovered 800 years later at Compostela, northwestern Spain. The site is now marked by the cathedral of Santiago de Compostela, since the 9th century the most popular Christian pilgrimage destination after Rome and Jerusalem.

Santiago de Compostela: Capital of Galicia, Spain; called Saint-Jacques de Compostelle in French.

Vercingétorix: Gallic chieftain of Arverni tribe, led resistance against Julius Caesar at Bibracte, surrendered at Alésia in 52 BC and was executed in Rome in 46 BC.

Vézelay: Village in the Yonne département of northern Burgundy, site of the 9th-century Basilica of Mary Magdalene, one of the legendary repositories of the saint's relics. After centuries of decline, Vézelay is again a pilgrimage site and important stopover or starting point on The Way of Saint James.

Way of Saint James: Network of pilgrimage routes across Europe to Santiago de Compostela, Spain, created starting circa 880 AD.

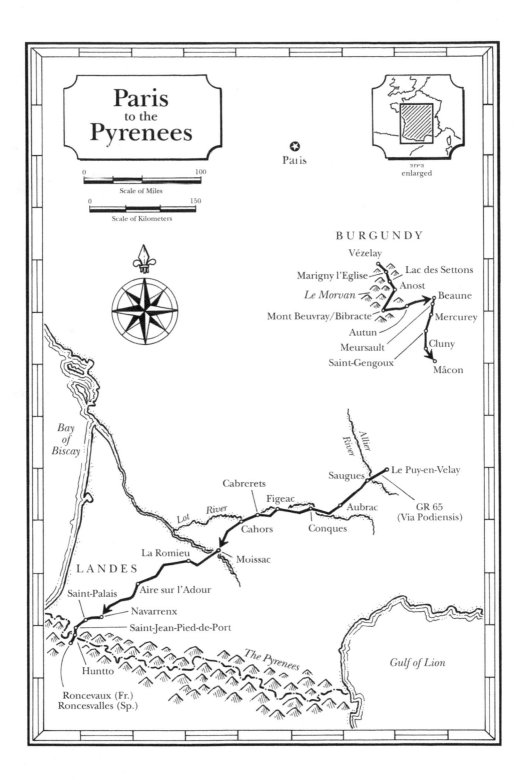

Paris
to the
Pyrenees

0   100
Scale of Miles

0   150
Scale of Kilometers

Paris

area
enlarged

BURGUNDY

Vézelay
Marigny l'Eglise
Le Morvan
Mont Beuvray/Bibracte
Autun
Meursault
Saint-Gengoux

Lac des Settons
Anost
Beaune
Mercurey
Cluny
Mâcon

Bay
of
Biscay

Allier
River

Saugues
Le Puy-en-Velay

Cabrerets
Figeac
Aubrac
GR 65
(Via Podiensis)

Lot River
Cahors
Conques

La Romieu
Moissac

LANDES
Aire sur l'Adour
Saint-Palais
Navarrenx
Saint-Jean-Pied-de-Port

Huntto

Roncevaux (Fr.)
Roncesvalles (Sp.)

The Pyrenees

Gulf of Lion

PARIS PRELUDE

We sealed our bargain in the shadow of the Tour Saint-Jacques, the flamboyant Gothic tower on the rue de Rivoli half a mile from where my wife Alison and I live in central Paris. The tower is all that remains of the celebrated medieval church and hostelry of Saint James the Greater from which pilgrims in their thousands for over a thousand years began walking south following the main European branch of The Way of Saint James—"The Way," for short—from Paris to the Pyrenees. That was where we were headed.

A few days before Easter, we strapped on our pedometers, booted up, and marched south from the tower through crowds of commuters and tourists. Crossing the Île de la Cité, we stopped for a moment of quiet reflection at Notre-Dame cathedral. Then we headed down rue Saint-Jacques, poking our heads into churches, former pilgrims' hostels, and the Paris residence of the abbots of Cluny—now Paris's museum of the Middle Ages where the enigmatic *Lady and the Unicorn* tapestries hang.

The French call The Way of Saint James *le Chemin de Saint Jacques de Compostelle* while the Spanish call it *El Camino de Santiago de Compostela*. Either way, this pilgrims' highway was built on top of an ancient Roman road that linked northern Europe via Paris to the heartland of Gaul and then continued south to Spain.

Straight and true like most Roman roads, today's rue Saint-Jacques still mounts past the Pantheon, then follows the edge of the Reservoir de la Vanne to the sprawling Cité Universitaire campus. It changes names four times. Beyond the university greenbelt on the pot-holed rue Henri-Vincent, my talking pedometer informed us we had walked 3.26 miles and burned 234 calories. Soon after this, we reached the point where The Way of Saint James dead-ends. It's no longer Paris's glorious roadway to Spain, but rather an off-ramp from the Boulevard Périphérique beltway, a six-lane moat isolating Paris.

As we pondered the snarled cement colossus, it seemed unlikely many pilgrims would flock to the Tour Saint-Jacques again. Questers no longer set out from Paris, we realized, a city of 12 million ringed by industry, housing projects, expressways, freeways, and railways that are lethal to even the fleetest of foot. Today's pilgrims nod at the Saint-Jacques tower and visit Notre-Dame for a symbolic bend of the knee. They then board buses or trains to other points along "The Way"—smaller, more welcoming locales such as Chartres, Tours, and Poitiers, or Arles, Le Puy-en-Velay, and Vézelay. After a sleepless night of anxious excitement, that's exactly what we did, hopping on the first train to Vézelay the very next morning at dawn.

PART ONE

❧◆❧

CAESAR'S GHOST

ACROSS LE MORVAN
FROM VÉZELAY TO AUTUN

"Here before me now is my picture, my map, of a place
and therefore of myself . . . much of its reality is based
on my own shadows, my inventions."
— M. F. K. Fisher, *Two Towns in Provence*

pilgrim . . . from Latin *peregrinus*, a wanderer, a traveler in foreign parts, a foreigner . . .
— *Webster's New Universal Unabridged Dictionary*

SAINTS ALIVE

The storied medieval pilgrimage site of Vézelay stretched lengthwise across a hogback Burgundian ridge like a patient on a psychiatrist's couch. At the head of the hill was the Romanesque repository of Mary Magdalene's relics. Our hotel stood near the former fairgrounds at the saint's feet. The simile seemed imperfect. I had heard much about the site's purported psycho-therapeutic powers, though no psychiatrist's couch I've seen is ringed by tall, crumbling walls, studded with belfries and surrounded by Pinot Noir vineyards and cow-flecked pastures.

As a seriously overweight freethinker with wrecked knees, a crazed individual proposing to walk 750 miles on pilgrimage routes, perhaps my vision of Vézelay was impaired by a skeptical outlook, and I was the one who needed a therapist.

A natty innkeeper and a sculpted wooden effigy of Saint James greeted us at the Hôtel du Lion d'Or. She wore a tailored winterweight pants suit. Saint Jacques wore his signature upturned floppy hat. It looked startlingly like the khaki-colored cotton sunhat the unrepentant optimist Alison had bought at a sports emporium in Paris. A ski cap would've been more appropriate.

I hated to disappoint James or the solicitous hotel manager, but Compostela by whatever name wasn't our goal. The Spanish section of the trail—from Roncesvalles Abbey in the Pyrenees Mountains to Santiago—is mobbed by hundreds of thousands of pilgrims each year. Their main preoccupation is to find food and a place to sleep each night, as we'd seen with our own eyes. Our goal was different. We wanted to cross France, not Spain, following age-old hiking trails, and do so unmolested by cars and other pilgrims, making the pilgrimage our own maverick way.

The truth is we weren't really religious pilgrims. At least I wasn't, and I could only speak for myself. Outwardly, the irrepressible desire I felt to hike across France had little to do with spirituality, a profitable concept whose meaning has never been clear to me. After twenty years of living and working in France, I simply felt the need to make my own mental map of the country by walking across it step by measured step and thereby possess it physically, intimately, something I'd failed to do through a car's windshield. I also needed to reinvent myself from the bottom up, restore something I'd lost, discover things I'd never tried to find, make an inner as well as an outer journey, and ask the big questions again, the What's-it-all-about-Alfie ones I'd stopped asking once out of adolescence. Among those fundamentals was, did I want to stay alive, or did I prefer to explode like an over-inflated balloon?

A quarter century of high living as a travel and food writer had demanded its pound of flesh. Many pounds, actually. I had become a hedonist and glutton. The cookbooks I'd written, the recipes I'd tested, the buttery croissants and fluffy mousses I'd savored in every imaginable locale, from bakery to multiple-starred restaurant, had buried me in radial tires, like the Michelin Man. I had also consumed gallons of wine, Calvados, Cognac, and even Inspector Maigret's *Vieille Prune*, a lethal eau de vie distilled from plums. Though I'd often tried to repress or control my gluttonous urges, change without crisis had not occurred.

Then one fine day, while eating my way through southern Burgundy, I'd keeled over and awakened to be told I was, in essence, a walking foie gras. I'd become a life-sized, green-hued liver, an organ afflicted by something called "steatosis." A second French doctor leaned over my hospital bed and nodded with undisguised disgust. He explained that steatosis means "marbled with fatty veins and pocked with fatty globules." I also had viral hepatitis, probably from food poisoning. I was, in short, experiencing liver failure.

Not that this was the first serious health crisis I'd faced in my nearly fifty-year existence—and ignored. A decade earlier, I'd been visited by sudden-onset optic neuropathy. It had gutted my vision, leaving me blind in one eye, my addled brain permanently dazzled by twinkling, spinning lights. But this tap on the shoulder with an angelic feather had not saved me. On the contrary. It had driven me to eat and drink even more, to forget my misery.

Still in Burgundy, trying to recover from liver disease, I vowed to change my life, seriously, this time. Really. Really. First I'd stop drinking and lose those saddlebags of fat that made me look like a pack mule. Second, I'd stay off computer screens long enough to see if my kaleidoscope vision improved. Third, I'd jump-start my jalopy and then slowly trickle-charge my batteries, and, who knows, perhaps bring a lilt back to my stride. Irreverent irony was my worst enemy. I was exhausted by flippancy and the forced cleverness of corporate magazine writing. Crossing France on foot, starting in Vézelay, was something I'd always dreamed of doing anyway, in part because Burgundy was so green and gorgeous, in part because of its historical associations with Rome and the ancient world, a lifelong obsession of mine. It seemed as good a place as any in which to force myself toward a new and improved lifestyle. I calculated that, if traversing Burgundy didn't kill me, I'd find some way to keep inching south until I'd crested the Pyrenees into Spain. Clearly, the best trails were the old Roman roads and pilgrim routes, where you could walk for miles without encountering a car. The only hitch as far as I could see was religion.

As a skeptic born and raised by skeptics in 1960s-70s San Francisco, a survivor both of the Haight-Ashbury and Berkeley's Telegraph Avenue, I felt queasy at the prospect of becoming an official pilgrim, with a pilgrim's *Crédenciel*—a handsome, fold-out passport issued and stamped by the Catholic church. The Crédenciel entitled you, among other things, to sleep in pilgrims' hostels along the way, for the price of a donation. But I couldn't face asking for one. I hadn't escaped the gurus and drug culture of California to wind up a Catholic in France; that was reason enough to devise my own unofficial pilgrimage, a journey into the past, to focus on the present, and, if I was lucky, to read the future.

Practically speaking, I planned to follow the 2,000-year-old Via Agrippa and pre-Roman, Gallic footpaths, routes predating Christianity, safe in the knowledge that, unbeknownst to most pilgrims, they underlie The Way of Saint James just as surely as Paganism underlies Roman Catholicism. I'd take the roads less traveled, the longer secondary routes from Vézelay via the ancient Gallic stronghold of Bibracte, then onwards to Autun, Cluny, and Le Puy-en-Velay. Julius Caesar and the Gallic chieftain Vercingétorix had battled along this route. Charlemagne had ridden down it for the epic Pyrenees battle against the Moors recounted in *The Song of Roland*. Cluny had been the second Rome, with the biggest abbey church in Christendom, and, despite the Internet and cellular telephony, all roads, at least metaphorically, still lead to Rome. Forget Santiago de Compostela, I told myself; if I could make it across France, nothing could stop me from one day hiking across the Alps into Italy and down the boot to Rome.

So here I was, a prematurely hobbled, sardonic miscreant, an admirer of Caesar who had long hoped the Vatican would be toppled by earthquakes, about to keep my solemn promise to myself and begin a cross-country quest in the company of Saint James. Originally my plan hadn't included Alison, a professional photographer with a busy schedule and a considerably less troubled psyche. But she'd insisted on accompanying me, possibly because she herself had a host of family-related issues to think through, and was also an avowed walk-aholic. Mostly, I knew, Alison wanted to come along because she feared I'd die of exhaustion, be murdered, or go back to gorging myself en route. My opposite number, she was afflicted not only by quiet optimism, altruism, and wisdom, but also by chronic slimness. She'd never put on weight even though she'd eaten as much as I had for decades, earning a living by turning roast ducklings and strawberry tarts into lovely still-life photos. Her athletic physique hid one minor flaw: an elegant, S-shaped backbone, the result, she claimed, of the wooden grade-school chairs of her youth. Two cameras, a hundred rolls of film, and a gross of digital photo chips was all she would carry in her small knapsack. I would play not only Don Quixote to her Sancho Panza, I would also be her pack-donkey.

COCKLES AND MUSCLES

The most appealing sign on Vézelay's steep, slippery, cobbled main street showed a familiar seashell and belonged to a *crêperie*. It was called Auberge de la Coquille—the scallop. A mouth-watering scent of melting butter, sugar, crêpes, and hot coffee blew toward us on the wintry wind. I studied the sign, hesitating. Would I ever be able to resist the temptations of gluttony and lead a normal life? There was scope for serious doubt. I was already feeling faint from hunger. We'd left Paris on a pre-dawn train. Stiffening my resolve, I hiked on, comforting myself with thoughts not of food but of history.

As any pilgrim knows, especially if he's read up on the subject, the French call scallops *coquilles saint-jacques*—shells of Saint James. The scallop shell symbolizes this enigmatic individual. But the scallop is also the generic sign of questers of all kinds, which is why I've always loved it. Never mind that before the pilgrimage route was built, the scallop, cockle, and conch denoted Venus, born of virginal sea-foam, immortalized in Botticelli's painting and countless myths. These shells had been signs of the divine—of fertility and love—for centuries before James joined forces with Jesus.

I felt inside the wet, clammy right-hand pocket of my windbreaker. Though an appealing shade of red and despite the manufacturer's claims, the garment was clearly not waterproof. There

I'd placed the misshapen shell I'd found years ago on Utah Beach, in Normandy, when we'd been on another kind of pilgrimage, to see the Normandy landing beaches on the fiftieth anniversary of D-Day, in 1994. Using raindrops to polish the shell, I thought fondly of my father, and Alison's, both recently deceased, both World War Two vets of the best, most skeptical kind. I kept at it, stroking the cockleshell, and soon enough we were out of range of Auberge de la Coquille's dangerously caloric scents.

"I've found the technique," I said proudly to Alison. "It's my first epiphany!"

STARRY SKIES AND COMPOST HEAPS

Despite our zealous desire to reach the basilica a quarter mile away atop the hill, the spring storm grew stronger, forcing us to seek shelter. In a cozy café we had several rounds of coffee and watched the rain turn to hail. I felt dazed and panicked. I'd pored over books and encyclopedias before leaving Paris. But somehow I hadn't been able to focus my mind on the actual reality of the journey ahead, or the cast of characters. All those unfamiliar names, dates, and places, and the thought of walking for nearly three months across rural France, without access to Google, now filled me with something akin to terror. I took out the concise biography of Saint James that I'd photocopied and, squinting, read aloud to Alison. This was a novelty. She's the one who usually reads aloud to me.

Alison sipped her coffee and agreed that it was easy enough to see how Iago—pronounced Yago—became the northwestern-Spanish equivalent of the Latin name Jacobus—pronounced Yakoboos. So Sant'Iago changing to "Santiago" was a logical step.

The origin of the winning name "Compostela" was less clear. *Campus stellae* meant "field of the star" and sounded euphonic, ringing like a Catholic retrofit to explain something unsavory.

8

The story goes that a Spanish shepherd saw unusual blazing stars pointing to a mound. Hidden by vegetation stood the ruined tomb of the saint, which the shepherd soon ensured was discovered by persons more noteworthy than he.

This was certainly more uplifting a tale than the other, possibly more credible origin-myth for Santiago de Compostela and the real reason for the spot's unusual-sounding name. According to modern archeologists, the tomb of two Roman patricians named Athanasius and Theodore, discovered somewhat inconveniently under the main altar of the Cathedral of Saint James, their names sculpted on it, seems to confirm the existence of an ancient Roman villa beneath the holy shrine. The rational explanation for the name is simple enough: the villa had become a cemetery or dumping ground—a *compost* heap—and the word "compost" had evolved into Compostela. I folded the photocopy and felt warm inside, encouraged by the thought that a humble compost heap had become a site of miracles, the source of hope and inspiration, misguided or not, for millions of fellow questers.

BONING UP

Possibly because I spent several formative years in the mid-1960s living in Rome, and was dragged by my mother into hundreds of places of worship there, as an adult I've actively stayed out of churches. It was with trepidation that I now approached the basilica of Mary Magdalene, a UNESCO World Heritage Site. Perched high on Vézelay's hill, it attracts about a million visitors each year. The façade is not handsome, despite the best efforts of architect Eugène Viollet-le-Duc, the 1800s over-restorer of France's monuments. He rebuilt the basilica as we see it today, rescuing a ruin while trying and perhaps not entirely failing to preserve its magic.

Tradition has it that the Saturday before Easter is a mournful day, anticipating Sunday's rising of Christ. Consequently there were no tapers to light, no flowers on the altar, and no singing. But we, the visitors shuffling down the soaring nave, made our untidy presence felt. Were pilgrims also allowed to be tourists, I wondered. And vice versa: Could tourists be true pilgrims?

We let the crowds thin before climbing down a steep staircase into the dark, damp crypt. I stumbled on the uneven stone floor. Behind bars in a niche was Mary Magdalene's reliquary, an ornate neo-Gothic arc of gilded silver borne aloft by angels and holy men. In the early 1000s, Alison reminded me, the abbot of Vézelay discovered the remains of Mary Magdalene somewhere inside the monastery, or so the story goes. What were they doing in Vézelay? To query their provenance was to doubt the miraculous nature of the discovery. And doubting raised the uncomfortable, associated question of how a saint had been made of a wild young woman of alleged loose virtue, a long-haired temptress who had dried Jesus's feet with her hair and might be on stage or in a padded cell were she alive today.

"Relax," Alison whispered, taking my hand. "You're trembling."

"I'm cold," I said. But the origin of my nervousness had little to do with the temperature.

I closed my eyes, allowing the presence of Mary's relics to bestir feelings of spirituality. More tourists crowded around, some with flashing cameras. I tried to meditate, beginning with progressive relaxation, but that didn't help either. I changed tack, and thought again of history. With Mary Magdalene's bones in its crypt, Vézelay had soared in status, becoming not merely a stopover on The Way of Saint James but the starting point and, for many, the goal of pilgrimages. Here we were, at Ground Zero, by the saint's bones.

Mary Magdalene's reliquary niche was designed to hold an entire skeleton. But I knew from my readings that there'd been a minor hiccup: the Vatican had de-authenticated the relics in 1295, and Mary's tomb had vanished. Happily some of the bones stayed behind and were placed in containers. We were in the presence of the largest portion of the relics. *Pop, ping, zing* went the flashes and camera lenses. Cell phones rang. A guided tour group tramped in. Feeling like a spy in the house of love, I was swept away by disbelief.

Another reliquary is on the ground floor, in the church's right transept. As we headed for the cloisters, we stopped to look at it. Crowned by a gaudy modern sculpture, the reliquary had been vandalized. A pocket-sized niche stood empty, a wire grate bent back. The miniature effigy of Mary Magdalene had been stolen by souvenir hunters in the early 2000s, the relics too.

"Are you sure you don't want to get a pilgrim's passport?" I asked Alison, feeling a twinge of guilt. She was a lapsed Catholic and, I reasoned, might want spiritual insurance while walking. "Just because I refuse to submit doesn't mean you shouldn't have one." But she firmly shook her head.

We found an unoccupied bench on the tree-lined road called Promenade des Fossés paralleling Vézelay's oval ramparts and enjoyed our first picnic as pilgrims, albeit unofficial pilgrims. Alison had picked up the local newspaper. It carried the Easter address by Archbishop Yves Patenôtre of nearby Sens-Auxerre. He noted that our lives overflow with unanswered questions regarding mortality and the loss of loved ones. The big question was why did humans have to die? Even Jesus had asked God why he had to die. However, according to the archbishop, the good news was, Jesus and God were still among us, in the streets—alive. The joy of Easter, alas, would always be mixed with the gravity of the human condition: finitude. Mortality. But, for people of faith, with the balm of hope that they too, in some way, would rise again as Christ did.

Lingering over my apple, I contemplated the apparent infinity of the scenery, and felt the irreverence drain out of me. Skeptic or believer, there was much to chew on in the archbishop's words.

I chewed on the words as we walked down a rocky path into the Valley of Asquins. Edging a thicket stood a tall wooden cross. We slid down to it, mindful that here, in the year 1146, the militant abbot Bernard of Clairvaux, not yet a mystic or saint, had harangued an assembly of thousands, from King Louis VII down, calling for a second Crusade to free Jerusalem from the Infidel—thereby restoring trade and Christian control of the Near East and Mediterranean. Petroleum and terrorism were not yet on the agenda. I squinted, imagining the sleepy valley alive with knights in shining armor, foot-soldiers, mercenaries, farmers, and priests. The assembled dignitaries could not fit into the basilica of Mary Magdalene. Anticipating the overflow, the abbot had erected a country chapel. It still stands and is named La Cordelle.

I was glad that the rain and wind had swept away other visitors. After the crowds at the basilica, we were alone at last, inside the chapel's mossy walled compound. The beauty of La Cordelle is its simplicity: un-faced gray stone walls and a floor of beaten earth. There was no noise from outside. Eyes shut, I felt the pleasant weariness that comes from rising before dawn, riding a train for several hours while seated backwards, walking for several more hours, talking to pious strangers, and wrestling with the ghosts of adolescent existentialism. I'd probably thought more and deeper about the human condition in the last six hours than I had in the last ten years. It had been quite a day. Perhaps "spirituality" was no more than an altered physical and mental state attainable by sleep deprivation or the fatigue of labor, prayer, or pilgrimage? Often, in my experience, it was the least likely candidates who had spoken the loudest about their spirituality and possession of religious feelings. Was I joining the choir?

What I really needed was another cup of coffee. Everyone knew that sleep deprivation was the favorite weapon of the medieval monastic orders, and plenty of contemporary sects, the kind that brainwashed adepts. I banished the thought and felt strangely

elated. Birds chirped. Rain pattered. The silence was not silent—
it hummed. We hadn't even begun to hike down to Spain. But
I felt I'd crossed a threshold. Maybe the walking would not be
necessary after all. Maybe we could call the whole thing off and
go back to Paris after Easter.

SACRED FIRES

The real challenge in getting to the 10 P.M. Easter Eve ceremony at
the basilica was not the rain, wind, or cold. It was overcoming the
desire for sleep that dogged us after dinner. We admired Vézelay's
lichen-frosted, floodlit old houses as we marched. Other diners
teetered along full of good wine. Bells rang out. The night was
full of other sounds, including the roar of a motorcycle engine.
Around the parking lot facing the basilica rode an adolescent boy,
his tricked-out, four-wheeled Quad motorbike scattering pilgrims
and other worshippers.

Darkness has its advantages. The basilica's homely façade had
undergone a transformation. Illuminated by spotlights, it hov-
ered and glowed, an amber-colored hologram against the indigo
sky. I thought for a minute about my confused state of mind and
realized I was wrestling holograms of my mind's own making.

Inside the enclosed porch, the darkness teemed. I could barely
see. A woman handed me two wax tapers with white paper hoods.
A choir of voices emanated from the basilica's nave. A figure in
robes appeared, his face lit by a flickering taper. He positioned
himself beneath the central tympanum, stooped, and lit a fire.

As if fed by gasoline, the fire exploded into a blaze. It cast
the priest's shadow upward, across the tympanum where Christ
reigned. A dog-headed man and the figure of Saint James glared
down at us. With flames leaping and shadows prancing around
him, the priest spoke. I could not make out what he was saying.
I grappled with slippery emotions, my mind jumbled with

thoughts of the primal fire, the eternal flame, and the campfires of my childhood. The priest tipped his taper and lit the candles of the men and women standing nearest. They lit others' candles. One by one, the twinkling points of light illuminated arms, necks, and faces, a throbbing canvas. And then a bell tinkled.

Unable to speak from the emotion, I pressed Alison's hand. As I lit her candle, her face leapt out of the darkness. I caught my breath as the basilica's giant doors yawned open. The faithful broke into song, their faces painted by childlike grins made strange in the dancing candlelight. I felt myself slipping into an intoxicating oneness with my fellow human beings, the torch bearers, the happy, the saved, the faithful.

But as the assembly filed from the porch into the nave, and the spotlights came up to enchanting harpsichord music, the stagecraft overwhelmed the authenticity. My cheeks burned with shame. I'd been hoodwinked. I'd hoodwinked myself. Shuffling forward, my candle before me, I felt like a walk-on in a cultish theater performance. The bone-china spell had broken. Toto had dragged open the curtains, revealing the Wizard of Vézelay. The words of an aged, atheist friend spoken years before welled up from memory. "If I had to do it again, I'd be a Catholic," she'd said with a wicked smile, "for the pageantry, the ritual, the marvelous hocus-pocus."

It was marvelous. With incense, bonfire, and candles burning, we took seats in the artfully lit nave—Plato's cave transmogrified by the Brothers and Sisters of Jerusalem, keepers of this extraordinary temple. I sneezed and felt at once foolish and guilty, a spy in the house of love all over again.

The Easter Eve sound-and-light extravaganza segued into the days of Creation. But my teeth chattered from the cold and my backside went numb at the thought of a French version of Intelligent Design. As the fourth day of Creation dawned, I rose silently from my seat and stole out of the basilica. The harpsichord's notes played up my spine, and the candles became voices roaring with skeptical fury.

Back outside in the parking lot, I watched the acne-scarred adolescent buck his Quad onto its back wheels, making it rear up like a horse as he rode around. I wondered how I could explain to Alison that I was not cut out to be a pilgrim after all. I'd been insane to think otherwise.

EASTER WITH ASTÉRIX

Dawn's surly light discovered us already at the breakfast table, our packs ready by the door. The sun's first rays had barely begun to tickle the town as we settled up and strode out. I'd had a change of heart in the night. Today was another day. I would hike. I would do it my way.

The Way of Saint James curls down into the Cure River Valley from Vézelay to a hard-driven village below it called Saint-Père-sous-Vézelay, our first stop on the way to Spain. Flanking the grass-grown dirt road were pastures and fields and confusing, competitive signage designed to lure pilgrims down the true path. But which true path? Yellow scallop-shell panels showed the Via Lemovicensis, the official Catholic pilgrimage route from Vézelay to Santiago—direct. Blue signs with a yellow scallop shell indicated the secular E-4 trans-European route, also to Santiago, but not as direct. Nearby, red-and-white bands painted on fences or trees tempted innocent hikers along Grande Randonnée long-distance trail number GR-13, which also led south across Burgundy paralleling the E-4 and then branching to Cluny. From there, you could hike any way you wanted.

I remembered what a wild-eyed pilgrim we'd met earlier had said to us. "There is no one route," he had insisted. "Any road to Santiago will do." At least for this short stretch out of town it appeared that all roads from Vézelay to Compostela ran together in blissful, competitive harmony.

At the bottom of the valley and a mere eight hundred years old, Notre-Dame de Saint-Père seemed undistinguished compared to the basilica. Mary Magdalene and Saint James stared out at us from niches on the façade. Inside, a colorful baptismal font from the 8th century and a stone altar from the 10th hinted at earlier origins. Our guidebook made things clear. Underneath the Gothic church there lie a Merovingian chapel and cemetery, and a Carolingian monastery for women, all built atop the ancient Roman village of Vezeliacum.

The monastery had been founded on the banks of the Cure River around 855 by a local robber baron turned pious Christian, Count Girart de Roussillon and his wife Berthe. But Viking marauders in kayaks paddled up the river, repeatedly raping and burning, so Girart and Berthe sent away the beleaguered nuns and set up a community of Benedictine male monks atop a fortified hill, and Vezeliacum became Vézelay. Alison tucked the guidebook into her pack between her cameras and seemed content.

Trained in art history and a lover of all things mossy and decrepit, she was already in heaven. "Let's see what's in there," she said, drifting off before I could object.

I trailed after her into the Musée Archéologique Régional, a dusty repository of local history. My eyes widened when I saw the man at the ticket counter. He seemed to be the reincarnation of Astérix without a horned helmet. The long, disheveled hair and thick, drooping mustache were lifted from a comic book or movie about the Gallic warrior. Astérix, as celebrated at the Astérix amusement park north of Paris, is an ambiguous character. Because he's based on the fierce Vercingétorix, the real-life Gallic rebel who stood up to Julius Caesar, he has gradually acquired a right-wing political cast. He's often perceived as a *Résistant* or freedom fighter, and portrayed as an anarchist battling the corrupt mainstream of world politics. On the macro level, he's the French David versus the global Goliath, a Gauloise-smoking Native Frenchman making his last stand dressed, nowadays, in denim and leather.

With tobacco-stained fingers the Astérix lookalike gently detached a museum entrance ticket, also valid for Fontaines Salées, an archeological site and natural salt springs, he said. With tobacco-stained teeth he smiled an unexpected smile. "Are you hikers?" he asked. He seemed suspiciously friendly. "Or pilgrims?"

Ignoring the distinction implied by the question—that hikers came a dime a dozen, and pilgrims were a more valuable commodity—we sketched out our plan to walk across Burgundy, and the rest of France, provided we survived, and said we were going to break in our boots on the Roman roads running south. We'd heard about the Via Agrippa, which ran somewhere nearby.

"The Via Agrippa?" he interrupted, excited. He ran his thick fingers across a survey map, showing us where to find sections of the Roman road, plus ancient ruins and a sacred spring. He seemed to know the area astonishingly well. Did he perhaps boast ancient ancestry, I asked? Astérix doubled in stature—to a full five foot-six. He said his forebears had been in this part of Burgundy since "time immemorial." He was, in a nutshell, a bona fide descendant of Vercingétorix—or another valiant chieftain with an unpronounceable name. Or so he thought.

We shed our packs and with Astérix at our elbows exuding nicotine, had a quick look at the display cases stuffed with broken statuary and rusted nails. Then we scuttled off to buy croissants and *pains au chocolat* before at long last hitting the road.

Following Astérix's instructions, we found the ancient Roman Via Agrippa on the east side of the clear, rushing Cure River. It was an auspicious start—a friendly Gaul and a Roman road south.

THE ROMAN WAY

Why was it people always thought in terms of *the* Roman road, I wondered, as if there had only been one in a given part of the Empire? The truth, of course, is more complicated. Wherever the

17

Romans colonized, they built many roads, often atop older roads, the way we do. "Street" and the Latin word for roadway—*strada*—derive from strata. In Burgundy, the pre-existing road network was Gallic. It linked hilltop towns the Romans called Oppida—or so claimed the book we'd brought along. And we had no reason to doubt its accuracy.

We found a bench on the riverbank and as we enjoyed our flaky, buttery pastries, Alison read aloud from the book. It was the subversively light, read-anywhere paperback entertainment we'd decided to carry with us: Julius Caesar's *The Conquest of Gaul*.

I'd read snippets of this masterpiece in Latin class back in high school, and had picked it up again while studying Political Science at UC Berkeley. But by now I remembered little, other than the fact that it is among the earliest reliable accounts of ancient warfare and of Gallic and Germanic history, religion, social structures, and lifestyle. Contrary to expectations, it also proved to be a page-turner. Already it was holding up our progress.

The introduction to Caesar's opus explained that the fast-moving military genius was highly appreciative of Gaul's fine roads and prosperous Oppida. In fact, without the pre-existing road network, how would Caesar have been able to march so quickly into Gaul? The Celtic tribes in Caesar's day already had been transformed by contact with Greeks, Etruscans, and Romans, and had an advanced if brutal civilization. They were less "barbarian," for example, than the hardcore Germans or the savages holed up in what's now Switzerland. The Gauls could no longer defend themselves against the Swiss-Germans and, taking Caesar at his word, it was these overly civilized Gauls who called upon Rome to save them from the future makers of the world's best chocolate and keepers of secret, numbered bank accounts.

The Gallic request for Roman aid fitted nicely with Caesar's long-term goal of "Romanizing" northwestern Europe as a bulwark against Teutonic hordes. So up he swept from the Forum, to fight for Gaul and, it turned out, to stay. And stay. The tale sounded like a warmup to the last few centuries' conflicts pitting France against Germany, with England and America—the New Romans—stepping in to save the day.

The day was long, but not long enough to spend it entirely with Caesar. Full of bounce and unfamiliar optimism, we headed south on the Roman-pilgrim's trail, following a bright yellow scallop-shell signpost. Though it made me feel unkind, I could not help thinking the road looked like any other rutted, muddy farm road. But as we trekked forward full of glee, the realization that centurions and perhaps Julius Caesar himself had ridden down it somehow gave the scenery a disconcerting, jackbooted gravitas.

TIME TUNNELS AND WISHING WELLS

We hadn't hiked more than a mile when we spotted our first famous landmark—the Fontaines Salées archeological site and salt springs.

"Do we have time for a visit?" I asked, checking my pedometer and watch.

"About three months," Alison reminded me. "Who's keeping track, other than you?"

Inside the ticket booth, a lean man sat reading a newspaper. "The Roman road ran by here," he said unprompted, as we showed him the tickets Astérix had sold us. "Part of it is underneath the paved road you just walked on. But the Romans were newcomers," he added with an air of mystery. "The Celts started using the salt springs around 200 BC." He sounded like an oracle, or an actor used to reciting the same lines. "It's older than that, though, much older." He raised a finger, wiggled it significantly, and returned to his newspaper.

A pattern of stone ruins hugged a lush, green hollow near the river. Walls a few feet high revealed what was, we learned, the

Gauls' circular temple to the gods of this mineral springs. The Romans had remodeled and expanded it. Enough had withstood the centuries to evoke the salacious rituals of old.

Frogs croaked in marshy pools as Alison read aloud from the site brochure. I couldn't help concurring that the Romans and Celts were Johnny-come-latelies. Archeologists had discovered nineteen wooden wellheads at Fontaines Salées, all fashioned from felled trees hollowed out with fire. Dendrochronology and carbon-14 revealed one sample to have been cut in the spring of 2238 BC.

2238 BC?

I repeated the date silently, counting backwards. That was 4,246 years ago, the end of the Stone Age or Neolithic. Here?

We wandered through the ruins, seeing them with new eyes. I was filled again with disconcerting enthusiasm. Salty water welled through the rubble. I peered into one of the submerged wooden casings. The bark was still on the tree. How had Neolithic peoples learned to glean and use salt to preserve food? Perhaps they weren't so primitive after all. Tadpoles swam among lazy bubbles. I couldn't help feeling lost in the bottomlessness of 4,246 years. It made Saint James seem a beardless youth. Was this where the wishing-well myth had originated? Had the pre-Celtic salt-harvesters invoked the spring's gods and the gods of spring? Had the Druids made human sacrifices here? Had Narcissus been mesmerized and fallen into his own reflection here? Here, this very spot? What a luxury it was to speculate. If that's what pilgrimages were about, then I was all for them.

On the way out, we asked the custodian if he knew of a shortcut back to the pilgrims' trail that would keep us off the asphalt and away from today's Gallic road warriors. He pointed northwest toward a place called Valbeton, as if we were familiar with the place-name.

A path ran uphill to a dirt road—another ancient road, he said. It was, the custodian added, the way Roland, Charlemagne, and

Girart de Roussillon had traveled to Spain. Girart de Roussillon was the founder of Vézelay, he reminded us. "Of course you've read the *Song of Roland* and know that Roland was killed near Roncevaux abbey, where The Way of Saint James crosses the Pyrenees and turns into the Camino de Santiago?"

"Of course," said Alison.

Well, I added, even though we were ignoramuses from the other side of the Atlantic, we were familiar with the personage of Roland and had even read the poem. I couldn't quote it to the over-educated ticket-taker, but I had read parts of the *Song of Roland*, an epic in late 11th-century French that sings the adventures of Charlemagne and his "right-hand man" Roland, Duke of the Marches of Brittany. It was the French equivalent of the Arthurian cycle, but older, bloodier, and less romantic. When I read it those many years ago, I'd skipped to the massacre scene near Roncevaux, where Roland blows his horn in extremis, in a Pyrenees pass. That's where we would be crossing the mountains in a few months, if all went to plan.

Yes, there was a plan. I checked my watch and compared it to the clock on my pedometer, realizing it was high time to hike south in haste. We had about ten miles to go before we'd reach our first overnight at a village called Domecy-sur-Cure, and it was already late morning. The lunch bell would soon be ringing in my belly, and if we didn't pick up the pace, darkness would enfold us, possibly in the middle of a fearsome forest where lions, tigers, and bears awaited.

GALLOPING SCALLOPS

As we bounded toward Spain like bee-stung hares full of hope and expectation, a mere month's walk from Cluny and our first major goal, I realized that for several years, Alison and I had been living in a kind of enclosed porch, like the one at the basilica of

Mary Magdalene, a pre-pilgrimage Limbo built onto the façade
of our lives. We were finally crossing into the nave, so to speak,
and it felt good. It felt wonderful, liberating, exhilarating.

We were not alone in our excitement. Climbing the grade on
GR-13, the secular hiking trail we'd selected, we spied a pair of
telescopic walking sticks flailing ahead of us and heard their click
on the rocky road. As we neared, I sensed the heavy breathing of
an unhappy camper. Uphill crept what looked like a giant snail
but was in reality a human of surprising proportions. She was
large, as pneumatic as a truck tire, and wore a bulky backpack.
As we came abreast, I also noticed her jack-o'-lantern smile. Not
much older than we, she'd somehow lost most of her teeth. Was
she on a pilgrimage to beseech Saint James for dental assistance?
Or was her journey about weight loss? She caught her breath long
enough to wheeze *bonjour.* We encouraged her with hand signals
and smiles, and climbed past, feeling like guilty hares leaving
the tortoise behind.

The mixed metaphors struck me as uncharitable, especially
given our Saint Jamesian surroundings. I didn't mean to make
fun of a fellow pilgrim, though I'd rarely seen a human so like a
snail and a Halloween pumpkin combined. Now that I thought
of it, she looked an awful lot like a tortoise, too. My knees ached
at the memory of carrying an extra fifty pounds around my
waistline, the pounds I'd managed to lose since catching hepatitis
and starving myself toward health. My heart went out to her,
furthering my misgivings about my mental metaphors. I couldn't
help wondering if there was some way to share the Good News
with her—that if a seemingly hopeless case like me could slim
down, perk up, and stride out, maybe she could too. All she had
to do was eat less, eat right, detox from the prescription drugs,
change her attitude, and get lots of exercise, without viewing any
of the above as a "sacrifice." Because if sacrifice was perceived,
then failure was guaranteed. The real trick, as she clearly knew,

seeing as she was out here, obviously suffering but with a smile on her face, was harnessing will power and self-awareness and. . . .

"Who are you talking to?" Alison asked.

"Was I talking?"

"It was either you or a ghost," she said.

"Caesar's ghost, maybe," I retorted. "Or Charlemagne's."

Charlemagne! The famous Valbeton lay ahead of us, pushing other thoughts out of my head. The dirt road turned into a trail that tipped up and ran over loose rocks. In my mind's ear I heard the hooves of Charlemagne's cavalry, but I failed to hear the blast of Roland's horn. At the crest, among swaying pine trees, we turned to cast farewell glances at Vézelay and the determined tortoise far below.

In the opposite direction, to the southeast stretched five ridges cloaked with fir forests and leafing deciduous trees surrounded by fields, pastures, and vineyards—and not a single paved road. Paradise!

The unassuming bowl beneath us turned out to be Valbeton. In theory it had been the scene of knights tilting on Charlemagne's round trip from Aachen, Germany, to Spain. Vineyards flanked the trail. Grapevines mossy with age grew on grassy slopes. The vineyards looked to be organic, a hopeful sign. In the distance, grape-growers burned cuttings and passed around a bottle of clear liquid, the contents of which they tipped into their mouths. We were on the section of trail we'd spotted earlier from Fontaines Salées. Thinking again of Roland, I looked down at my boots and, thunderstruck, stooped to pick up an old cow's horn.

"Roland's horn?" I asked, turning it over. The pattern of Alison's lips indicated to me that this wasn't the famous Oliphant. A bone, then? And not from an animal. "A human tibia, perhaps?"

Alison recoiled. "Roland died on the Spanish border and was buried in Aix," she said, shaking her head.

"Roland died on the Spanish border and was buried in what the French call Aix-la-Chapelle," I retorted. "That's Aachen, in Germany, Charlemagne's capital. They brought his body back to Aachen on this trail. Don't you see?"

If it wasn't Roland's horn, I reasoned, maybe it was one of his lost bones. Or maybe it had belonged to another knight who'd died at Roncevaux. Girart de Roussillon, for instance. Why not? His body had been brought up this trail to the abbey he founded at Vézelay, hadn't it?

Before Alison could call me a fantasist, I knocked the mud off Roland's bone and dropped it into a zip-lock bag. "Specimen one."

"Are you planning to carry that horse bone across France to Spain?"

"I might," I said, stowing it before she could reply. "At least as far as Cluny. This is how relics are born."

VILLAGE IDIOTS AND THE FRENCH DESERT

Steep, rock-strewn and slippery, secular hiking trail GR-13 snaked down from a plateau into Foissy-lès-Vézelay. The rock-built village of leprous old houses seemed hacked and lifted from the Appalachians, the red-necked heartland of Americana. Hunting dogs howled from fragrant farmhouses. Chickens clucked, reminding us of the etymology of "Gaul"—the name comes from "galli," meaning roosters in Latin and Italian. A few fearful locals scrambled for cover at our approach, shotguns at the ready. To say Foissy hadn't yet been gentrified is gross understatement. But conversation was worth the risk: I was dying for a coffee. Our *Topo Guide*—a guidebook with topographical maps—sited a café in the village square.

The café was closed, naturally. Ditto the church and everything else. This certainly wasn't Paris. According to the literature, we'd officially entered the Morvan, an unsung enclave of rural France where amenities are few and people are on the far side. We looked for the exit and caffeine.

A pair of pale eyes behind lace curtains tracked us along the main road, past several ramshackle hovels. I noticed the houses were for sale. As we walked by, a tall, blond man stepped out, speaking in something like English while a shortish real estate agent with a perceptible non-Gallic complexion waved his hands. Never fear. The gentrifiers were coming.

South of the village, a tractor blocked the unpaved forest road. Alison scrambled around it and came face to face with a beaming individual we immediately recognized as the proverbial village idiot. He seemed glad to see us, a carefree man of perhaps forty years with large, rough hands. A yellow corn-paper Gauloise cigarette wiggled on his lower lip as he talked. And talked. And talked. He was herding cows, he said. His real job was gardening.

An ungenerous big-city friend once told me that throughout France, the postwar process of rural abandonment caused by the decline of the family farm had left few "normal" people in the countryside. They were flanked by fossils and the feeble-minded—young, healthy, ambitious people fled to the cities. One famous sociologist had written a book in the late 1940s titled *Paris et le désert français*. It wasn't about cakes but about desertification and the effect it has had on the countryside. However, I'd read recently that the direction of the flow was finally turning. More people were leaving cities for rural France. Expense, pollution, and stress were making big cities, even Paris, less palatable. Apparently, the seniors and mentally retarded of France's backwater deserts would soon have more for company than wealthy Dutch and Englishmen with vacation properties. Whether these rural-dwellers were happy about the moneyed invasion was another question, one still to be asked in France. Judging by the results of gentrification in prettified Paris neighborhoods such as the Marais—not to mention in rural

America—the natives of today's Gallic heartland were unlikely to be universally thrilled.

CONFESSIONS AU LAIT

The roadside café in the village of Pierre-Perthuis was called Les Deux Ponts—the Two Bridges. It turned out to be a stylish country inn despite its hayseed surroundings. The owner busy behind the bar said his name was Philippe, and that he had chosen Pierre-Perthuis for its nearness to the tourists and spiritual charge of Vézelay, and for its pair of handsome, historic bridges. "I work fifteen hours a day," he added gruffly. "We love it, but. . . ." He was too tired to speak, other than to inquire as had Astérix whether we were plain old hikers or bona fide pilgrims. I told him about our trek, two skeptical pilgrims following the Via Agrippa in Caesar's footsteps; Saint James was too recent for my taste, I added.

As if electrified with painful pleasure, Philippe raised his eyes to the ceiling. "In 1979 when I was eleven years old. . . ." he began to recount.

With his school cycling club, Philippe had ridden a thousand miles from Le Puy-en-Velay in France's Midi to Santiago de Compostela—part of the same route we would follow once we had made it to the southwest of France. "I couldn't appreciate it back then, not in a spiritual way," he added with wistful urgency, drying and re-drying a cup and saucer. "Now I could, and would love to, but we're too busy. Too busy. Maybe when we retire we'll walk it, like you, from the basilica of Mary Magdalene." Philippe said the bike ride had been a physical challenge, but what he wanted now was the time to step back and take stock. He wasn't sure what religious feelings he had, but *spirituality* fascinated him. There had to be more to life than materialism, than foie gras and Domaine de la Romanée-Conti, he opined. Sometimes he felt trapped in it, in the world of food and wine and entertaining. "Trapped," he repeated.

As I listened, an eerie kinship with Philippe grew. I silently counted backwards. Philippe said he was thirty-seven and had another twenty-five years to go until retirement. Unexpectedly he stopped drying the dishes and looked at me with disquieting intensity, waiting for his wife and Alison to wander out of earshot, into the dining room. "I can't help asking," he whispered. "Do you know why you're doing the pilgrimage?"

"Do I know why?" I stumbled for words, prepared to toss off the usual vacation-responder explanation about losing weight, an atheist out for a lark. That's what most of the people I knew seemed to expect from me, and I supplied it. No one except Alison had asked me why I was really doing this, what my deepest motives might be. Either they didn't care or didn't dare, which was fine. Who could blame them? Relationships were superficial by and large, and most people just wanted easy answers, good news, and directions to the best restaurants. Why was I walking for three months? I'd asked myself that question many times, and had come up with far too many partial answers. Maybe there wasn't one single answer, I said to Philippe. It was a multiple-choice exam question where all the responses are right.

Before leaving Paris I'd met many pilgrims and been told that the unspoken agreement among them was never to ask the "why-question." That was between you and God, or whatever you took Him or It to be. Had Philippe forgotten? "Do I know why," I repeated, buying time. I stirred my café-au-lait and stared into middle distance.

"Yes, the real reasons, the deep ones," he goaded. "What do Caesar and the Via Agrippa have to do with it?" His bloodshot eyes burned. "Why can't you just say you're a pilgrim if you are one, and I think you are, even if you're not religious?"

I stuttered and then realized my lips were moving of their own volition. I told Philippe that the trek was about breaking away from distractions and stripping away the unnecessary things in life. There was my bad health, for a start, and we were both exhausted psychologically by a variety of matters; but there was also something else, something about coming to grips with ghosts and Hitchcockian family issues, spirituality and religion. I'd never been able to get my mind around belief in a God or gods, and in recent years, evangelism and neo-Paganism had estranged me from my family, especially my mother and two elder brothers. I no longer spoke to or saw them. My brothers' midlife discovery of religion had spurred my ageing, widowed, eccentric mother to rediscover the pantheism of her ancestors. She was a Roman, literally, not an ancient one, but a contemporary Italian war-bride who had never forgiven my GI father for transplanting her from Rome to California. He had died recently and, shortly afterward, she had set about turning his garden into a sacred sculpture grove dedicated to Pan, reminding bemused visitors that her eldest son, the one who'd become a militant evangelical, was named for Dionysius, and that if she could, she would feed Christians like him and his evangelical wife and children to the mountain lions, which roamed her garden at night.

My mother had also hidden my gentle, quietly atheistic father's incinerated remains in a suitcase in her closet. I was pretty sure it was the same suitcase they'd taken ship with in 1950 from Genoa to Los Angeles, and reused on our tragicomic return journey to Italy in 1965, when she had unsuccessfully attempted to leave my father and bring up her four children as Italians. The ashes now awaited her own death, incineration, and transfer to a twin-portrait urn she had made and fired in her own kiln. She was, I explained to the astonished Philippe, a sculptor and teacher of art, trained at the fine arts academy in Rome. She also had the charisma of an Etruscan soothsayer, a neo-Pagan or Druid priestess, and was revered by other eccentric artists on the Mendocino County coast of California, where she lived.

"A Druid for a mother?" Philippe nodded gravely, as if he could possibly understand. "What about your wife?" He raised his chin toward Alison, who was across the dining room. "What does she think? Is this a spiritual quest for her?"

I shook my head. "That's complicated, and she hates it when I put words in her mouth."

It struck me as miraculous that Alison had put up for years with my hereditary anticlericalism and church-bashing, my hedonism and over-indulgence. It confirmed my fears that she was a closet martyr. As a fallen or lapsed Catholic and the daughter of a diplomat, however, she was too smart and too well drilled in politesse to be pinned down about issues such as non-belief. When we had met in 1987, she had alarmed me with talk of walking to Santiago de Compostela for cultural reasons, saying it would be all right for atheists, meaning the pair of us, to undertake the journey. Now she eschewed "atheist," preferring the softer, fuzzier "agnostic." It left wiggle room for spirituality and last-minute changes of heart. We had both lost our fathers recently, I told Philippe, stirring my cold coffee, and both of us needed to come to grips with finitude, mortality, and the big issues we had dismissed in our youth.

Philippe smiled wanly, looking all at once stricken and elated. I thought he might laugh or weep. Before he could say anything else, Alison wandered back from the dining room with Philippe's wife. We finished our coffees, shook hands all around, and at the door to the café wished each other farewell, like old friends about to part forever.

WET HEART OF DARKNESS

Pierre-Perthuis is named for a natural rock arch—a *pierre* worn through by the Cure River. Past the crumbling fortified gateway and a 12th-century fortress stands a compact church. It was locked.

"What if I'd wanted to light a candle?" Alison asked, half joking.

The encounter with Philippe had shaken me. I was glad to be distracted by the wide, wonderful world and the pressing need to walk.

From a modern bridge spanning the river valley we spotted the rock arch and a sturdy humpback bridge of stone. The older of the two bridges was built in 1770—recent by French standards. It stood at the confluence of the Cure and a swift-running stream. A few hundred yards up the stream another, more ancient span marked where the Roman road and pilgrim's path continued south. Decisions, decisions. . . . The riverside Grande Randonnée trail looked even more appealing than the pilgrim's route. So we backtracked to it, crossed the humpback bridge, and strode south through woods sprinkled with white, star-shaped wildflowers.

By something like a miracle, no paved road runs along the Cure. The setting has magic. Cliffs and outcrops rise through interlacing bowers of branches. The river rushes noisily over rocks and around boulders. I imagined the trout jumping, and stopped to peer into an eddy, my mind tracking back to the Sierra Nevada mountains of California and fishing the Yuba River. The mossy shoreline and overhanging willows, even the aspen and birch trees, seemed familiar, and their heady, earthy scent came with memories attached, as if I'd been here before.

Curling itself into a shepherd's crook, our riverside trail mounted. Through the trees, keyhole views showed tantalizing snippets of the river and, away and across it, a dark, hooded church set in pastureland. Seen from a panoramic point atop cave-pocked cliffs, the village of Cure looked to have been lifted from the land of dreamy dreams. At the top of an abutting hill stood our first Madonna. Her name was Notre-Dame de la Lumière— Our Lady of Light. It seemed an unusual name, but maybe not in the rainy forests of the Morvan. According to our *Topo Guide*,

"Morvan" is the modern French transliteration of a Celtic word meaning dark mountain or black forest.

A pink millhouse watched over an old bridge at the foot of the village. Ahead, the medieval towers and walls of a manor signaled that Cure had once been strategic. Approaching the manor, we saw what looked like thick, tangled tentacles spreading in the air. They were the lichen-grown, many-times-pruned limbs of sycamores—limbs so shagged, contorted, and knobby that it was hard to recognize them.

My own knobby knees sprang to mind, and then Wotan, the demigod beloved of Wagner. For reasons beyond my ken, Wotan immolated himself head-down on the sacred tree of Scandinavian and Germanic myth, sacrificing his own life—though as a demigod he could've claimed immortality—to give knowledge to mankind. It was a Germanic vision of Pandora's Box merged with Prometheus and the Garden of Eden and then transferred to the real Black Forest, the one north of the Rhine. Somehow, in my agitated mind, the mythical tree now seemed to be standing before us, upside down, its roots in the air. But I'm no Wagnerian, and I struggled to express my contorted imaginings.

At first Alison seemed to be only half-listening, more intent on taking photos. "I see stumps, severed arms and legs," she said suddenly, tilting her head. Granted, she loved Goya at his darkest and most brutal. But coming from the mouth of an uncomplaining, indefatigable woman of at times maddeningly positive outlook, her words surprised me. "Limbs with gangrene," she added, pointing to the moss. I staggered back. "We've lived together for twenty years," she continued, "and I didn't know you were familiar with upside-down Scandinavian mythological trees." She finished me off with a quizzical smile that showcased her perfect teeth. "Had you mentioned Saint Martin and the Druids' sacred tree, the one he ordered to spin around and fall on the Pagans, I might have followed you. But Wagner and Wotan?"

Why had she married me, I wondered? Quiet and mysterious, Alison's large blue eyes and handsome, youthful exterior masked a secret world visible only through keyholes, or reflected by "back-bearings," as the spymasters used to say—or in her moody black-and-white photographs, many of them studies in decline, decrepitude, and decomposition.

BLACK FOREST CAKE WALK

It was early afternoon by the time we lumbered into Hôtel de la Poste. We suddenly remembered we hadn't eaten lunch. Actually, I'd been ravenous, and had gotten used to the gnawing sensation. It was like dieting on steroids.

Under the heading "time-warp," on-line dictionaries and GPS-enabled apps might consider linking to Hôtel de la Poste, a combination café-hotel-tobacconist's shop in Cure. But, I wagered as we stepped inside, causing a bell to tinkle, no computer or handheld electronic device has ever passed the threshold, and a link would be difficult to establish.

A pale-skinned woman of middle age with a carrot-colored permanent appeared from a back room and whispered hello. We saw from a receipt on the counter that her name was Madame Danielle Schwer. That sounded anything but Gallic and seemed a good omen.

In a corner of the room, a grandfather clock ticked. A real, living grandmother, Schwer's mother-in-law, it transpired, padded through the semi-darkness around the red linoleum-topped wooden tables and bentwood bistro chairs. "You've come all the way from Vézelay already?" Danielle asked, taking refuge behind her counter, in case we really were crazies. She emanated vulnerability. Shameless and hungry, I confirmed that we'd hiked to Cure without finding fuel en route, and wondered if there were some way of conjuring a sandwich. "I only cook for hikers who can't get into town," she apologized. "But I guess I could make you an omelet, if that's all right."

"Praise be!" I exclaimed, clasping my hands together.

The mineral water Danielle brought us was gone within minutes. Our gulps and the plop-plop-plop of sweat accompanied the bubbles in the water, the ticking of the grandfather clock, and the shuffling of grandmother Schwer's slippers. A buttery scent drifted in. My stomach roared as the omelet came out. A black sheepdog three feet high at the shoulder followed it, his nose in the air. "It's mushroom omelet," Danielle said. She seemed to be whispering again. "He's Lucky. Lucky is very gentle, so don't be afraid." She pronounced the dog's name "Look-E."

Danielle wished us *bon appétit* and took up her post behind the bar. She tuned a radio, raising the volume of a crooner's voice. It covered the sound of our feasting. We fell upon the omelet the way heroes fall on swords. Perfectly cooked and folded, it tasted of fresh egg and was bursting with parsley and baby-button mushrooms—from a can, but who cared? Somehow the flavor was incredibly delicious.

"I got the eggs from the neighbors," Danielle confirmed. "They're the real thing."

You could tell. It was a treat, and Alison said so. "Where are the chickens?"

"Next door," Danielle answered shyly. "I fear you'll hear the rooster in the night."

With drooping eyes Lucky watched us, slobbering. His tail swept like a rag-mop, keeping time with the clock and the warbling 1950s music. We asked about the village and the hotel's history. The riverside manor we'd seen, Danielle said, was originally an abbey, a very old abbey built before the year 1000 "or something like that." The same family had owned it since 1790. They were prominent. Danielle stiffened. "Not much else to tell. My in-laws bought the hotel in 1936. It hasn't changed, except

that my father-in-law and husband both died a few years ago."
She paused. A veil fell over her eyes. "The clock was here when
they bought the place. It ran for seventy years. Then it stopped
one day, just like that. The same way they did."

I swallowed hard. A childhood earworm began to play in my
head. *And the clock stopped, never to run again, when the old man
died. . . .*

The bell on the door tinkled and a client teetered in. He lifted
his cap and said *Messieurs-Dames* as if he were appearing in a
vintage movie. Ruddy-cheeked and past retirement, the man
clutched two empty wine bottles. Danielle filled them with bulk
red from a tap, slid two packs of cigarettes across the counter,
and lightened the man's wallet by fifteen euros. She waited until
he had gone before asking us if we'd like coffee. "Several," I said,
"strong and black."

Like the hotel's other three bedrooms, ours didn't overlook the
scenic river valley. The window opened instead onto a muddy
parking lot. Our room was simple—clean, functional, and compact, devised for the traveling salesmen and modest vacationers of
old. We washed up in cold water and stared at the bed, tempted.
But to walk the three-mile Roman road from Cure to the Château
de Bazoches as we'd planned and make it back by nightfall, we
would have to leave right away.

Astérix back at the history museum in Saint-Père-sous-Vézelay had marked a thin straight line on our map. It ran from
the modern highway at Domecy-sur-Cure to the Château de
Bazoches. That line was the Via Agrippa, the freeway of its day
linking the once-important Roman cities of Autun and Sens.
Danielle showed us a shortcut. "You won't be muddying your
boots on the Via Agrippa," she said enigmatically, and watched
until we had rounded the corner uphill.

We climbed through pastures alive with newborn lambs and
anxious ewes. The lambs were cotton swabs, the ewes cotton balls.

Their chorus of bah-bah-bah encouraged us onward into the rain. At the top of the rise, we found the high-power electric lines and turnoff Astérix had described.

As anyone who's walked on the Via Appia Antica outside Rome knows, the thing about most ancient roads is they're pretty straight, and they've been pilfered almost to oblivion —everything stolen or destroyed from the paving stones on up to the temples, monuments, and cemeteries. You've got to spur your imagination to see the vanished taverns and fortresses and pottery works that once lined them, and the tunic-clad workers and slaves, the plump patricians and battle-scarred warriors.

As we walked along the raised roadway, I understood the meaning of "straightedge" and "rectitude." The Romans cut to the quick. It was clear why Danielle had mentioned a lack of mud. The road was in perfect condition, topped with compacted gravel, clear trenches on either side. Pilgrims and tradesmen had taken over from the Romans, apparently. Now forestry workers maintained the historic highway.

In thick woods near the château, we came across oaks as old as Mary Magdalene, towering mother trees with round shaggy heads high in the sky. Moss dripped from crumbled walls built of rough-hewn boulders. Behind the château loomed a chestnut tree as broad as a California redwood. I tried but couldn't spread my arms wide enough to embrace it.

"Saint Martin's or Wotan's tree?" Alison teased.

"Both," I said. "And Caesar's too. A trinity tree!"

It may once have been a major thoroughfare, but the Via Agrippa is now the back way into Château de Bazoches, a major attraction. The medieval castle and a gabled 18th-century manor attached to it were besieged by tour-bus loads of visitors. We bought tickets and gazed at the 350-year-old Lebanon cypress growing on the panoramic terrace. It seemed a seedling compared to the trees we'd seen in back. The view took in the angular village church of Bazoches. Pilgrims once made it their first or last stop on The Way of Saint James.

The trapezoidal, turreted fortress of Bazoches was the favorite residence of military engineer Marquis Sébastien Le Prestre de Vauban, born, so we learned, in 1633. For historians, the château is a secular pilgrimage site, restored and filled with period pieces, tapestries, maps, and books written by or dedicated to this remarkable, energetic genius. As shown in the portrait that stared at us in the great hall, Vauban was a big, blue-eyed man. He appeared to have had a quizzical nature, meaning he seemed to be asking those gazing up at him why the job hadn't been finished. Which job? Why, clearly, the job of modernizing France, Vauban's lifelong project.

With knees like pruned sycamore stumps, I followed Alison, limping and clomping through the château's magnificent salons, smelling beeswax but not dust. I learned that, in a career spanning fifty years, Vauban built or rebuilt a hundred fortresses and thirty walled citadels scattered across what he termed *le Héxagon*—the hexagon-shaped territory of France. As King Louis XIV's Maréchal or Field Marshal, he became the most successful general up to then in French history, and France's most famous military hero until Napoléon Bonaparte. Like Caesar, Vauban spent much of his life immersed in politics and court intrigue but he was a thoughtful man with a mission in life, not your average court sycophant. I glanced from the windows of the château back toward Vézelay, wondering how he could tear himself away from this place, and realized that's precisely what we needed to do unless we were planning to spend the night.

ETERNAL RETURNS

Marching back to Cure in the plentiful rain, three thoughts drummed in my head. The first was that while finitude clearly applied to all living things, some trees seemed to be pretty well immune to mortality. Second, and related to this, I couldn't help noting how similar Vauban's genealogical trees—displayed prominently in the château—were to the living giant oaks and chestnuts we were passing again on the Roman road. Vauban's family had owned the château long before he inherited it in the late 1600s. His descendants, the Chastellux family, own it to this day, in a way perpetuating the great man, carrying forward both his professional and genetic heritage.

As the product of a family of itinerant mongrels, it was hard for me to imagine being rooted anywhere for eight hundred years or more. Much more, in the case of Bazoches: naturally enough, we soon learned, given its location abutting the Roman road, the château sits atop a Roman fortress. That also explained the unusual, trapezoidal shape. Who knows upon what the Romans built their fortress: a trapezoidal, Gallic village?

Third and more disconcertingly, I'd learned that Vauban wasn't Louis XIV's yes-man but rather he was a reformer, an idealistic urban planner and critic of the *ancien régime.* Written in secret, his visionary 1698 *Projet d'une dixme royale* called upon plutocratic French aristocrats and clergymen to give up their tax-free status and institute a revolutionary system of proportional taxation. In his travels, Vauban had seen the misery and dangerous malcontent of the peasantry and city-dwellers packed into teeming slums. Greed and unequal income distribution threatened the kingdom, he wrote, foreseeing *le déluge* that in 1789 swept Louis XVI and Marie Antoinette to the guillotine. He believed the geographical and political unity of the nation had to be preserved for the good of mankind. To Vauban's mind, France was the heir to Rome. Louis XIV was the new Caesar, a leader who could pull together France's many nations—from the Flemish speakers of the north to the Basques of the south—just as Caesar had brought Gaul and North Africa into the Roman Republic, albeit in its dying days.

But Vauban's subversive treatise was leaked to the king in 1706. Unsurprisingly, instead of thanking his loyal servant, and welcoming his plan, Louis condemned Vauban and sent him home a broken, embittered man. There was no Brutus in this story, but the fates of Vauban and Caesar were similar—stabbed in the back by the men they loved and trusted.

Vauban's broken heart is no longer in Bazoches. Whatever was left of it after rotting for 102 years in a sarcophagus in the village church was removed to Les Invalides in Paris. Since 1809 it has reposed in a cenotaph—a funerary monument that does not contain a complete body. Apparently the obsession with relics and body parts survived the Enlightenment and French Revolution, infecting the otherwise anticlerical Napoléon Bonaparte, who lionized the tragic Vauban and wanted his heart to be nearby him in Paris, capital of the revolutionary French Empire.

With evening upon us, we tramped back into Cure past the bleating cotton balls and swabs. Had Vauban read the classical writers, Caesar in particular, I wondered? Caesar admiringly described un-take-able Gallic earthworks very much like those Vauban designed 1,700 years later to protect French strongholds, seemingly following to the letter the descriptions Caesar gives for their construction in *The Conquest of Gaul*. The two men shared much, despite the centuries separating them. A populist, though also a demagogue and dictator, Caesar, like Vauban, struggled against the oligarchs in an effort to make the dying Republic and budding Empire a better, safer place. The Republic was dead, Brutus's murderous betrayal vain. Centuries later, as Rome slid toward the anarchy of Late Antiquity, many commentators laid equal blame for the decline on the Germanic hordes and the Empire's greedy plutocrats and tax system, the system Caesar had tried to reform before it weakened the Empire beyond the point of return from wild income inequalities, the need for perpetual warfare and economic conquest, and a military-industrial complex ante literam. It sounded depressingly contemporary.

History doesn't repeat itself, naturally, and individual experiences clearly do not recur. That would be too easy. So forget Nietzsche and his "eternal return." But as I walked and pondered our current economic mess and our astronomical income inequality, the words of 19th-century French wit Alphonse Karr sprang unbidden to mind. They seemed even more appropriate than Nietzsche: "The more things change," Karr wrote, "the more they stay the same."

As we stepped into Hôtel de la Poste, my talking pedometer announced that we had covered 11.33 miles since Vézelay and burned 1,215 calories apiece. Alison's old-fashioned, silent, German-built model put the figure at 14 miles. In either case, we had trudged long enough for our first full day. Our mushroom omelet was a distant memory.

Dripping and bespattered despite the mud-less Roman road, we paused at the threshold to the hotel's dusky dining room. In it sat what looked like a large tortoise, placidly munching lettuce, sipping water, and gazing out of the windows as night filled the river valley. "*Bonsoir*," said the tortoise. "You passed me this morning going up the grade from Saint-Père-sous-Vézelay."

I was taken aback by her recollection of us, and felt chastened for my unkind thoughts about the tortoise. At the same time, a momentary feeling of dread assailed me. We were so tired that we could barely speak and had looked forward to a quiet evening of solitude in our time-tunnel hotel. Guilt welled up like the water at a mineral springs: why not embrace the moment and share our lives with the lonely, ungainly tortoise?

HYDROLOGY AND WET-NURSES

By the time the fresh, pink Cure River trout had arrived pan-fried in butter, we'd learned many things. Our fellow diner was from

Auxerre in northern Burgundy. She'd lived in Paris for ten years and, since leaving, hadn't gone back once or missed The City of Blight, as she put it. We couldn't help wondering why she felt embittered about Paris, but the thought left us as she poured out her passion for the Morvan. An avid hiker, she knew the Morvan's trails in rare sunlight and frequent darkness. "I carry a flashlight, food, a gas burner, water, and a tent," she said through missing teeth. "In the Morvan, you never know where you'll find supplies or a bed."

The remark reminded me of the wilderness treks I took as a teenager, not something I needed to repeat in France, even without rattlesnakes and bears.

The garrulous tortoise's knowledge of the Morvan turned out to be encyclopedic. It was hard to imagine that someone who appeared to be so marginal and unkempt could in fact be so well educated and articulate. Her low, quiet voice accompanied us through succeeding courses as night fell and the rushing river grew louder. While we savored cheeses and dessert, she gave us a potted geopolitical, demographic, natural, economic, and cultural history of the region we would be crossing for the next ten days.

The Morvan isn't a mountain range, but rather a granite plateau that stretches south from Avallon about 45 miles to an abrupt end at Saint-Léger-sous-Beuvray. Erosion, said the tortoise, munching a slice of bread, and geological "movements" make the plateau feel mountainous. At just under 3,000 feet, the Morvan's peaks weren't exactly the Himalayas. However, because they frown over gorges and valleys, there is drama in the landscape.

The Morvan had always been remote, impoverished, and sparsely populated, she remarked. In the 19th century, most wet-nurses in Paris were *nourrices morvandelles*, driven from places like Cure to the big bad city, their breasts swollen with milk that they couldn't afford to give to their own children. These *nourrices* also reared Parisian children at home in the Morvan. Such farmed infants were nicknamed *les petits Paris.* Bucking worldwide trends, the Morvan's economy had actually worsened in the last century as timber resources and mines ran out. The whole depressed region had been declared a park in 1970 in hopes of promoting tourism and stemming the demographic outflow. The results were unexpected.

"Fewer fulltime residents than ever," noted the tortoise, "and lots of vacation homes and nonresident foreigners. You'll see. The Morvan has the highest ratio of secondary residences in the whole of France."

Meanwhile, she advised, we should prepare ourselves for trails that were little more than riverbeds filled by constant rainfall. The Morvan holds another dubious record: it is France's wettest region, with rain or snow falling on average every second day. "That's why the Celts liked it," she grinned, a jack-o'-lantern now. "There was plenty of clean water, sacred springs everywhere, wood for building settlements and fortifications." She raised her water glass, indicating the wine on our table. "They didn't grow grapes, you know— the Romans brought in the wine. And that was the Gauls' downfall. With one amphora of Greek, Etruscan, or Roman wine you could buy a Gallic slave. Not even the Druids could resist. They enslaved each other and sold each other off for wine. Celtic peoples have a genetic predisposition to alcoholism."

This wasn't the first time I'd heard the claim, and, unfortunately, it rang true to me. I found it refreshing that a French person would speak so candidly, without fear of being un-PC, about her ancestors.

The shy owner of the hotel leaned on the door jamb. She remarked that many of her clients were indeed heavy drinkers.

When it came to demographics, the hotel's name, "de la Poste," spoke volumes. It would soon no longer make sense: the post office across the street was set to close. Since her arrival in 1961 from nearby Saint-André-en-Morvan, the number of farms in Cure had spiraled down from fifty to two. "They were subsistence farms, and the produce was good," she explained. "Now they're big, subsidized sheep and cattle farms, factory farms."

Sadly, she didn't see the irony. "Poste" referred not to mail but to the stagecoach inns that had once dotted the Continent. They'd disappeared. Now the post offices were disappearing too, and the little old hotels misnamed for them.

Danielle also told us how the local Madonna of Light got her name—from water. Abundant rainfall percolated through decomposed-granite soil, forming creeks and giving rise to the Cure and the Yonne rivers, both big tributaries to the Seine. Starting 150 years ago the powers-that-be in Paris had built reservoirs and hydro-electric plants to control the Seine and electrify the capital, using the Morvan's resources for distant city folk. The Madonna was there to commemorate the electrical substation hidden in tunnels beneath the mountain we would be hiking over in the morning.

"She's also there with her magical powers to protect the area from flooding," added the tortoise with a sardonic grin. "If you believe in such things."

"Plenty do," said Danielle.

"Oh, they believe in that and a lot of other things," said the tortoise placidly, without a hint of sarcasm. "Everyone around here is searching for something—a saint's relic, a Druid's sacred dolmen that has nothing to do with Druids, a hilltop with the right orientation and magnetism for building a Buddhist shrine. The beauty and quiet isn't enough, not for them." She shrugged and smiled. "To each his own."

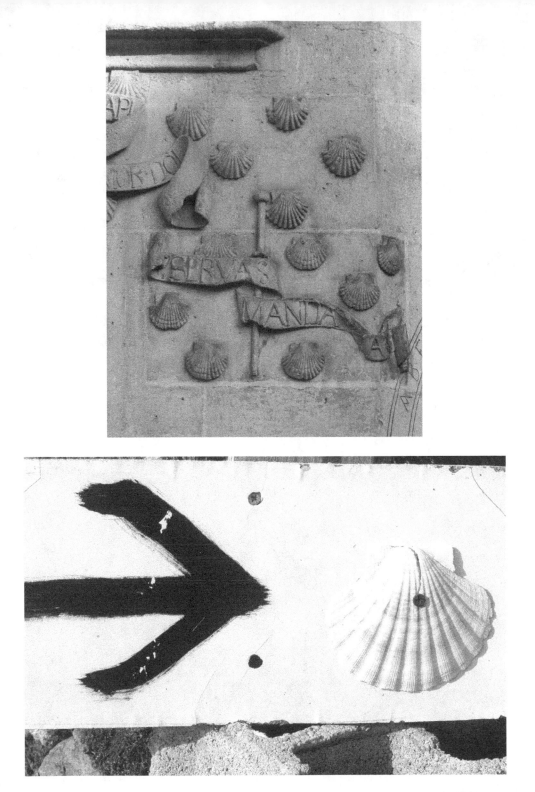

TOP: Cockleshells on façade, Cluny Museum, Paris. BOTTOM: Arrow and cockleshell sign on pilgrimage route.

TOP: Roman road to Bazoches, Burgundy. BOTTOM: Path bordered by hedgerows near Marigny, Burgundy.

Vineyards near Vézelay, Burgundy.

ALL IMAGES THIS PAGE: Signage along pilgrimage route, Burgundy.
ALL IMAGES OPPOSITE PAGE: Stone walls along pilgrimage route, Burgundy.

THIS PAGE TOP: Wooden fence with blue ties, Burgundy. THIS PAGE BOTTOM: Red cheese box, Burgundy. ALL IMAGES OPPOSITE PAGE: Charolais cows, pigs, and goats along pilgrimage route, Burgundy.

Branches and gray sky, Morvan, Burgundy.

PILGRIMS' PROGRESS

A cocky rooster provided our 6 A.M. wake-up call. There wasn't room for us to do our usual morning exercises, so we cracked stiff joints and went out to stretch our legs and explore the village.

The church was closed, but the churchyard stood open. The tombs seemed well cared for. An inscription on one related to a woman who'd lived from 1911 to 1992 and had won the *Médaille d'or de la famille française*—the Gold Medal of the French Family. It spoke of the demographic politics applied after the decimation of the populace in World War One, a policy quietly continued today. This particular mother had borne many children, been subsidized by the government, and awarded a medal for her exemplary breeding. Her maiden name was the same as that of the current owners of the most important piece of property in the village, a family, we were given to understand, not well-loved nowadays.

Carved on the obelisk-shaped village war memorial were the names of dozens of soldiers from World War One, three from World War Two, and one deportee—probably a Jew or undesirable sent to the death camps. Every French village has a similar memorial, usually an obelisk, the age-old symbol of power. In France it also symbolizes the secular state. The memorials told the same story of slaughter in 1914–1918 that led to the *débacle*, capitulation, and Nazi Occupation of 1940. World War Two had been a continuation of World War One, the so-called Great War. Great for the arms business, among others.

Not everyone in France had capitulated and collaborated. The Résistance had found its homeland here, in the Morvan's impenetrable black forests, which in 1944 stood between retreating Nazis and safety in Germany.

As we settled down to our *petit déjeuner,* the grandfather clock in the hotel dining room rang eight times, not once, not twice, but thrice. "It's always ahead by half an hour," Danielle reassured us. "If it runs on time, I'll start to worry."

We tucked in and tanked up on watery coffee. I was sorry to be leaving but, for many reasons, elated to start walking again.

Outside, the stolid tortoise awaited us. "Will we see you tonight at Marigny l'Eglise?" Alison asked encouragingly, referring to a village several valleys south.

The tortoise shook her head. "I probably won't make it that far." She measured her words. "I'm in no rush. After Marigny my route diverges from yours." She cracked her jack-o'-lantern smile. "Do you have water and lunch?"

Water we had. But there were no provisions in Cure. "Lunch?" Alison mused.

"My wife doesn't actually need to eat," I said. "She's a stag-horn fern. Anyway, the *Topo Guide* says there's a café in Saint-André-en-Morvan. That's a couple of hours down the trail. We'll be all right."

The tortoise smiled wider, shook our hands, and lumbered in to breakfast.

Upstream from the pink millhouse, the Cure splits, rushing around isles of poplar and birch. I drank in the scent and remembered Danielle's parting comment. I'd asked about our destination, Marigny l'Eglise, ten miles south and six miles beyond the village where she was born. "I've never been to Marigny," she'd said wistfully, as if that were the most natural thing in the world. "I've never even walked over the hill back home to Saint-André."

To me that seemed astonishing. Was it lack of curiosity? Clearly Danielle wasn't lazy. Maybe she just didn't like to walk, or didn't have the time or feel the need.

Time we had made for our walk, though it might ruin us financially. Time, in the form of calendar days, appointments, e-mails and telephone calls, was already beginning to melt, like Salvador Dalí's pocket watch.

I thought of the many other deep-rooted Europeans I'd met over the years, people who stay close to home, who hardly know the village across the valley, let alone the one over the ridge. How different we were. No matter how long I lived here, I would never be like them, at least not in the realm of being root-bound. Having winged my way from San Francisco to San Diego, New York City to Providence and Boston, and from there to Milan and Rome before settling, for the last quarter century, in Paris, my understanding of permanence was slight. And here I was, on the road again, and as happy as the proverbial bivalve.

"DONKEY HOTEY"

Our looping trail mounted through spongy woodlands, following a kidney-shaped reservoir carved into the hillside. Water ran down spillways and rose underfoot from springs. In the hamlet of Narbois a homeowner clipping his hedges seemed startled to see us. He said there were in his village precisely fifteen inhabitants, three vicious dogs, 237 cows, a pair of lively jackasses, and, as we could see, views galore.

We coasted downhill and came upon the donkeys—in flagrante. When the male caught sight of us, he dismounted and brayed. Gnashing his long, yellow donkey's teeth, he did his damnedest to scare us away. "Springtime for jackasses," I said, capturing his bray on my digital audio recorder. I played it back, thinking he'd find it amusing. But the donkey went berserk instead, bucking and braying while galloping along the fenced roadside, his eyes rolling and nostrils foam-flecked.

"Goodness," I exclaimed as he tried to nip me. "Don't be a horse's ass."

"That was cruel," Alison scolded, struggling to stifle laughter. I wasn't sure what she was referring to: the teasing with the audio player or the fact that I had interrupted the donkeys' passionate embrace.

"Oh, put your gums away," I joked. I played the recording again, and both of us bent double with absurd hilarity. "Whenever we get tired or worried," I said, mopping the tears from my eyes, "I've got a secret weapon: Donkey Hotey."

SAVED BY LES PETITS PARIS

It might've been the rain or an attempt to confound hikers. The trail markings suddenly disappeared. We navigated by sight. Approaching the perched village of Saint-André we noticed someone had vandalized several stone crucifixes marking trail junctions.

At the top of a looping grade we entered Saint-André-en-Morvan, the place Astérix at the start of our journey had described to us as "quintessential Morvan," something we simply had to see. The rain petered out and a surprisingly scorching sun blazed down. Another toppled crucifix stood near the village café, which doubled as a general store. The door was locked. I cupped my hands and called out. A young man thrust his head from the building next door. "It's closed," he said. "The owner had to leave." He drew shut the window. I called after him. He reappeared, hesitant. "No, there's nowhere for you to get coffee or food anywhere." This time he pulled the shutters noisily and slammed the window. A bolt slid into place behind the door.

Great. Very friendly.

"The guidebook says there's drinking water in the square," I sighed. We started climbing. "Inventory time. We have energy bars and some fancy chocolates," I called out. Alison was taking her 345th photo of the day. She seemed unconcerned. The walking stag-horn fern. Air and water. But the water was now gone.

A medieval church clamped its stony shell to the hilltop. It had an unusual open narthex, the same kind of enclosed, hooded porch as at Vézelay. Carved into the plaster walls were crude representations of churches, as if pilgrims or school children long ago had wanted to draw their own village church. Iron bars kept us out. We peered through at a barren nave. Once upon a time, in the bad old days, peasants and serfs were not allowed into country places of worship. They had to stand in the narthex or on the porch, lest their muddy clogs and unclean souls pollute the holy, land-owning atmosphere within.

"This time I really did want to light a candle," Alison said.

Mild alarm bells rang. Candles? I was more concerned about water and food.

Up in a pasture behind the church, a lone cow mooed. A fountain played on the square. A sign read "not potable." The words of Astérix came back to me. *Ah, Saint-André-en-Morvan, plus Morvan que ça et tu meurs.* Any more Morvan than Saint-André and you die.

"Food we can do without," I grumbled. "We have to find water." I stalked among the houses thinking, they've pulled up the drawbridge.

"They're afraid of us," Alison said, amused.

Granted, I could understand someone fleeing at the sight of me—the dark hair, perpetual six o'clock shadow, the trucker's hat and big black mountaineering glasses. But Alison? With her silvery hair, dangling cameras and ready smile, she might indeed inspire terror in a mouse, but a Frenchman?

I caught sight of a woman villager who hadn't run away in time. Leaning over the garden wall, I held up our water bottle, trying to look and sound meek. "We're pilgrims," I pleaded. "The café is closed, we have no food or water, please let us refill our water bottles."

The woman blushed the color of a red delicious—par-blind as I am, even I could see that. "Who is it?" questioned a worried voice from inside the house. A man came out and goggled at us—unexpected outsiders.

"They're pilgrims, and the café is closed," said the woman. "It's typical."

The man looked up wryly. "Hold on," he said. "We'll get you some water." He stood guard while the woman disappeared. Presently she returned with a bottle. By then the man had told us his family came from the village, though he'd grown up in the big city. Paris and the Morvan were tied by an umbilical cord, he explained, practically repeating the tortoise's words, because of the wet-nurses and foundlings of yore. Over the last century, most *morvandiaux* emigrants had found work in the City of Light but lived with one foot in their village. "Out-of-season people aren't used to visitors," he added by way of apology. "They're not mean, just shy."

"And distrustful," snorted his wife. "I'm not from the Morvan and can't get used to it. No one talks. People say Parisians are unwelcoming?" She peered at us. "I have half a frozen baguette," she seemed to remember. "And some cheese. Otherwise what will you eat? There's nothing for miles around. Nothing. And no one else is likely to offer you anything."

The energetic *Parisienne* came back with bread, cheese, and, since I'd already finished the bottle she'd given us, more water. Our gratitude was boundless and sincere. We waved and made to leave. But the man kept talking. There were three hundred people left in the *commune*—the territory covered administratively by the village, he said. It was five miles square. In other words: vast. His mother, he said, was in a retirement home nearby. It took three hours to get here by car from Paris, because of the traffic. And he gave us a detailed account of the shortcuts to take, and places to stop en route to shop.

"It's good to talk to someone," he said, winding up his tale with a reluctant smile. "The minute we get here, it's total isolation."

We thanked the couple again and walked south, thinking aloud about isolation and poverty. Once upon a time, the Morvan had survived thanks to breast milk and foundlings. Now it was retirees. The newly bred and the nearly dead. By the looks of them, this pair of seniors was pretty spry. The village was lucky to have them.

DRUIDS AND FLYING FISH

At the bottom of an erosion-sculpted valley rushed a clear creek called Le Saloir. We crossed on a wooden footbridge. Mossy boulders and budding trees stood on both banks. It was a perfect spot for Druids—the priest-class of ancient Gaul. Where were the Druids of today? Did they drive farm vehicles or live in Paris and own holiday homes in the Morvan?

Allegedly, the proto-Impressionist painter Jean-Baptiste-Camille Corot painted upon these banks, inspired by Saloir Creek and its ruined millhouse. It was hard to tear ourselves away. I stared into the swirling, sparkling water and felt the kind of dizzy, falling sensation you get when you've looked at a computer screen too long, a sensation worsened, in my case, by eye problems. What a joy it was to be away from laptops, the Internet, and the New Paradigm.

On the slippery uphill grade south of the creek, a sign dangled from a lichen-shagged tree. "Farmhouse B&B, go to the monument, turn right, 500 meters," Alison read aloud, her head tilted back. The "monument" had to be the obelisk to the dead of the World Wars. In France there was no need to specify.

"Lunch or coffee at the B&B," I said brightly.

Over the ridge we spotted something strange. A black cross had been painted on a freshly sawn tree trunk. String and yarn decorated the lower branches of a large fir tree, and rocks had been piled into a triangular mound. "Druids or a Satanic cult?" I wondered aloud, checking my pedometer and then marking our map.

Alison shrugged. "Bored teenagers probably."

"Probably," I repeated. "But what if?"

"What if what? You think they're neo-Druids? What about your mother, and her off-the-wall friends? They're not dangerous."

This was true. Lunacy did not always indicate redneck-style violence. We picked up the pace and, at the five-mile point, my pedometer squawked in synthesized global-English. I looked down at my boots and noticed something. Belly-up in the road was a dead fish. In the middle of nowhere. On dry land. A fish? I studied the lowering clouds. "A flying trout," I said. Alison pretended not to hear. "Fly fishing gone awry?"

A few hundred yards later, entering Chastellux-sur-Cure, we came upon a washhouse. Spring water gushed into a basin where the womenfolk once did the laundry. I was about to plunge my cupped hands in and drink when I saw the school of fish. Mystery solved. Washing machines had spawned trout.

Across the river valley half a mile as the fish flies, the turrets of Château de Chastellux rose majestically. A castle has been at Chastellux since at least 1116 and, according to our *Topo Guide*, it still belongs to cousins of the owners of Bazoches, a many-branched, well-rooted clan whose most celebrated member was and is Vauban. A recent forebear named François-Jean de Chastellux (1734-1788) fought in the American Revolution. He even wrote a memoir of his travels in America. Long out of print, the book was replaced in the mid-1800s by Alexis-Charles-Henri Clérel de Tocqueville's evergreen *Democracy in America*. Democracy in America was sometimes notional: I couldn't help wondering if in Tocqueville's day chads had dangled from ballots, and the Supreme Court had been for sale. But that too was now ancient history. I preferred to think of eternity and finitude—and lunch.

Crenellated and straight out of a Disney fantasy, chez Chastellux looked to be in good shape. We couldn't help wondering if it, like Vézelay and a hundred other French monuments, had been Viollet-le-Duc'ed—meaning, restored beyond recognition by that indefatigable architect, friend of King Louis Philippe and, later, Napoléon III and his enthusiastic empress Eugénie. What would Walt Disney have done without Viollet-le-Duc? Whether or not you liked the Frenchman's Romantic over-restorations, you had to admit that he, like Vauban, had been a tireless preserver of culture. Who even half his stature could France put forward today, Alison wondered aloud. The ensuing silence deafened me.

"Better to be low-born and lucky," I couldn't help saying as we eyed the castle, "than high and mighty. Imagine owning a drafty pile like that and having strangers sauntering through your living room. It's the only way to get a tax break and subsidies."

The truth was, I'd rather live in a reconverted barn and drive an old rust bucket than own a château and a Rolls. Owning things had never been my thing: I was perfectly happy with the pair of boots on my swelling feet, and the sweater, raincoat, and poncho I was wearing. The poncho was essential. April? It was as cold as the lower reaches of Dante's Inferno, and wet and windy too, and we were both fairly hungry by now.

We hadn't actually expected anyone to answer the telephone or the door at the farmhouse B&B. And no one did. With grim satisfaction we gazed upon our *petit Paris* picnic before digging in. Defrosted camembert never tasted so good. For dessert we made Toblerone chocolate-and-baguette sandwiches, shivered under the rain, and felt footloose and free, glad to be rootless wanderers. All was well in this, about the best of all possible worlds. Except for one thing: there was no coffee. My head ached already.

OF LIGHT & DARKNESS & CAFFEINE-STARVED BRAINS

For a plateau, the Morvan certainly felt hilly. Up and down we hiked, from one ridge and deep, encased creek-bed to another. When at last we crested a rise higher than others and intersected with the "GR Tour du Morvan" hiking trail, we knew what watery body lay below us.

51

The Lac du Crescent is a good-sized reservoir holding fourteen million cubic meters of water, according to the literature. This tidbit was meaningless to me and possibly others unfamiliar with cubic meters by the million. This particular Crescent Lake was something I ought to be familiar with, however. Not only does it generate electricity for Paris. It also stabilizes the Seine's flow, ensuring that in summer the river doesn't run dry, and in winter stays within its UNESCO World Heritage Site banks and out of our cellar. We also drink its contents.

The view troubled me. The reservoir seemed low, almost empty. And this was the rainy season. Perhaps a postmodern Doomsday had snuck up on us in the night, and the water-table had dropped beyond recovery? Had we reached the drippy tipping point? More likely, we were headed into another dry spell and heat-wave. The one in 2003 had killed 30,000 Europeans and devastated agriculture and forestry. The prospect of another roasting, parched summer brought to mind climate change, which led my enfeebled brain onto SUVs, Kyoto, and home—meaning California. Members of my family owned SUVs. I loved my whacky family but not their gas-guzzling cars.

Increasingly dizzy from lack of coffee, we decided to rest where the panorama embraced the muddy reservoir and green slopes cupping it. Among friends, I sometimes refer to Alison as my seeing-eye wife. She reads to me because my eye-power is limited. Essentially I'm a Mr. Magoo, James Thurber's stumbling, bespectacled hero. We spread a poncho on the grass, got out our Caesar, and drank deep from our water bottles. I wondered if any of the liquid in them had come from Lac du Crescent, and if the millions of cubic meters below would get to our sink in Paris before we did. Alison reminded me that on average, by the time it passed through our spigots, Paris's water had been filtered by the kidneys of five human beings living upstream. With that thirst-quenching thought in mind, she found where we'd left off in *The Conquest of Gaul*, and began to read aloud.

In the year 58 BC, Caesar reminded us, the Helvetii—a Germanic-Celtic tribe in what's now Switzerland—crossed into Gaul looking for greener pastures. They joined other marauding tribes to wreak havoc on local Celts, including the Aedui, who were "friends of Rome" and happened to live in this part of Burgundy. These soft, victim-Celts, led by a chieftain named Dumnorix, called Caesar in to quell the invaders—or so Julius claimed.

When they could no longer sustain the Roman charges, Alison read, *the Helvetii resumed their retreat. . . .*

As I gazed over the countryside, my mind's eye followed the hedgerows through sunny pastures and shadowy woods. Caesar and his legions had galloped by long before the reservoir had been built, before the Gauls' virgin woods had been felled with the efficiency of a Weyerhaeuser. It was an ancient, layered, complex landscape. The more you read and queried, the more you realized that the foundations, the lowest layers of the Morvan's saga, were strife, hunger, bloodshed, and a nightmare existence.

Some documents found in the Helvetian camp were brought to Caesar, Alison continued, *a register of the names of all the emigrants.*

The total of fighting-age men, plus women, children, and old men, came to 368,000, Caesar noted, *comprising 263,000 Helvetii, 36,000 Tulingi, 14,000 Latovici, 23,000 Rauraci, and 32,000 Boii . . . a census was taken of those who returned home, and the number was found to be 110,000.*

I asked Alison to re-read the paragraph. Then I subtracted 110,000 from 368,000. That came to 258,000 dead or enslaved. In a single battle? Even if the count was off, even if only one tenth of that number had died, it was still a massacre of unimaginable proportions.

This seemed to me a two-headed revelation. First, I'd never known that body counts were important in Antiquity, and wondered now whether the Romans had sent out messengers to tell families their loved ones had died. Caesar doesn't mention the tally of dead Romans and mercenaries, only that of the enemy.

The second revelation was that Caesar, too, outsourced to security contractors and shied away from showing or talking about body bags. The parallels to modern warfare and public relations were uncanny.

But to return to the Helvetii—our modern-day Swiss—and a peculiar irony of history, it suddenly struck me that the infallible pope, heir to Caesar and the divine-right emperors that followed him, is guarded by none other than Swiss guards.

Alison read several more pages, but the rain had gotten going again and the book was getting wet. No sooner had we packed and started walking than a Mirage fighter jet appeared, a dart on the horizon. It roared toward us, its black silhouette piercing the cloudy gray sky. Within seconds it was overhead, a hundred yards above us. Instinctively I ducked. The heat of the jet's flames seemed to singe my hair. The crackling, hoarse thunder deafened us. "Jesus J.," I blurted. "Good thing we're not superstitious."

"Superstitious? You think someone is listening?"

Of course not. No one was watching or listening to us. The Mirages were merely engaged in low-fly exercises. The French did them daily, flexing their muscles, swinging the slingshot, one eye on the arms market, the other on the global Goliath in Washington, D.C. Precisely because the Morvan is depopulated, no one complains about low-flying fighter jets; and when they do, *tant pis!* Too bad, and so what?

For the next hour I barely noticed the gentle sylvan scenery. It was hard to believe that in this gorgeous backwater, a place tourists will kill to visit, the natives had experienced millennia of misery. Theirs was a heritage of blood. They'd bred canon-fodder for the Great War of 1914-1918. Hundreds of thousands had perished. Long before that, their Celtic ancestors had suckled spear-fodder— the warriors and drudges Caesar described, men sent out for slaughter by pitiless Druids and head-hunting tribal chieftains. The rule back then was burn your village before your enemy could take it. Burn and fight, or flee before superior force. Few straggled. Those left behind would be hideously tortured and disfigured, skewered alive or enslaved by the newcomers—either rival tribesmen or the Romans, who were charitable in comparison.

We crossed a modern causeway, pausing to admire the lake's blue waters, so worryingly low. Then we found the dirt road to Marigny and started to climb. The road looked suspiciously straight, like the Roman road to Bazoches. Had Caesar ridden up it? Had I always been obsessed with Caesar and Rome? If so, why? The answer seemed straightforward enough. It wasn't merely my Roman genes and the idyll I'd experienced while living in Rome as a child. My fascination stemmed from the eerie, disturbing similarities between the Roman Empire and contemporary America.

Reading between the conqueror's lines, Caesar operated much like contemporary Russian or Sicilian Mafiosi or African warlords. What the Romans wanted were recruits and a cut—protection money, a slice of the tax action. They called that "paying tribute." If you paid tribute and respected Rome's laws—including ritual sacrifice to the gods and, later, to the divine emperor—everything would be all right. Blond or black-haired and brown-skinned, it didn't matter: you were a friend or citizen of Rome. Rome would civilize you, give you Latin, straighten and pave your roads, provide a new pantheon of gods, and teach you how to build with hewn, straight-edged stone. Not hypocrites, Caesar and his minions didn't call the process "spreading democracy." He called it Romanization.

HOME SWEET ROME

As we lumbered skyward on what was proving to be an interminable straightaway, I thought of the Biblical metaphors of pilgrimage and the kind of civil and military engineering Caesar and

Vauban had perfected. The concepts were related. The straight-and-narrow was all-important to Roman commerce and conquest. Rectilinear roads and hewn-stone cities divided into quadrants along the east-west *decumanus*, and north-south *cardo*—the word that gives us cardinal points—were the objective correlatives of rectitude, rightness, correctness. The Celts' roads and bosky trails were different. They'd looped and woven, like their hedgerows and the randomly scattered wooden houses they built in watery, wooded, dark places. The Romans worshipped light. The Celts worshipped darkness. Their most powerful god—according to Caesar—was named Dis, the god of night. They even measured time by night, not by day.

Another thought swam up from the depths. It was the orderly, hierarchical spirit of Rome that infused the Catholic Church. As the Empire unraveled, the pontiff took over from the emperor—who was also known as the Pontifex Maximus, a semi-divine "bridge builder" between man and the gods. That's precisely what "pontiff" meant. The divine-right, Catholic kings who ruled France for over a thousand years, from the breakup of Rome to the French Revolution, had been Caesar's heirs. In tandem with the Vatican they'd continued the pontiff's bridge-building work.

So, was it the spirit of the Celts—the dark, meandering anarchic spirit of pre-Roman, pre-Christian days—that had infused the French Revolutionaries and *their* heirs, the militant secularists of today?

Maybe.

No wonder, I told myself, turning to look back to where Alison was framing her 516th photograph of the day. No wonder loony French nationalists simultaneously embraced First Nation causes and admitted to institutionalized anti-Americanism. America, the New Rome. That's how they saw us.

In the twenty-plus years I'd lived in France, I'd rarely encountered a Frenchman of whatever political persuasion who actively disliked individual Americans. A certain kind of Frenchman resented *America* and what it stood for. Why? Simple: what could be more objectionable to a descendant of the anarchic Gauls than the distant rule of the bright, brash, pushy New Rome? What the tribal Celtic Frenchman saw, filtered through a long and bloody history unfamiliar to the rest of the world, were the proselytizing, puritanical, plutocratic militarists whose neon-lit, grid-block cities, straightaway Interstates and oligarchic multinational corporations smelled of the corruption of Late Antiquity.

America: the New Rome and its military-industrial, neo-Mafioso Empire, an empire with global reach. Is that what they saw?

My head hurt. I needed coffee.

We continued to slog uphill on the straight, putative Roman road as more rash thoughts sprang to mind. My temples and eyes ached. I was an addict, a caffeine junkie. It occurred to me, thinking back to what the tortoise had said in the dining room, that we and the Romans had something else in common. They'd used wine as WMDs—Weapons of Mass Drunkenness. An amphora bought you a Celtic slave. More recently, we had used narcotics and prescription drugs to the same effect. Clearly, the mafia was us. We'd morphed from guys with submachine guns, into legitimate businessmen. We'd diversified into pharmaceuticals, defense, fast food, entertainment, gaming—into corporate America's myriad incarnations, some good, others iffy, still others downright dangerous.

My temples throbbed harder with every step. Luckily, before I could embarrass myself with further outlandish thoughts, I spied the steeple of Marigny l'Eglise. My fatigue-induced, delusional ranting ebbed. Once we'd slipped off our backpacks and washed up, the soft-spoken innkeeper at our B&B put us on a coffee drip, and all was well again. No one had heard my thoughts. No one was listening. There was no military-industrial complex, democracy and freedom of expression were safe from marketers, and I did miss Google. Unfortunately, the B&B was not equipped with either a computer or an Internet connection. I couldn't download or upload the sounds I'd recorded—the Cure River rushing over rocks, the bells of Vézelay, birds, cows, Mirage fighters, and Donkey Hotey braying and gnashing his teeth.

NÉO-RURAL REALITY CHECK

"We're *néo-ruraux*," said the proprietor, a tall, thin, dark-haired man in his forties. He was also named Philippe, like the man at Pierre Perthuis, and he'd visibly survived trauma. Much of his lower face had been removed, it wasn't clear why. With his wife Armelle, Philippe had left Paris in the year 2000 to reinvent himself in a rural setting, much as the tortoise had. "Something healthier, saner than big-city life," he added softly, pouring more coffee.

In Paris, Armelle had been a manager. He was in publishing—an editor at the defunct, formerly prestigious Presses Universitaires Parisiennes. That explained the quality of the books in the century-old house they'd transformed into a B&B. The plank floors shone, the understated contemporary furnishings offered genuine comfort. A sculpted Buddha's head on a pedestal appeared to be listening to us. Were the couple spiritually inclined, I wondered, like the other Philippe we'd met? Had they sought enlightenment and discovered Druids, or the big and little wheels of the Buddha?

I didn't dare ask, fearing we'd wind up in the land of crystals, horoscopes, and Druids and New Age solutions to the crises of middle age. So once Alison had disappeared into the kitchen with Armelle and the couple's newborn baby, I quietly queried Philippe about the local inhabitants, wondering if they had welcomed him. He shrugged. "To them we're foreigners." There were 342 residents left in Marigny, a *commune* spread over many miles.

However, Philippe and Armelle had befriended the other six neo-rural Parisian colonists who'd also bought rundown properties in the village and restored them. "The mayor is nice," he added. "He lived in Paris for years and understands."

What the mayor understood was the "neo" phenomenon—the neo-ruralists, neo-nature-lovers, neo-pilgrims, and neo-retirees, who together were bringing life back to abandoned French regions. "People like you," Philippe ventured, "people who need to recharge their batteries, reinvent themselves, not necessarily for religious reasons but because they feel an irresistible need to re-energize in a rural context." He turned his head, making an unnecessary effort to hide the disfigured side of his face. I felt deeply sorry for him, but stopped myself. He seemed to be regaining his health, he had a lovely wife, a newborn son, a wonderful house, and his spirits were high. There was no need for me to pity him.

"You haven't embraced Buddhism, by chance?" I raised my finger toward the bust. "I understand there's a major Buddhist community in Burgundy." Something about Philippe's detachment and quiet optimism reminded me of two childhood friends in California. After lives of sun, fun, and skirt-chasing, one had become a Buddhist, the other a Quaker.

Philippe shrugged again. "I'm not sure. You begin to seek answers and make changes at a certain point. Sometimes it's too late. For me, it may have been in the nick of time." He paused and watched me nod my head—his words sounded familiar. "I'm not sure I buy the reincarnation story, and I have difficulty imagining a primordial Buddha manifesting himself on earth for our benefit. It sounds a lot like Christ the Messiah, doesn't it?"

I nodded. The similarity had occurred to me before, but I really didn't know enough to draw comparisons. Buddhism predated Christianity by about five hundred years. It was conceivable the Christians had taken elements not only from Judaism and

Paganism, but other religions too. "I studied martial arts for a long time," I confided, "I meditated and did yoga, and listened to our karate master talk about some fairly arcane subjects, but nothing ever stuck."

The truth is, when Alison and I did karate and yoga, my knees hurt so much that the pain had overwhelmed everything else. My congenital skepticism had also helped keep me at a distance from spiritual evolution, if such a thing existed.

"It sounds as if you might be seeking something," he said, "though you don't seem to know it, and probably wouldn't admit it, which is fine. I was like that, a rationalist, a certified Parisian secularist intellectual. It's fashionable to disdain religion, and there are plenty of good reasons to do so. I snorted at spirituality, preferring philosophy and ethics. Sometimes you need to wander. The meandering seems pointless, but it isn't. Nothing is wasted, nothing is pointless, and nothing comes from nowhere."

The silence held us for a full minute. "I think I know what you mean," I started to say, filled with dread and unexpected urgency, the same earnest need to talk that I'd felt back in Pierre-Perthuis with the other Philippe. Since leaving the Bay Area nearly twenty-five years earlier, I was no longer accustomed to the touchy-feely confessional, and I disliked the idea in any case. Dissecting spirituality, whatever it was, had never thrilled me. "Alcoholism and obesity are like that," I said at last: "there's always a cause, though it's hidden."

"There's a cause in the personal and the wider sphere, from problem-drinking to war and terrorism. We all have trouble facing ignorance. You see, for me atheism was easy—you don't believe in God or the church, that's fine, most of the world doesn't believe in the same God, and the church is corrupt and retrograde, burns heretics, believes in miracles, and so on. But then you ask yourself, are you the hardcore kind of atheist, the real, authentic scientific skeptic who can say with confidence 'It all started in the primal sea, from nothingness' and believe in nothingness? That may be. But good luck explaining to yourself where nothingness came from and how all of this," he spread his arms, "came from nothing. I'm not sure science really claims to know everything. Science knows it has limits."

Armelle called from the kitchen, bringing us back to earth. Philippe smiled with difficulty, cupping his jaw, and said he had to help prepare dinner. They were expecting a crowd tonight.

SAINTS ALIVE

From our upstairs bedroom I pulled back the curtains and watched the rain pour down. Mist shrouded the tower of the out-sized church. It rose over the rooftops and was by far the biggest building in the village. Would the bells toll all night, waking us over and over, as they had in Cure? In Paris, near our apartment, the bells of Saint Paul's church ring on the half hour, 24/7. How is it they get away with disturbing the peace like that? And why were religion and spirituality such taboo subjects in France, I wondered? Everywhere else I'd lived, people handled faith without undue drama. Everyone was a nominal Roman Catholic in Italy, for instance, and swam in it like anchovies in the Mediterranean. Most Americans wore their beliefs like comfortable, elasticized jogging clothes—exception made for the radical Christian right. The French were different. The practicing Christians I knew—not to mention Jews, Muslims, Animists, Buddhists, and others—were careful, sometimes secretive, about acknowledging their faith, especially the Protestants among them. Religious persecution had marked them. The French Revolutionary heritage of anti-clericalism had survived, and the cult of the secular Republic had supplanted religion. A Frenchman's first allegiance was expected to be to the Republic, not God, whatever name God or the gods or their messengers might bear. Paradoxically, that didn't stop the church bells from ringing at 3 A.M., or prevent Christmas,

Easter, and Ascension from being holidays. Now that I thought of it, almost all Frenchmen's names are saints' names, often in surprising cross-gender combinations such as Jean-Marie for a boy or Marie-Pierre for a girl. Until the end of the 1990s, French law actually forbade the use of names not belonging to Old Testament figures or saints. And to this day, no religious symbols, including the cross, can be worn ostentatiously or displayed in public offices, hospitals, or schools. To me, the arrangement had always seemed like a civilized fudge, an imperfect but functional compromise to carry forward the rival French traditions of Christianity and Republican statist secularism. It codified not freedom *of* religion, but rather freedom *from* religion. The French had had their violent Wars of Religion in the 1500s and 1600s between Protestants and Catholics, and at least in modern times had succeeded in avoiding anything like the Troubles of Northern Ireland. Why wasn't the compromise working anymore?

Clearly, the cult of the secular Republic hadn't foreseen globalization or the arrival of five million Muslims. Some wanted to wear headscarves in public schools—something that was strictly forbidden by law and frowned upon by nearly all French people—and a few swore allegiance to radical Islam. I couldn't help regretting how a few thousand uncompromising Islamists were driving otherwise civilized Frenchmen toward intolerance, xenophobia, racism, and unsavory nationalism. As far as I could tell, what most French appeared to desire was not racial or religious tension but the freedom to name their children after soap opera and reality show stars, wear religious symbols as fashion statements, benefit from subsidized, secular education, retire early, and buy SUVs—the ultimate symbol of aspirational materialism in a country where gas typically costs about $10 a gallon.

As if summoned by sympathetic magic, I watched as a very large SUV pulled up to the B&B. Out of it emerged three children, two adults, and six suitcases.

HIT THE ROAD, JACQUES!

The rain had stopped. Weightless, we left the B&B and walked the quiet, soulful streets of Marigny, my mind re-running my conversation with Philippe. Two intense Philippes in the space of twenty miles? I was glad this wasn't fiction, because I would be inclined to disbelieve.

Marigny seemed to be the objective correlative of my psychological state. Half the village was for sale, the other half shuttered. Both grocery stores had gone out of business. The café was no longer. A chill wind blew past two manor houses, one rebuilt in a wild, 19th-century neo-Gothic style. Horse-head sculptures and lanterns protruded above the door of what appeared to be an eccentric carpenter's workshop on the main square. Tacked to the door, a sign read:

Notice to inhabitants. There's nothing more unpleasant to those who work than the presence of those who have nothing to do. Claude.

"Fortunate man," I said, "if nothing in his life is more unpleasant than being pestered by talkative retirees. In any case, it suggests there are humans in this village."

The *mairie* or town hall of Marigny occupied an unremarkable building near our B&B. There was no doorbell. We took Monsieur le Maire, Jean-Claude Jacquinot, by surprise. Alison deduced his name from a sheet of paper tacked to a billboard. The mayor swiveled and raised his large frame upon hearing us. "Not many people drop by," he said, shaking our hands. Since we were staying at the B&B and seemed harmless, he rooted out the church keys from a deep pocket and held them out.

I'd read in a history book that "Jacquinot" was one of the French last names designating a pilgrim who'd reached Saint Jacques de Compostelle. When might the mayor's ancestor have accomplished the feat, I wondered aloud, and was the mayor religious or *Républicain*? Now that I thought of it, weren't the multiple variations on "Jack" in English derived from Saint Jacques? Millions of Englishmen had crossed the Channel and traversed France to the Spanish shrine. We had "man-jack," "jack of all trades," "jack of hearts," "you're in the groove, Jackson," we even had "hit the road Jack, and don't you come back no more no more no more no more." Jack was the commonest of first names and part of many last names, a diminutive of John, I'd always thought, or, perhaps, in reality, derived from Saint John's brother, James the Greater.

Dust impregnated the stifling air inside the church. Cobwebs encased the broken-down confessional. My eyes made an inventory. Two dead organs sat in the transept, the keyboards missing teeth; this made me think of the tortoise. Plaster peeled, drifting like autumn leaves to the dusty floor. Panes gaped in leaded windows. There was no sign of Saint James, yet Marigny straddled the pilgrimage route. I stood underneath a wall-mounted sculpture of Joan of Arc. It was one of those dime-a-dozen gaudy representations of the woman-child warrior made during the 19th century's Catholic Revival. Joan's sword gleamed. She was a church militant, like Saint Michael the dragon-killer and Saint James, also known as Saint James the Moorslayer. In the 1400s Joan drove out the English occupier, just as, in the Middle Ages, Saint James had driven the Moors out of Spain. He's often shown wearing scallop-shell armor, and got his nickname, "the Moorslayer," because the Christians of Western Europe happened to be at war for 700 years with the Muslim occupiers of the Iberian Peninsula. That long-forgotten struggle that ran and ran was called La Reconquista. James is still Spain's patron saint, and Spaniards are still resisting Islam, nowadays in the form of illegal immigration and terrorism. I'd always found the political side of warrior saints offputting, but then, whether you liked it or not, perhaps the church needed an army to protect it, like all institutions of power.

"A Revival in need of revival," I remarked, trying not to sound flippant.

Alison didn't hear me. She was determined to light a candle, and was delving into every recess looking for one. But there were no candles to light.

MITTERRAND'S MEGALOMANIA:
BURY MY HEART AT BIBRACTE

Mayor Jacquinot of Marigny l'Eglise told us he'd spent his adult life in Paris, and had only recently retired and moved home. "I was an electrical engineer," he said. Did he know about the reservoirs and why they were so low when it'd been raining for months, I wondered? "No, no, no—it's not climate change," he chuckled. "It's kayaks. Whenever there's a white-water kayak or canoe race down the Cure River we release water, lots of water."

Alison and I caught each other's eye. "Isn't that kind of wasteful?"

"It's good for tourism," Jacquinot replied, raising his stout shoulders toward his large ears and blushing ever so slightly. "And anyway, when the reservoir drops really low you get a treat. You can see the medieval stone bridge at the bottom."

Jacquinot rose up on his toes like an excited boy. He told us the reservoir's murky secrets. Not only did a humpback bridge sometimes emerge from the waters, like the monster of Loch Ness. There was also a submerged farmhouse.

"We're talking the 1930s," Jacquinot said, increasingly familiar. "They dynamited everything in the valley that could interfere with boating. One old guy refused to leave. He holed up in his farm. The firemen came in rowboats and pulled him out of the hayloft. I've seen photos. His house is still there, on the lake bottom, seventy years later."

The pigheaded farmer's family lives nearby, the mayor added. From their house they gaze at their "underwater farm." Ever more cheerful, the mayor pulled out huge, detailed survey maps from centuries past, unrolling them across a table. He pinpointed the submerged bridge and farmhouse, and told us more than we thought we'd ever know about hydroelectric generation. "That guy with the farmhouse, he's typical of the Morvan," the mayor went out of his way to explain. "You hold out, you resist. This has always been a leftwing, pink territory—first we had the Celts, then the Protestants and Revolutionaries. That's why the Résistance survived here in World War Two. The villagers and farmers joined them in the woods or helped from home. Anything to fight the Nazis. And that's why Mitterrand set up shop here, too."

The mayor, we knew, was referring to controversial former French socialist president François Maurice Adrien Marie Mitterrand, alias the Sphinx. A conservative aristocrat and member of the collaborationist Vichy Government, Mitterrand had somehow changed sides, joined the Résistance at a convenient juncture, emerged from the Occupation a hero, and become a councilman and then mayor of Château Chinon, one of the Morvan's largest towns. Even after becoming president of France, he remained mayor of Château Chinon, a clever way to maintain his association—however tenuous—with the French Résistance, which had lived its greatest hours in this area.

It also explained why Mitterrand's name was pasted all over certain towns and villages, I realized, and why Mitterrand had created the Résistance Museum in Saint-Brisson, and the Museum of Celtic Civilization at Bibracte on Mont Beuvray. To the nationalist and socialist mind they were powerful symbols of French identity. We'd be visiting both in coming days.

"While we're at it," the mayor added, "the Résistance myth and Mitterrand's mayor-ship of Château Chinon are why he legally could have been buried in Bibracte." Jacquinot paused significantly. "You're familiar with Bibracte—the lost city of the Gauls? It's where Vercingétorix rallied the tribes, and planned our last stand against Caesar. Like your General Custer."

In France, said the mayor, you have the right to a grave in your own back yard, garden, or whatever piece of land you happen to own. So Mitterrand in an access of megalomania made the central government in Paris buy the top of the Gauls's sacred Mont Beuvray from the Burgundy regional authorities, then he sold himself a plot in Bibracte, atop the mountain, near the spot where the heroic Vercingétorix had given his spiel against Caesar.

"You're joking?" I couldn't help saying.

"Oh, no, it's no joke. You see, by owning the plot up there, the president had the right to build himself a tomb. He wanted to be immortalized in a sacred Gallic site."

Beautiful. It was a gorgeous Mitterrand story, and a gloss on so much that was profoundly, incomprehensibly French.

I asked the mayor if he thought Mitterrand had imagined himself Vercingétorix reincarnate. Jacquinot played with the ring of keys before answering. "Who knows? The scheme didn't work. People cried bloody murder and Mitterrand wound up buried in his home town, Jarnac." He paused and grinned maliciously. "Do you know what a *coup de Jarnac* is? You've read *The Three Musketeers*? In fencing, Jarnac means an unfair thrust." He made a downward, poking motion aimed at my calves.

It was, I realized, what we call a low blow.

RUSSIAN CELTS AND ROAMING ROMANS

Staring out from a shelf at our B&B was a vintage hardcover with the winning title *Histoire de Bourgogne*. Presumably this was a history not of Pinot Noir wine but of the Burgundy region. I plucked it and headed for a pre-prandial nap. Beyond the flowing draperies of our bedroom rose Marigny's church spire. I plumped the pillows and squinted with heavy eyelids.

Written in the 1950s by a certain Charles Commeaux, the book recounted Burgundy's early history, the part leading up to Caesar's arrival. It told of waves of nomadic hunter-warriors who had swept in from the east around 500 BC, or so the author claimed, their ancestors having left what's now western Russia sometime between 800 and 1200 BC. Go West, Young Barbarian! These so-called "Celts" had promptly set about exploiting the happy natives of Gaul, members of the older, sedentary, pacific, agriculture-based Halstatt Civilization, which didn't sound very French either. The warlike Russian Celts' modus operandi was much like that of the brutal Romans who followed them and the even more "barbarian" Germanic tribes who came after. In fact, with their beheadings, live burials and burnings, raping and pillaging and serious hygiene problems, the Celts sounded considerably worse than Caesar, more on par with Attila. As to Caesar himself, he came off as being less dasdardly than dashing, as portrayed in the pages of the book, despite his thinning hair. What color eyes did Caesar have, anyway? I blinked, trying to recall the painted statues I'd seen. The pages of the book blurred. I blinked again.

Instead of seeing Caesar's eyes, I saw his nose, a Plasticine nose, with my forefinger outside it and thumb up a nostril, pinching the modeling clay. My hands felt youthful. Atop them arthritis-gnarled fingers nudged and directed. As I pinched and smoothed, my mother's fingertips flattened my clumsy work and reshaped it with broad, confident strokes. "You're putting in too much detail," she said gently; "rough out his features first, and then go back."

Art history books lay open, ranged around her basement studio. Black-and-white photos of busts depicting Caesar filled the clay-encrusted pages, each held open with a clothespin. And then I was standing in Latin class, a clothespin and the bust in my clay-crusted hands, saying to my teacher, "Here it is, my year-end project, it's finished. We modeled the Plasticine first, rubbed it with Vaseline, made a two-piece plaster mold, and poured 'cast-rock' into it. Yes, ma'am, it's the first head I've ever made, ma'am, and no, it isn't perfect, and I'll never try again, and yes, my mother helped me and yes, she helps me with my Latin, but she's Italian and she doesn't pronounce it the way you do, and that's why you don't like me. The nose and ears have too much detail, ma'am, the chin is weak, I agree, the forehead does look like a monkey's forehead, yes, ma'am." Miss Nelson the Latin teacher curls her lip at my Caesar, the same way she curls her lip when I read aloud from Cicero. Miss Nelson pronounces it Sissero, in that sticky southern accent of hers, and she pushes her glasses up her broad, flat nose over and over again. She says wheny, weedy, wiki, turning Caesar's v's into wimpy w's in that syrupy Louisiana voice, threatening to flunk me if I won't give up that vulgar "church Latin" in her classical Latin class. Veni, vidi, vici, I say back to her. Go ahead and flunk me, go ahead and—

"Wake up," Alison whispered, nudging me. "It's dinnertime. They're waiting downstairs."

GETTING TO KNOW YOU

In France, a *chambre d'hôtes* is what we'd call a B&B. When the establishment also serves dinner, *table d'hôtes* is tacked on. We no longer have an equivalent in America or England. Our hostelries and inns of old must have been something like a *chambre d'hôtes-table d'hôtes*—unpretentious hospitality in the family home, with everyone around the table. It's literally potluck: you never know who you're going to meet and what you're going to eat.

We'd been promised a mixed salad, pork roast, and homemade fruit pie. Philippe and Armelle unexpectedly eclipsed themselves. There wasn't room at the dining table and, more urgently, four-month-old Victor cried for his supper.

"Victory," Philippe joked, coin purses of fatigue under his eyes.

The company was mixed—a global mix. It included an outspoken Swiss couple employed in high tech and their trio of lively children, and a diminutive but talkative French computer scientist, his large, trumpet-throated Taiwanese wife, and their sonorous offspring. The Franco-Taiwanese were the proud owners of the SUV I'd seen earlier. All our fellow guests were smart and curious, the adults especially so once lubricated by Pinot Noir.

Chit-chat swerved into serious talk of politics and religion— the twin taboos. The Swiss man said friends of his had walked the Compostela pilgrimage. "Not for religious reasons, but to see whether they should marry and have children. If they could get along while hiking for months, they could weather any storm."

"It is reportedly wearing," the Swiss wife chimed in, sizing us up like specimens in a Petri dish. "Very wearing. What precisely are you expecting to get out of it?"

Alison turned away, pouring wine for another guest. I was slightly taken aback by the woman's mercantilist nature, but didn't want to be impolite. I remembered a saying a pilgrim in Paris had taught me. It ran something like, "You need three weeks to get into a pilgrimage, the first for your legs, the second for your mind, the third for your spirit." We'd only been hiking a few days. I'd already shared my innermost secrets with the two Philippes, and didn't feel like being interrogated by this angular Swiss woman. "I'm not sure we're expecting to get anything; we're hoping to be pleasantly surprised," I said at last, more defensively than I'd meant to. "Just having the time and space to think, and get back in shape, would be enough for me; so if anything else comes in the bargain, that'll be great."

With dainty fingers flying, the French computer genius said he was happy to be a materialist, a scientist, and a believer in technology. "It's the only thing we can truly hope will save us from the messes we've made." He steered us away from Compostela and, his cheeks flushed with wine, gave us a disquisition on the labor issues behind recurrent French strikes. His wife from Taipei provided a potted history of Taiwan. It sounded strangely similar in points to the history of France, with tensions between

First Nation activists and waves of mainland Chinese "invaders." It was the Gauls and Romans, and the Franks and Germans, all over again, on the other side of the world. What terrified the Taiwanese nation, she said, was the prospect of rule from Beijing, which appeared to be increasingly the de facto reality.

Eventually, when our fellow diners had established their intellectual credentials and sent the children to play in the living room, they turned to us again. Their vigorous curiosity could not be ignored. We contributed a few anodyne anecdotes about freelance life in Paris, and ran through our maverick hiking itinerary, which threw all of them off course, and reignited the question of religion and science. It would've been easier to hike with everyone else on the mainline route, I agreed, but that wasn't what we were after. The Frenchman heartily endorsed non-religious walking, and for a moment waxed philosophical. "Admittedly, technology isn't always the answer. The car, for instance, appears to have given us freedom," he said. "But it has destroyed sociability. It has left villages like this one empty and ruined the small, provincial merchant class. Everyone drives to a shopping mall on the outskirts of town."

"Just wait until Wal-Mart gets up to speed," said the Swiss man snippily. "We lived in America for two years. Plenty of giant churches and tele-evangelists, but no more unions, no more holidays, and taxpayers subsidize the corporations."

The evangelization and Wal-Mart-ification of the world provided plenty to hash over, and however much I sympathized with our fellow guests' points of view, I refused to go down that road. It wasn't just my profound desire to remain positive, or the negative, preachy tone the Swiss man had adopted. The walking, wining, dining, and talking was making my head spin. When the apple pie arrived, I saw pillows as the happy aftermath. Alas, our tablemates had no intention of letting off their captive American audience, who must be made to reckon for the failings of the American Dream. The philosophical Frenchman turned twinkling eyes upon me. "And how did you wind up in France, if I may ask?"

"You may," I said, "but it's a long story, and past our bedtime." The tale threatened to add a Wikipedia-style coda to what was already a long day.

"Oh, we're in no rush," he insisted. "It's early. We won't let you go until you tell us something about yourselves; it's a tradition at *chambres d'hôtes*."

Since Alison routinely balks at the inevitable question of roots, and since they weren't letting us go, I dove in, explaining that I was a native of San Francisco, had lived in Rome as a child, and, having finished political science and Italian literature degrees at UC Berkeley and Brown, in the early 1980s had moved back to Rome and from there to Milan. After two years and a failed marriage, I'd headed north to Paris to start over again. That's when I'd met Alison. I'd stayed on, an accidental Parisian. "The rest is mystery," I concluded.

"And you?" asked the pink-cheeked Swiss, turning to Alison. I couldn't help thinking of the Helvetii and the pope's Swiss guards. The Swiss couple may well have been descendants of survivors of that horrific battle and so, perhaps, were we all.

Alison remained silent, suffering as she always did when the center of attention. A child of the foreign service, she had happened to be born in Paris and brought up there—plus Ankara, Karachi, Washington, D.C., and Rome, then Paris again. You never knew which origin myth she'd choose. Sometimes she came from Little Rock, her father's birthplace. Sometimes from Montreal, her mother's. And sometimes from San Francisco. Never from Paris. That's because, despite her French citizenship and passport, and decades lived in France, the French consider her a foreigner. Wisely, she prefers to view herself as an individual without national affiliations.

"I'm from Arkansas," she said at last, and then skillfully changed the subject to beddy-bye.

THERE OTTA BE A LAW

Crottefou is the name of a hamlet in the Cure River Valley, our first stop a few miles south of Marigny. The name means "mad dung" or "crazy droppings"—presumably of horse, cow, or mad dog. Happily the restored houses we admired held little resemblance to the place-name. Chainsaws whined in the distance. They approached and were, of course, not chainsaws but dirt bikes. Several flew past at breakneck speed. I silently hoped the riders would indeed break their necks, pronto. It was not a charitable, pilgrim-like thought.

Tacked upon the village billboard was a petition. The locals demanded that the Prefect of the Département ban off-road vehicles such as dirt bikes on GR-13, our secular pilgrimage trail. Said vehicles had allegedly been trashing the trail and terrorizing residents for several years.

South of the two-lane highway dividing the hamlet we found another billboard. On it was the Prefect's reply: to wit, the people's will had been done. In the Crottefou *commune* off-road vehicles were heretofore banned.

The elation I felt was disproportional to the problem at hand. But my loathing of noisy, smelly, brutal, and pointless off-road vehicles is visceral, especially when riders choose to destroy historic hiking trails in parklands, as opposed to, say, riding around reclaimed dumps or toxic waste sites, battlegrounds scattered with cluster bombs, and abandoned coal mines—ideal settings for motorsports.

On the south bank of a lovely creek, the star-shaped flowers familiar from previous days spread around budding saplings, ancient oaks, and extravagantly mossy boulders—the kind favored by Rip van Winkle. The site's beauty was distressing. I blinked at it, trying to fix it in my mind's eye.

Before we left Paris, a photographer friend had e-mailed me with his secret technique for visually embedding scenery. I'd printed out Russ's words and pasted them in my pocket diary. I reread them now. "At particularly beautiful spots," he wrote, "I practice an exercise which cements the scene in my brain. Look at the view, close your eyes, and try to reconstruct it. You'll find lots of gaps in your mind's eye. Open your eyes again and learn what you missed . . . little things, like where the horizon intercepts the barn, what's in the foreground . . . keep doing so until you could sketch the scene in a closed room. You'll have it forever. I can still see a view from a hotel balcony in New Zealand, and a street corner in Prague."

Standing in the magical grove, I tried to embed the moss and trees and morning light playing on the old winding road. It was a tough exercise. Luckily, I remembered Russ's suggested alternative. "Have Alison take a picture."

There was no need to "have her" take a picture. Wild motorbikes, let alone wild horses, couldn't stop her from taking thousands of pictures. And anyway, she famously never responded to obligation.

Further upstream, the trail turned into a road named rue des Maquisards. It crossed an island at a putative village called Les Iles Menéfrier-La Chaume aux Renards, where a roadside memorial to the French Résistance bore a plaque: "Here 2,000 patriots of the Maquis Verneuil fought for freedom, 1944."

Bushels of history hid underneath that single, straightforward line of prose. During the war, each Résistance unit had been identified as a "Maquis-something." Often the something was the codename of its leader, or a secret location. The fighters called each other "maquisards," a reference to the Corsican outback—*le maquis*—where the French equivalents of Robin Hood or Billy the Kid hid out in thick, Mediterranean scrub.

There was no sunny scrub here. This was Druid-land—dark and wet and moody—and, perversely, I found the Druids almost as fascinating as the ancient Romans. Was that because they had somehow managed to create a sophisticated quasi-religious dogma, set themselves up as mediators between men and the gods, and keep the other social classes in subjection and fear? They seemed a fine illustration of the power of negativity, the strength of superstition, the fruitfulness of scare-mongering and so, like Caesar, were uncannily modern once you scraped away the primitive surface. Their creepy presence could still be felt, clinging to the waterlogged timbers in the creek, the mossy trees and the boulders cloaked by lichen-frosted shrubbery. I shivered. I simply couldn't grasp how anyone in the 21st century could embrace the revived cult of Druidism and propose to be a "neo-Druid." Yet there were hundreds, perhaps thousands of apprentice Druids all over France—and the rest of the former Celtic world. There were Druid festivals, and Druid summer camps, Druid sing-alongs and probably Druid barbecues. The phenomenon suggested to me the desperate search for "spiritual" communion with God or the gods, the profound need to find an explanation, a solution, a reason for being. Perhaps that was our common trait, what ultimately distinguished us from other animals. We had to find an explanation, no matter how imperfect or ridiculous.

La Chaume aux Renards, where Gauls had once bowed under the Druidic wand, where maquisards had once hidden from Nazis, turned out to be a less-than-spectacular youth hostel today. Worse, its café was closed. Somehow we hadn't expected to get a cup of coffee. Druids never drank the stuff.

Opposite the hostel, a sign on the trail stated that dirt bikes and Quads were not allowed on this section of GR-13. The chains blocking the trail reinforced the words. Again we heard the distant whine of two-stroke engines. As in Crottefou, battle had been joined. I couldn't help feeling elated.

In a feisty, Druidic mood now, as we worked our way uphill, I began pulling deadwood onto the trail to slow the next pack of illegal dirt bikers. My hands turned black with mud, and my palms prickled from slivers. At the top of the rise, I looked back with satisfaction. It was almost as good as Druids' work, or, better yet, beavers' work. Branches and fallen trees now clogged the trail. I imagined the bikers having to slow, stop, dismount, and clear a path, making them think for at least one precious moment about the ecological madness they were indulging in. I winced with satisfaction. But my temples throbbed and my eyes ached more than usual. I'd been full of righteous wrath, of anger at the bikers, and anger made me very unhappy and unwell.

"Less coffee and less anger," I said to myself, hurrying to catch up with Alison, "and less Druidic nonsense." She seemed blissful, taking her still-lifes of moss and lichen. She glanced back and down at my handiwork and, much to my surprise, gave her approval.

We hiked diligently onward, with another five or six miles to go before we reached the Pont du Montal, our destination for the night where I'd reserved a room. But first we had to get across another valley and make it to Le Vieux Dun.

THE PAST IS PRESENT

According to our *Topo Guide*, Le Vieux Dun, a hilltop hamlet, was already very *vieux* when Caesar rode through. Its reclusive inhabitants appear to have preserved an atavistic memory of the invasion. Village dogs barked. Bearish villagers barricaded themselves. Shutters and doors closed before we could reach them. Was this the essence of Burgundy? I couldn't hide my disappointment. We'd been expecting something very different. Perhaps, I told Alison, trying to lighten our mood, perhaps the water engineer at Marigny was wrong, there really was a drought, and thus they didn't want to refill our water bottles. Happily, I'd brought along an extra bottle from the B&B plus fruit juices. We would not die of thirst because of the unfriendly locals, though we might suffer for several hours.

Some commentators ascribe the fearful, distrustful nature of the French and their pathological attachment to the past to regicide—the murder of divine-right king Louis XVI. By killing God's representative on Earth, and destroying the church and aristocracy with a slice of the guillotine's blade, the French, the theory goes, lost their grounding. They cut their own tap root. The return to kings and emperors Napoléon I and III in the 19th century, and the creation of paternal Statist governance thereafter, are merely incomplete attempts at re-rooting.

That could be. Pop psychology sometimes hits the mark. The source of widespread French fearfulness and the petty aggressiveness or morbid shyness that springs from it may, however, go back to the chieftain Vercingétorix and the resounding military defeats at Bibracte and Alésia, or perhaps to gallant Roland's slaughter at the hands of the Basques—an event later blamed (for political and religious motives) on the Moors, who were innocent. It seemed to me after over two decades in the country that whatever the origin of this unpleasant French trait, what the French themselves now recognize and describe as negative *passéisme*—the obsession with the past and fear of the future—was here to stay. The homely village of Dun seemed like *passéisme* incarnate.

"Dun" is one of those Indo-European root words that crops up in both Latin and Celtic, and usually means hill or fortified heights or, an easier guess, "dune" as in sand dune. There are dozens of place-names in France with "dun" in them, the most famous being Verdun.

Wherever it once stood, the Celtic-Roman fortress of Le Vieux Dun which we'd read about escaped our ken. We searched for it but soon gave up. Without the help of the natives, we were lost.

Having also given up trying to replenish our water supplies, we headed east beyond the village and found an unlikely picnic spot—the bramble-tangled graveyard around an abandoned chapel. Out of punctilious respect, before sitting down on it, Alison was careful to choose a tombstone whose owner's name had worn off. She possessed an admirable ability to overlook the nastiness of the local populace wherever we went, and also magnanimously avoided sweeping associations between historical and current events. "You have an overwrought imagination," she said, handing me a carrot. "Just eat your lunch."

RECTITUDE VERSUS ROMANCE

Flanking the trail from Le Vieux Dun to the forest-hamlet of Bonaré, which lay several miles down the road, tall hewn stones stuck out of the undergrowth. Were they Roman paving stones, we wondered? Some might even have inscriptions on them, I told myself, trying to get a closer look. But probably not. Most of the ancient tombstones and milestones of France were hauled long ago to provincial museums where they fill dusty rooms seen by few. Might it have been better to leave them where they were, on the roadsides, evocative memorials to a mysterious, moss-grown past?

That, I knew, was a romantic notion based on the supposition that civilized, sensitive people would have civil sense. In other words, it was nonsense, the objective correlative of the romantic agony—the eternal struggle between reason and hope. Everywhere in Europe where monuments have been left in place, they've been stolen or vandalized, usually both, or knocked down in the name of progress. For every sensitive romantic, there are ten insensitive brutes of the opposite persuasion.

Our trail, in part trashed by off-road vehicles, rejoined the Cure in another deep, dark, enchanted forest cleft. Upstream we spied a B&B on the riverbank in a particularly scenic spot, where water cascaded from all sides. I closed my eyes and concentrated. But I couldn't evoke Pan or Mary or play my friend Russ Schleipmann's visual memorization game, for a very simple reason. Three trail bikes sat on trailers attached to SUVs with Belgian license plates. I was furious, and saw red everywhere despite the green.

Upstream another quarter-mile, we reached the Pont du Montal—a bridge at a crossroads and our day's destination. Tacked to a corkboard in the entrance to our modest motel, called the Chalet du Montal, were posters advertising "extreme off-road tourism." One company was based nearby in Dun-les-Places. There was no escaping the motorsports set.

A tall, thin, blue-eyed Dutchman showed us to our room and said his name was Huub Broxterman. He repeated it several times until we got it more or less right. A young retiree, Huub bought the motel in 2002. His target clientele was Dutch and Belgian. "Americans don't know the Morvan yet," he remarked amiably.

In our riverside room it sounded as if a waterfall ran behind the bed. Through the open doorway we watched the white water in the Cure froth and foam. Dams upstream must be releasing water for kayakers, I joked. No sooner had I spoken the words than a raft appeared, loaded with yelping kids. It floated past, bouncing over rocks. Another raft and then a canoe and kayak followed. This time the passengers were Africans. I heard a scream, a plop, and the sound of thrashing, and dashed out of the room to the river's edge to pull out a teenage boy. He hesitated, trying to get out of the water on his own, and finally accepted a hand. His wary eyes stayed fixed on me, as if he expected a kick. I asked if he'd hurt himself. He shook his head, mortified, and without a word limped downstream.

Later, in the dining room, Huub explained to us that under-privileged kids from Paris's grim suburbs are sometimes taken to the Morvan to experience "wilderness."

It was a great idea, I agreed, also wondering aloud what most Europeans make of real wilderness, the American or African kind, where human beings are potential links in the food chain. I'd never seen a truly wild place on the Old Continent. Neither, it turned out, had Huub.

VERCINGÉTORIX, MITTERRAND AND VON STÜLPNAGEL

The Morvan Park headquarters are in a spacious farm compound at Saint Brisson, a mountain village about four miles from the Pont du Montal. After resting up for a while, we hitched a ride there. Towering old trees rose over a landscaped courtyard. In their shade stood the bust of a mature man, portrayed like a Roman emperor. His name was Paul Flandin, a founder-member of the French parks federation and president of the Parc du Morvan from its inception in 1970 to his departure in 1992. We'd seen and heard the name Flandin before, in Cure, and wondered now how many political mysteries and real estate deals lay buried under that bust.

Another inscription outside a two-story building informs visitors that on June 26, 1983 President François Mitterrand inaugurated the site's Musée de la Résistance. We stepped into the Spartan, nondescript building. The ground floor offered a potted history of the Morvan, from Celtic times forward, gently aiding the visitor in constructing a mental bridge from Vercingétorix to other French war heroes. Propaganda? Perhaps.

Despite my years in France, I still fumble when I get "Vercingétorix" in my mouth. With my digital recorder in hand, I asked an affable woman at the ticket counter whether she'd mind providing the proper pronunciation. Surprised but game, she obliged, repeating "Vercingétorix" three times.

I duly repeated the name as I climbed to the museum's upstairs displays. Vercingétorix, Vercingétorix, Ver-cin-gé-to-rix. It didn't sound anything like Mitterrand.

From a document on display, I soon learned that the Italian Risorgimento freedom fighter Giuseppe Garibaldi had ridden to the rescue of the French at Autun, on the Morvan's southern edge, in 1870, during the Franco-Prussian War—the prelude to World Wars One and Two. Garibaldi's was a little-known twist on the Caesar saga, a friendly Italian attempting to save France from Germany. He'd failed, of course. The logical fallout to France's disastrous defeats became clear a few steps up the staircase. There, an original Order of General Mobilization dated September 2, 1939 faced out. It filled me with foreboding. This was not going to be entertaining.

In a display case, a German aviator's gloves and Nazi propaganda leaflets—produced to demoralize the French—flanked yellowing documents, photos, and maps. Evocative objects told the tale of the French *débâcle*, the Occupation and the rise of the Résistance. The line between Occupied and Free France ran across southern Burgundy. We would be crossing it down the road. We'd also be passing through half a dozen "martyr villages" destroyed by Nazi reprisal raids against the Résistance. I read the list of names: Dun-les-Places, Montsauche, Planchez, Anost, Glux. Tomorrow and tomorrow and tomorrow, I said to myself, checking our marching plans.

Clandestine newspapers such as *Défense de la France*, founded on Bastille Day, 1941, had attempted to give the lie to German propaganda. So, too, had courageous historians. A quote by the 17th-century philosopher Blaise Pascal reprinted during the Occupation was displayed prominently above one Plexiglas case and seemed topical: *Je ne crois que les histoires dont les témoins se feraient égorger.* "I only believe stories whose witnesses would be willing to have their throats slit."

Victor's justice came with a victor's version of history, from Caesar's *Conquest of Gaul* to the present. I wondered what Goebbels & Hitler's version of World War Two would have been, had they prevailed. Luckily, sometimes the good guys win. Sometimes no one wins and the world loses, and sometimes the good guys turn bad.

A notice to French citizens by the Nazi Occupier caught my eye. It was signed "Von Stülpnagel, General der Infanterie."

Von Stülpnagel? At last we meet.

How to explain the exquisiteness of that name? In moments of great frustration, my father, a wartime Jeep driver, encryption man, and, later, correspondent, would sometimes blurt "Don't be a Stülpnagel, for god's sake!"

I'd always wondered what a Stülpnagel was. Now I knew, and could see the results of his actions: death, destruction, genocide.

Amid the wind-up radios, field telephones, and tattered codebooks were photos of Allied parachute drops. In 1944, the RAF and the U.S. Air Force routinely dropped large canisters filled with communications equipment, dynamite and sabotage manuals, guns and first-aid kits, to assist the Résistance and the OSS units who joined them.

The vintage canisters on display looked like elongated, oversized propane tanks. Other photos showed artillery pieces and Jeeps being dropped in Operation Houndsworth. I peered at the Jeep. It looked exactly like the one my father had driven in the war. But didn't they all?

In a snapshot taken at Autun in September 1944, crowds of Résistants and citizens gathered around an American Destroyer tank, celebrating the liberation of the city. I stared at that photo, wondering how after the Nazi Occupation the French themselves could continue to occupy Indo-China and Algeria and fight colonial wars to try to hold them in the 1950s and '60s. I wondered what wrong turn had taken us into Vietnam, Iraq, and Afghanistan, not as the good guys, but as hated occupiers.

Before leaving the museum, Alison spotted another snapshot, this one taken on the Pont du Montal, theoretically across from our hotel. It showed a Panzer tank de-tracked by the Résistance. Derailing Nazi trains, blowing up power stations, and trapping tanks were the kind of hit-and-run actions the Résistance had done best.

"Notice anything?" asked Alison.

I thought for a minute. "Yeah: no Chalet du Montal; our hotel wasn't there."

BURGUNDY SNAILS GO DUTCH

"The hotel wasn't built yet," Huub explained that evening when we told him about the photograph of this spot at the Musée de la Résistance. The back wall of the dining room was decorated with black-and-white photos of the chalet from the 1940s and '50s. "Built in 1948," he said proudly, rapping the dining-room wall with his knuckles.

The river's rapids, the forest setting, even the knotty pine décor, old tables and chairs, appeared unchanged since the 1940s, corresponding to the vintage prints. I was glad there were no Nazi tanks outside. The problematic presence of leather-suited, chain-smoking motocross riders in the bar area paled in comparison.

We asked Huub about his background. He told us he'd retired just in time, from a job as an administrator. He'd been in charge of ensuring that authors and artists received royalty payments on copyrighted material. What a quaint notion, copyright. By purchasing the Chalet du Montal, Huub joined the other two thousand Dutch families who've moved from cramped Holland to the spacious Morvan since the year 2000. All told, about eight thousand Dutch households totaling twenty thousand individuals—and growing by the hour—now live in Burgundy. They often outnumber the less fertile native French, those, that is, presumably descended from Vercingétorix or the local chieftain, whose name we confirmed was Dumnorix.

Huub had hired a young Frenchman to be his chef, so while the Burgundy snails in puff pastry sounded daunting in Dutch as *slakken à la Bourgogne*, they turned out to be tasty.

The Dutchman's explanation for why he chose the Morvan dovetailed with what we'd heard and read elsewhere. Holland's population density is something like four hundred inhabitants per square kilometer—among the highest in the world. In the Morvan it's eleven per square kilometer—among the lowest in Europe, on a par with the Himalayas. Ironically, as Holland clamps down on inbound immigration, it is sending record numbers abroad—to places like Burgundy, where the non-Europeans are few. Property prices are relatively low, and there's an anything-goes, Far West feel to the place—by European standards. It isn't exactly Montana or Texas. Bureaucracy abounds. Huub explained that the park area is parceled into 105 *communes*, each with a mayor, totaling a mere 37,000 residents.

"That's why they come," Huub said, motioning to the group of motocross riders. "Trail riding is illegal in Holland and most of northern Europe so they come down here. It's advertised on the Internet—come to the Morvan and do what you want, no one will arrest you, it's wide open and empty." Huub shrugged. Much of his business came from such people, he admitted.

"No one complains?"

"Oh, they complain. Bitterly. But each mayor has to rule on off-road use in his *commune* even though this is a regional park and the GR-13 is a cross-country, European pilgrim's trail." Huub glanced around. He lowered his voice. "You can imagine the chaos, it's so French. Nine of ten people here are against this invasion of motor-sportsmen. The ten percent who are for it claim it's good for business, and believe me it is good for business. In a few years it'll be over, they're going to outlaw it in France and that's fine by me."

Because I didn't want to raise my blood pressure I said I understood. In a minor way it was the Occupation all over again, and here I was agreeing with a Dutchman collaborationist—a pleasant, decent, literate guy like Huub forced to go along.

VICHYSSOISE À LA MITTERRAND

Reflections, reflections. . . . Perhaps I'd merely been inattentive. At the Musée de la Résistance built by President François Mitterrand, nowhere had I seen it mentioned that François Mitterrand's codename was "Morland." Nor were the details given of Morland's earlier, pre-resistance role in the collaborationist Vichy government. Perhaps it was unfair to expect it. The museum wasn't really about Mitterrand, was it?

It appears to be a documented fact and is widely reported in the French press and in biographies of François Mitterrand: in 1943 he secretly left France, presumably with the help of the Résistance and Free French, in order to meet Charles de Gaulle in London. De Gaulle loathed him, suspecting ulterior motives. De Gaulle wanted order imposed on divergent Résistance movements. He understood France's historical weakness as fractious tribalism. In response, Mitterrand reportedly claimed that a central command was not possible. The political divide between right and left was too wide. The best compromise the insurgents could offer was an agreement that neither anti-communist nor pro-communist militancy would be tolerated among the maquisards.

It's said that after Mitterrand left London, a furious de Gaulle exclaimed something like "That man should be eliminated."

The two men's rivalry continued into the postwar period. De Gaulle still distrusted Mitterrand, who'd morphed by then from a Vichy Catholic of aristocratic lineage into a Résistance hero and spokesman for the budding new socialism of the late 1940s. Mitterrand's brand of *socialisme* turned out to be old-fashioned prewar patriarchal Statism wrapped in pink, but the nation only discovered that years later, after he became president in 1981 and ruled the country like a monarch for fourteen years. That is gross simplification, I had to remind myself, contemplating the forest beyond the dining room's picture windows. French politics are a deep, dark, tangled wood populated by wily, cynical beasts. The odd thing is, more than a decade after his death in 1996, François Mitterrand remains a hero, especially in the Morvan. Perhaps, I told myself as we headed downstairs to bed, perhaps he was an authentic hero and his boosters know something we don't, something witnesses would have their throats slit to back up.

DOMINE, QUAD VADIS?

As dawn tickled us with pink fingers, Alison announced she was determined to see Dun-les-Places, one of the area's martyr villages. Over breakfast, Huub said it was only 800 meters out of our way. That meant half a mile in each direction, an added mile on the already long day we'd planned. But I, too, was curious. So we backtracked and detoured. To avoid the main highway, we took a dirt road southwest. Half an hour and one and a half miles later we spied the village. Between us and it rose a cloud of buzzing dust. The dust sounded like a swarm of stirred bees. There were no bees. They were Quads, their motors revving. Since we had strayed from the pilgrim's route, I had no right to object. We stood aside. As they passed, I thought I recognized the wary-eyed black teenager who'd fallen off his raft into the Cure River the day before. The riders were helmeted. I couldn't be sure.

"Did you see how slowly they drove by?" Alison asked, trying to calm me. "One of them even waved."

So had a certain number of Nazis, probably, as they flew overhead during the war, smiling and waving as their bombs fell merrily to earth. Had Picasso been here then, he'd have painted another *Guernica*.

The Luftwaffe and Nazi armored columns bombed and shelled and burned Dun-les-Places for three days, from June 26 to June 28, 1944. The Allies had just landed in Normandy. The events were invisibly linked. In preparation for the landings, the Résistance and Allied "special forces" had stepped up attacks in the Morvan. For each attack, there was a Nazi reprisal.

Proud and pigheaded, after the war the French rebuilt martyr villages like Dun, and all these years later you could still tell: they were ugly and haunted.

Huub had mentioned that the late Danielle Mitterrand, the former president's widow, reportedly a bona fide *Résistante* born and brought up in Cluny, had made a yearly pilgrimage to Saint-Brisson and Dun-les-Places. The monument upon which Danielle would place her wreath each year lists the names of those who died in the monstrous Nazi attacks. In front of the monument is a massive 19th-century church built of granite. Behind the monument, a weathered, sculpted cross sits atop a hewn block—probably a recycled pre-Celtic standing stone. Nearby rise two obelisks. The collection of carved stonework seemed to cover about four thousand years of credence—and bloodletting.

Empty stood the square and empty the church. It felt remarkably outsized. My footsteps echoed as I walked around the ambulatory looking for signs of Saint James. I found none. However, Alison was at last able to light a taper, for whom and for what purpose I wasn't aware.

On the main highway into town, two tall, pneumatic, brightly colored balloon-banners wiggled in the breeze, looking like giant condoms and advertising a Japanese motorcycle manufacturer and exciting Quad excursions. This was the phoenix that had arisen from Dun's ashes.

HAM SANDWICHES AND BARBED WIRE

Around noon, as we crested a clear-cut mountain en route to our hotel for the night at Lac des Settons, Alison detoured down a logging road where a teenage boy on a motocross racing bike revved his steed. Click. Bzzz. Immortalized on cellulose film and in pixels. The site was not scenic. Logging rarely is. An unseasonably hot sun drove steam up from the trashed forest floor and its row upon symmetrical row of Douglas fir stumps.

Beyond the stumps and the rutted logging road we came upon a refuge, la Maison forestière du Breuil. Flanking it was an observation tower, a murky pond, and a deer park surrounded by a tall wire fence. The enclosure looked like a misplaced petting zoo, its occupants half a dozen tame, tired stags with mottled coats. One of them had blue eyes. The eyes followed us. The stag licked himself like a dog and seemed to be asking what on earth we were staring at. I asked myself the same question, and wondered what on earth this so-called "park" was all about, other than commercial timberland, off-road vehicles, and miserable penned animals.

Happily, the trail zigzagged down and away to a lush river valley. We found a dreamy picnic spot on an island surrounded by rapids. Moss grew mattress-thick. The fir trees were tall, spaced at random, and seemed noble with their lichen beards. Our surveyor's map gave the place-name: Port des Épines. It sounded familiar. I checked our picnic bag. The bottles we'd bought at Dun were labeled Épines spring water. The creek's name, however, was not Épine but Vignan, which explained the absence of a mineral water bottling plant.

The setting reminded me of Little Yosemite Park in California, and a backpacking trip I took in the summer of 1975. The principal difference between then and now, there and here, beyond the salt in my formerly pepper hair, appeared to be the lack of bears. Also, on the riverbank stood a fairly impressive pre-Celtic dolmen. A dolmen is a horizontal slab of stone—this one about the length of a compact car—propped up by smaller stones. Dolmens, like their phallic counterparts, the menhirs or standing stones, served some unknown sacral function in prehistory. This particular stone was not blood-stained. It looked suspiciously well placed and in good condition. But it might well have been authentic.

Perhaps the sunshine and fatigue were to blame. We both started to laugh. The shared, ludicrous vision of park rangers and a crew of Astérix lookalikes manhandling the huge stone slabs gave both of us the giggles. Had they meant to create a Druid theme park?

Our hilarity was short-lived. The motocross band that roared by us as we climbed the next hill seemed hell-bent on caffeine. I attempted to calm my nerves with deep breathing, but the stench of two-stroke oil interfered. When it dissipated, the scent of fresh clear cuts and sappy fir returned.

The motor-sportsmen seemed to be everywhere. A few miles south in a field near the town of Gouloux, an ageing, blue-cheeked farmer in a worn suit-jacket doffed his cap at our approach and returned our greeting. He explained that he was retired, like most of the area's inhabitants. He'd come out to look at his cows, now officially owned by his son. "The law says I can't raise them or I'll forfeit part of my pension," he said quietly.

The cattle he spoke to—between words with us—were of the Nivernais or Charolais breed, he explained. The choice of appellation depended, he said, on whether you were a native of the Nièvre *département*—he pointed down at the ground—or the Charolais region. This he indicated by a wave of his hand at the mountainous south. The cattle's official name was a bone of contention in this border area. "So I just call them *race blanche*," he said philosophically—white breed.

The odd thing was half of his white-breed cows were brownish. "They're mixed, not on purpose but because it just happens," he said. He seemed to blush, but it was hard to tell because of his bristly, sun-rouged complexion. The breed always bred clear after a few seasons, he added. The white hide was like the root stock of a fruit tree or a grapevine. Sooner or later it returned to its wild base.

"Seen anyone go by on a motorcycle?" he asked, his friendly manner changing. "I'd like to string barbed wire across the trail and get those . . ." he refrained himself from strong language. "When you're old you can't jump clear of them. So you just stand there and hope they slow down." I told him I'd been contemplating piano wire or heavy-duty fishing line strung strategically at helmet level. The farmer seemed surprised. "Sabotage?" His eyes flashed, and he crouched instinctively, glancing around. Then he shook his head and straightened up. "No. It might hurt a hiker or a child." Without further ado he nodded good-bye, put his cap back on, and spoke to his brownish-white cows.

Half a mile later, the trail reached a two-lane highway. Several cars were parked there. They had Belgian license plates, and Quads on trailers hitched behind. I couldn't help thinking that it was people such as these who fueled the oil addiction, people who perhaps unwittingly drove the West toward the geopolitics of war. Clearly, this wasn't a great day for spirituality.

On the edge of the parking lot, the sun beat down on a menhir-style monument. It wasn't the usual monument to the dead of the World Wars. Erected in 1995, it commemorated a local legionnaire named Gabriel Léger, one of only 15 French survivors of the 1845 Battle of Sidi-Brahim, in Algeria. That was when France invaded and set up a colony in Algeria that lasted until the 1960s. Apparently the man's family and former "chasseurs"—French army units who'd fought in the Algerian War—had paid for the memorial.

"Touching to remember Monsieur Léger after 160 years or so," I remarked. "You don't think this has anything to do with the National Front, do you?"

Alison's eyebrows seemed to rise unbidden halfway up her forehead. Some extreme rightwing veterans of the Algerian War, many of them associated with the National Front, a political party, were in the forefront of anti-immigration, racist politics in France. "Very touching indeed," she agreed. "Shall we keep moving? Something about this place gives me the creeps."

In the Algerian War, "only" 30,000 Frenchmen died. The estimated 360,000 Algerian-French soldiers, the countless Algerian freedom fighters and civilians killed, were rarely mentioned. With 35,000 *communes* in France, each with an obelisk-shaped war memorial, that meant there would be fewer than one "real French" name per obelisk to commemorate this colonial war the nation has yet to face up to. It is France's Vietnam and Iraq combined, a bad, ugly war that will continue to divide the nation until the French admit the horrors they committed in the name of colonial power.

We hiked another half hour or so, until the sight of a cow-sized wooden clog hanging on the main street of Gouloux stopped us short. The clog signaled the world-famous Musée de la saboterie, which I naively assumed was a museum of sabotage: this was the heartland of the French Résistance, after all. It turned out to be a workshop with vintage tools and a boutique selling clogs—*sabots*. We peeked in at the riveting displays. "I suppose," I couldn't help saying with malicious disappointment, "that if you threw a clog in the works, it would slow down any machine."

Naturally, no one was around to sell us a ticket. This was another dreary, half-abandoned village. We picked up a brochure and kept walking. But the going was slow. I soon realized why I was so tired. We'd added three miles to our itinerary with our morning detour to charming Dun-les-Places.

Dragging myself up a hill, I pulled over into a shady thicket. Cattle and two water troughs stood in the pasture behind. "We could fill our bottles here," I said. Then I did a double take. I stood up and pointed. The troughs looked very much like the para-chuted supply canisters we'd seen in the Musée de la Résistance. These had been cut in two with a torch. I couldn't help wondering how many canisters like it were rusting away in the woods, some, perhaps, still filled with dynamite or guns or chewing gum, con-doms, spreadable SPAM, and cigarettes.

Several hours later, having gotten lost twice, we emerged from the deep, dark forest, staggered past a mini-golf course, and limped down to Lac des Settons. Despite the Quads, it had been a long, mostly lovely day, and the effort now seemed worth it.

Three things immediately struck me as marvelous. First, the *lac* looked like a real lake, not a reservoir. Second, pedal-boats, sailboats, and vintage steamers were out, transforming the scene framed by lakeside cafés into an Impressionist canvas, and I had not expected a Renoir in the Morvan. Third, at the western end of the lake rose an impressive dam. It looked like the granite rampart of a fortified city, with a citadel on one end, and a watchtower toward the middle. It seemed taller than a towering fir and longer than an aircraft carrier. I couldn't help punning, "I'll be damned."

I had phoned ahead from our last lodging to ask for directions. As instructed, we crossed the causeway looking for our hotel. A weathered plaque midway across, near a crucifix and Madonna, informed anyone who cared to know that the dam had been inaugurated on May 15, 1858. That was the heyday of the Second Empire, when Napoléon III had ruled France. It explained the hewn granite paving on the causeway, the elegant ironwork, the Paris-style lampposts and attention to detail throughout. The same kind of Second Empire workmanship had made Paris's parks magical retreats within the capital. The only thing that seemed missing here was a toy train station. I wondered if steam engines had ever puffed their way along the lake, and whether Renoir or his companions had arrived with easel and paints and worked from our hotel. If only we could find our hotel.

We were somewhat fatigued after eight hours of up-and-down hiking. Neither of us could get a bead on the elusive Hôtel Les Grillons du Morvan and, as usual, the natives weren't much help. We made two distress phone calls, and the instructions given by the panting, breathless voice on the other end led us back over the dam twice. The granite was beginning to feel unattractive underfoot. After a third call, we realized that one of the hotel's owners assumed we were coming from the south, while the other thought we were coming from the east, though we'd stated in several languages that we'd be arriving from the north. Sunset was upon us. Our hearts sank the farther we walked away from the sparkling lakeshore. We'd hoped to stay in a lakeside room.

Finally, down the main highway, and far from the lake, we found the hotel. No one seemed to be manning the desk. We called out and no one answered, so we unsaddled ourselves and explored what felt like the French retort to a Victorian inn, with neo-Baroque and New Age overlays. The lobby harbored knick-knacks, eclectic, shabby-chic furnishings, and a gutted TV set transformed into a Buddhist shrine. Brazilian lounge-lizard music played. It matched the mauve, purple, pink, and scarlet color theme. As my bafflement and exhaustion ebbed, I began to have an inkling of why we'd been misdirected. There were probably sorcerer's crystals and magnets hidden away. Even a compass would lose its bearings here.

In the fullness of time, our hosts emerged from a back room decked out like vacationers deplaning from Hawaii. They wore wide grins. It was springtime. We'd interrupted something intimate. That explained the panting.

Our shabby chic room was done in shades of lilac scented with lavender, or perhaps it was the other way around. I threw open the window, and in poured fresh air and the sound of cascading water. Below us, the Cure River, released from captivity in the reservoir, gushed from the dam down a spillway, through woods to a holding pond and then onward to our sink in Paris. It wasn't the shoreline hotel I'd imagined, not that it really mattered where we stayed, but I was beginning to take a liking to the place.

In the dusky garden I drank a cold beer—my first of the year—while equally unwisely demolishing a bag of cheese puffs. Junk food never tasted so good. I ordered another of each and wolfed and drank before Alison could show up and stop me. This was very bad, I knew, and I resolved to get back on the straight and narrow instantly. The unseasonable heat was extraordinary.

Quand avril se met en fureur, il est le pire des laboureurs, said the owner, Claire Gillard, presumably quoting from an almanac. Certainly it had been a furious April day—far hotter than normal and possibly not good for the vegetation. That was the gist of the saying. The unexpected hot spell hadn't done much to improve my personal hygiene or wardrobe, which was increasingly wrinkled and rustic.

BEN HUR, BLUEBERRIES AND LES DEMOISELLES DENÈFLES

While resting in our lavender room, Alison read aloud to me from the local newspaper. It was only mid-April, but celebrity director Robert Hossein's planned interpretation of *Ben Hur*, to be held in September in Paris's gigantic soccer stadium, the Stade de France, had already pre-sold 150,000 tickets.

Had France always been as obsessed as I was by enslavement, ancient foes, and the Roman Empire, I wondered?

Posters in the hallway advertised the area's attractions, starting with tree-climbing and tree-draping, whatever that might be. Others ran the gauntlet to Paint Ball, Saint James pilgrimages on the scallop-shell route, river rafting, a prehistory park, Quad/motocross, a summer bagpipe festival in Autun, and an accordion festival in Saint-Léger-sous-Beuvray. Autun also offered a

Gallo-Roman spectacle in its Roman amphitheater, with chari-
oteers and a sound-and-light extravaganza. Rome? Again?

Yet another poster tacked to the wall announced that Lac des
Settons was 1,054 kilometers from . . . Rome . . . and a mere 210
kilometers from Paris. The spirit of Imperial Rome might be with
us, but the Eternal City and the City of Light felt several million
miles away, and I for one did not miss either.

Between courses at dinner downstairs we learned many things.
For a start, the Lac des Settons area was renowned for its timber,
which had once been bound into rafts and floated from here to
Paris. The area also reportedly had great beef and wild bilberries.
The berries grew in the woods, whatever was left of them after
the timbermen had done their work. We also confirmed our suspicions that our hosts Claire and Fabien were not ye olde locals
but rather Parisian *néo-ruraux*. Trendy castaways, they'd moored
themselves here in 2003. Fabien had been the creative director
of a magazine, Claire a corporate consultant. She was now a self-
taught and surprisingly passionate if somewhat baroque chef.
The secret to their easy insertion into the prickly Morvan lay in
Claire's childhood, spent with grandparents on the lake and in
nearby Autun. Tired of the stress of big-city life, they'd hoped to
open a B&B but happened instead upon this abandoned hotel,
an architectural hodgepodge from the mid-1800s. Like the lake,
the hotel had a checkered past.

As suspected, Lac des Settons turned out to be the Second
Empire's "wilderness" counterpart of Paris's 1850-60s parks. This
required further explaining from our hosts.

For decades, Claire told us, little steam trains called "Tacots"
linked the lake and Paris. They took wet-nurses up, and brought
down foundlings and tourists. Settons was the prototype Second
Empire resort—entirely artificial, yet so skillfully made that you
were taken in, or might actually prefer it to Nature. Its pragmatic
creators had envisioned the lake as a reservoir for Paris, a staging

ground for logging, and a vacation spot. By now it had become almost natural, with a century and a half of settling. In the 1990s, a massive clean-up, new sewage system, and ban on motorboats had brought the water quality back to 19th-century levels.

That was reassuring. Our Paris drinking water awaited us below. In the meantime I ordered a bottle of imported San Pellegrino, not a good choice for locavores and the environmentally sensitive, with the excuse that I needed bubbles to be happy. The bubbles helped us get through the long wait as dinner was prepared and served, with doses of history between courses.

For decades, the hotel had belonged to three unmarried sisters from Paris, known locally as Les Demoiselles Denèfles—a polite way to say "the old-maid Denèfles sisters." They'd had "artistic leanings," explained Claire, and one, a professional painter based in Montmartre, had probably painted the naïf landscape mural in the dining room. During the war, the sisters took refuge here and helped the Résistance. They also hid Spanish civil war refugees and Jews in the attic, under the rafters. The hotel had been built in stages. It was a compact but disorienting labyrinth of hallways and rooms. Part of the attic had been rendered inaccessible by poorly planned additions, and the Nazis never discovered several secret rooms.

That night we slept lulled by the cascading water. It was good to know that, like the lake, the hotel had been reborn. For once, a tale of rebirth filled me with joy.

HIP HOP RAPTURE

Dawn's fingers were at it again, tickling the lake as we trooped south along the western shore, heading for a municipal hostel about fifteen miles south in the middle of nowhere. All was still and idyllic and too lovely to be real. Wavelets lapped, ducks and geese quacked—and then the gardeners at a lakeside villa set to work with leaf-blowers and gas-powered hedge trimmers.

As I'd noticed time and again on our walk, the trouble with silence is, it's fragile, easily shattered and quickly forgotten. Cities have no place for it. Once gone, no one knows what it sounds like. Silence has a sound, as the song suggests. A rounded, vibrating three-dimensionality.

My personal pilgrimage was starting to feel more like a quest for silence than anything else.

The Cure River is the principal source for Lac des Settons. But as we discovered by walking its length, many small creeks drain from the hills into its waters. We crossed a swampy spot and at one point I thought I saw the nibbled, piled workmanship of the region's notorious wild beavers. They not only build dams. They chew up cabins, telephone poles, and anything else vaguely wooden they can get their teeth into.

When you stopped to think of it, the lake itself, and the Morvan's other reservoirs, were in fact the results of beavering. No wonder the Celts worshipped the Beaver Goddess, Bibractis. She must've been a toothsome lass, able to fell trees with strong incisors, and control the course of streams with her tail. Every civilization needed water, and in one like the Celts', dependent upon wood for fuel, defense, and housing, you could do worse for protection than hire a beaver.

Wild narcissus rimmed lovely meadows, accompanying us on our woodsy climb past the hamlet of La Chaise toward hilltop l'Huis Prunelle, where we'd reserved bunks for the night. We found the predictable crucifix at a crossroads and followed signs to what's called a *Gîte communal*. As far as we knew, the hostel was the only lodging for miles around.

"Do you hear what I hear?" Alison asked.

I cocked my head. Something thumped. Techno? Gangsta Rap? "Oh, boy," I sighed.

The surreal quality of the scene awaiting us at the top of the rise took us both by surprise. In the hostel's yard, a boombox blared.

Three large rear ends jiggled, hopped, circled, and swayed side by side in mesmerizing rythym. The posteriors belonged to three large, beaming female adolescents whose ancestry suggested not Vercingétorix but rather the Queen of Sheba.

Seven pairs of hiking boots lined the rim of a wellhead in the hostel's yard. On a blanket spread upon the dazzling green lawn sat a woman slighter than the girls, of adult age, possibly thirty years old. She cupped her hands and shouted. The volume came down and the manager of the refuge appeared, a young Frenchman barely out of adolescence, his cheeks prickling with the kind of patchy stubble no designer would lay claim to.

Our dormitory room offered military-style bunks, a writing table, and a lovely view. The boombox thundered again. "You're the only ones in this room," shouted the manager. "There'll be a family next door. The group of kids is on the other side of the showers. It'll be quiet—no music at night."

We took a tour of the Spartan facilities. A Franco-African teenager was busy with a rubber squeegee, drying the floor of the shower room. He looked familiar. But I couldn't place his face.

"It's Craig," I said moments later. "My nephew in Los Angeles. That kid has the exact same facial expression."

Alison seemed unconvinced. "Could be," she waffled. "What's really surprising is the girl, the one dancing in the middle of the group. She looks like your niece Tina. Tina listens to that music and is built like her." Admittedly it was a jarring taste of home and family so far away.

Back outside, the dancers had paused. Two boys stood nearby, awkward and gawky. One was as pale as a Charolais—or Nivernais—bull while the other was as black as the dancing girls. We said hello and nodded. I couldn't help staring at the girl in the middle of the threesome. She did look startlingly like the problem adolescent Tina, my sister's daughter, now adult and thoroughly delightful. I wondered if the girl also wore a stud through her tongue, gorged herself on junk food, and drove an SUV, as Tina once had. Probably not. This child was too young to drive. The multi-ethnic, multi-racial group seemed an accurate reflection of the reality of modern France. Certain nationalistic French may fancy themselves the descendants of Vercingétorix, but in fact the country is now a fondue or perhaps a *salade mixte* of nationalities, in much the same way as America.

It was only mid-afternoon, but it occurred to me that something was missing from the picture, something which could cause pain later. "Nope, no restaurant here," said the manager, fumbling with a rumpled pack of cigarettes. "People who don't bring food with them usually eat in Planchez." He pointed. "It's four kilometers that way by road." That made eight kilometers round trip. Five extra, unexpected miles.

Together we went into his office, found a detailed survey map, and traced a path to food in Planchez. "You can take the shortcut on the Roman road," he said, trying to sound encouraging. "I'll phone and make sure the restaurant is open." That was nice of him. And, yes, there was a Roman road nearby, clearly marked on the map as *Voie romaine*. It ran part of the way to the restaurant.

The chain-smoking manager turned out to be an avid hiker. He was twenty-four years old, had worked for ten years as a baker's assistant and then reinvented himself. "No bakeries around here anymore," he coughed. On his map I traced the Cure River until it disappeared under a blue water-drop symbol. Was this the fountainhead, the source? "The source of the Cure is a couple kilometers from here in the opposite direction," he confirmed. Then he told me exactly how to get to the sacred fountainhead, reminiscing along his garrulous way. "Must be climate change," he surmised; "the water used to be waist-high when I was a boy."

"You mean five years ago?"

He blushed. "Ten or fifteen years ago you could swim in the river. Now. . . ."

"And what's this?" I tapped the map.

"The Bibracte-to-Alésia hiking trail," he said. "Have you heard of Vercingétorix?"

"Vercingétorix?"

Somehow the Gallic warrior's route didn't appear on my map, so the manager made a photocopy of his. If we took the Gallic road from the Source de la Cure, he suggested, with a slight detour we could catch the GR-13 pilgrimage route again a few miles further on. "You can walk in the footsteps of the Gauls," he added, his eyes twinkling.

BEAVERS, MEDLARS, AND VER-CIN-GÉ-TORIX

The woman on the blanket was named Sylvie and she came, she said, from a small village in Côte d'Ivoire—Ivory Coast. She'd lived in France for over half her twenty-seven years and was an *éducatrice spéciale*, a remedial, special-needs instructor. Her charges were the six kids we'd seen with the boombox. They came from a "problem" housing unit on the southeastern side of Paris. It was called La Cité des Néfliers.

"A little mixed up but basically good," Sylvie said. "The girls are doing a Hip Hop performance next week, so they're rehearsing."

The girl who looked like my niece plonked herself down on the wellhead next to the boots. She asked what we were doing here.

"Walking across France," I said.

"You're *walking*? Why don't you drive or take a bus?"

Sylvie laughed. "They're pilgrims."

"What's that?"

I showed our maps and *Topo Guide*, and explained what a pilgrim was. "From here," I said, "to here." I started to tell her about Caesar, Vercingétorix, Saint James, and the pilgrim's route. Her eyes widened.

Murus Gallicus/Gallic rampart, Bibracte, Burgundy.

Vineyards, Cote d'Or, Burgundy.

TOP: Formal garden and vineyard, Mercurey, Burgundy. BOTTOM: Vauban parterre, Chateau de Bazoches, Burgundy.

TOP: Village square, Marigny l'Eglise, Burgundy. BOTTOM: Town square and *Octagon for Saint Eloi*, 1991, Richard Serra, Chagny, Burgundy.

Red fire hydrant on street corner, Meursault, Burgundy.

ABOVE AND OPPOSITE PAGE ALL IMAGES: Blue Madonna statues overlooking vineyards on the Cote d'Or, Burgundy.

Cathedral forest spring, Saone-et-Loire, Burgundy.

"You *must* be crazy," she blurted, bursting out with laughter. "Aren't you kind of old to be doing that?"

Uncanny. She even sounded like Tina. The intonation was identical.

We chuckled at her words. She was right. It *was* crazy to walk across France. And we were, I realized, over thirty years older than she, fossils in comparison.

"How far did you walk today?" she asked.

I showed her the map and Lac des Settons. She whistled backwards as only the French can do, sucking air.

"Do you want to walk with us to the source of the Cure River?" I showed her the map. "There's an ancient Gallic road—right here. The manager says it's only two kilometers. That's four, roundtrip. A breeze."

The girl's eyes widened. "You're going to walk *more*? No way. Walk?"

"And tonight we have to walk another four kilometers to get dinner. Each way."

She hooted, bounded up, and called over her dance partners. "These people are out of their minds," she said. "I'm joking, of course." She batted her eyelashes at her instructor.

A shiver ran down my sciatic nerve. It was Tina. A doppelganger. That was the very same expression and playful, irreverent tone Tina had used when I told her by telephone about our hike. Was this child a distant cousin of Tina's long-dead father, Albert Oates, alias the Cyclops? The Harlem gangster who'd made good in San Francisco's Haight-Ashbury, by marrying a nice, mixed-up middle-class girl with a clotted-cream complexion and a misguided sense of social justice? Albert the Cyclops was a Black Panther, bloated from drink and scarred from street fights, who wore bottle-bottom glasses that seemed to enlarge and merge his angry eyes. What my smart, pretty older sister had seen in him, I would never understand. But she'd had the smarts and the courage to leave him and take the kids with her as soon as she could. When the Cyclops had dropped dead from cardiac arrest aged thirty-five, I'd danced a jig to celebrate. Happily, all that was ancient history.

I sighed, watching the girls dance, all smiles and sass. What future would they forge for themselves in the Cité des Néfliers? It's hard to grow up with fear and hatred in your heart, no matter what the color of your skin.

An hour later, we were still talking with Sylvie and the girls. The boys huddled across the yard, glowering and eavesdropping. The one who'd been upstairs in the shower room appeared. He signaled meekly. Now I recognized him. He was the kid I'd helped out of the river. He'd also been among the helmeted kids on the obnoxious Quads near Dun-les-Places. I waved back.

"Yeah, we did rafting and Quads," confirmed another of the dance trio, a girl whose dream it was, she said, to become an air hostess.

"But the thing we liked best was the cows," said the third girl.

Sylvie explained that these children had never seen a cow before. Or a horse. Or a field. Though born only minutes from downtown Paris in the Cité des Néfliers, they'd never been beyond their housing project, and were equally unacquainted with the City of Light. I asked the first girl if she knew what a *néflier* was. She shook her head. So did the others. I called over the boys and asked them. They shrugged.

"It's a kind of funny-looking fruit tree," I said. "It has small, brownish-orange fruits that are mostly seed. We call them loquats in California. The English call them medlars."

None had known that their housing project was named Loquat City, a baffling discovery.

"The only thing to do is tear down the projects and start over again," said Sylvie. "The problem isn't money or racism; it's isolation." Sylvie had never experienced prejudice or racism, she claimed. She and her parents had spoken little French when they arrived. But they'd integrated, studied, found work, and were happy. She considered herself French, no hyphen needed. "The problem with juvenile delinquency is purely individual," she added. "Most kids in those places are normal. They just don't think they're French, but they're not African either, I can tell you. And though they come from poor families, they think life should be served to them on a platter." She shrugged. "In my humble opinion, the worst thing the government did was abolish the draft in the mid 1990s. Is it a coincidence that that's when the rioting and all the Islamic fundamentalism started? Before that, people were forced to mix, to rub shoulders, and to work."

I turned to the Tina-doppelganger. She was listening intently. "Are you French?" I asked. She made a face but didn't answer me. "I've got a French passport," I volunteered, "but I've also got a problem with pronunciation. Could you help me with a very difficult French name that only the French seem able to say properly?" I got out my digital recorder. "It's something like Vercingét . . . Vércint. . . ."

"Vercingétorix?" she asked, pronouncing the Gallic warrior's name with ease. She rattled off a brief history of the Gauls, confirmed she thought me crazy, and then declaimed "Vercingétorix, Vercingé-torix, Ver-cin-gé-to-rix" in flawless French. I played it back to everyone's delight, and played back the woman at the Résistance museum, and the donkey near Saint-André-en-Morvan.

"You pass the test," I said. "Very French."

We listened several more times, the kids rolling over themselves, laughing, repeating *Vercingétorix, Vercingé-tor-ix* and *Jules César.*

SPRINGS ETERNAL

When the baker had been a boy those many years ago—the distant 1990s—the Cure River rose majestic from these hills and tumbled into Lac des Settons. Or so he claimed.

103

I wanted to see the geyser where our tap water in Paris came from. I wanted to find a water nymph or beaver goddess, a medallion, woolly mammoth tusk, or olifant. We would just have to hike those few extra miles to the Source de la Cure.

Lost already as we hiked down a lonely dirt road behind the hostel, we passed the umpteenth roadside crucifix. This one was made of wood, not stone or iron, and had a niche carved out of it in which sat a plastic Madonna statuette, protected by a wire grate. Behind the Madonna spread swampy woodlands. "Here we are," I said brightly. The woods were called Le Bois de Cure. Our trail plunged into them like a knife in water.

Half an hour later, we stopped to study the photocopied section of surveyor's map. By now we should've been up to our waists in water at the Sources de la Cure. But it took us a good twenty minutes more of wandering to find the small wooden sign by the logging road pointing into thick forest.

The ancient Gallic trail made famous by Caesar's *Conquest of Gaul* lay just beyond the Cure's putative fountainhead. That made sense. Vercingétorix and his fearless men would've needed a watering hole. But there was no sign of water. I scampered and slid into the underbrush. At the bottom of a ravine, a trickle of water welled. The Cure was a leak, a hole in the leafy forest floor. I rinsed my fingertips, wished the water *au revoir* in Paris, and couldn't help looking around for votive offerings left for Bibractis, the damp-eyed goddess of the springs.

"Maybe it gets waist-high a little farther along," I said hopefully as we hiked back to the hostel. "The water table must've fallen, like my arches."

CHRISTMAS IN APRIL

Because there was no food at the hostel, that evening we tramped for miles, famished and rattle-boned, through scented

Christmas-tree plantations on the Roman road from l'Huis Prunelle toward Planchez and dinner. Plastic pots with knee-high conifers peppered the hills. As night fell, I feared we'd have to settle for ham-on-baguette sandwiches at the first café, if we could find a café, and then slog back feeling our way in the dark. Naturally I'd forgotten to bring our flashlight, and felt not only stupid but also irresponsible.

At 7 P.M., we found ourselves on Avenue François Mitterrand, in the center of the narcoleptic "martyr" village of Planchez. It too had been destroyed by the Nazis and rebuilt in haste. The Restaurant-Hôtel le Relais des Lacs appeared before our eyes. A mirage? We knocked the mud off our boots, tidied our clothes, and succeeded in rousing a chambermaid. It was early for dinner, she said, eyeing us. The Morvan was not the maid's native land. She seemed glad to alternate English with her rough French, and said her home in Istanbul did feel rather distant.

We had the place to ourselves. All the better, since we were underdressed and musky. This looked like a serious provincial gourmet restaurant, with starched gray and blue tablecloths, blue candles in silver candlestick holders, and oversized wine glasses. A prim hostess busied herself. There had been a change in ownership, she said. The new boss was a mysterious-sounding Parisian named Philippe Morinay. Another Philippe?

Plied with bite-sized delicacies to keep us from swooning, soon we were into serious gluttony, of the kind I'd long excelled at but had foresworn. There was no need to diet, though, when walking twenty miles a day, I told myself, ordering rack of lamb with roasted garlic, leek tops, carrots, and a caloric, unctuous potato casserole. Alison opted for the whole roast squab. It barely had time to alight before she polished it off. So much for the baguette sandwich.

As we enjoyed our pudding-like *fondants au chocolat* dessert, a contingent of Belgians arrived, already lubricated and broadcasting the scent of hoppy beer. Caesar had skirmished with the Belgae, the fierce Celtic ancestors of our fellow diners. Two thousand years ago, they'd swept swords-drawn from Germany into Holland, Belgium, and France, dragging behind wagonloads of womenfolk and children, terrorizing, looting, and eventually taking over and melding with the locals. Now they spoke passable French, arrived natty in luxury cars, and bore thick wallets. Everyone seemed happy.

I glanced at the clock. It was 8:30 P.M., the start of dinner for most Europeans. We eavesdropped and divined that François Mitterrand had stopped here many times during his regularly scheduled Burgundian Résistance pilgrimages. From our hostess we learned Mitterrand was polite and *correct*—wonderful French understatement meaning "okay" when "great" is needed. But my attention span began to slip as the many miles on our meters tugged down my eyelids.

Dapper, tanned, and radiating ease, the establishment's owner Monsieur Morinay surveyed the dining room. He wondered why we were lodged in the dreary municipal hostel when he had thirty rooms upstairs. We hadn't known of his hotel, I explained. When he heard we had no flashlight and had already walked twenty miles, he gallantly offered to drive us back. It was a long walk but a short ride. Very short, it transpired.

En route at 100-plus kph, the dashing Morinay talked nonstop and solved a riddle that had perplexed me all evening. What were a glitzy guy and a restaurant with blue candles doing in an isolated village like Planchez? "Nothing to do with Druids or spirituality, is it?" I asked. He chuckled. He too had grown tired of the stress of the Paris area, he said. The allure of the Morvan and the tourist-rich lakes of Setton and Pannecière appealed to his business sense and love of sailing.

This was disappointing news. Here was another urban refugee. "You've moved to the mountains to sail?" I gripped the armrests of the car as we slid around a corner. "This looks like Christmas-tree heaven, not the French Riviera."

"It's the live Christmas-tree capital of Europe," Morinay chuckled again. "From late October to Christmas Eve, this road is bumper-to-bumper with trucks. The plantations extend all around. They work around the clock." He pointed to floodlights, now dark, and a trucking facility.

I blinked, thinking of Santa Claus and Roman roads and how, during the Empire, relay teams of oyster-runners had carried baskets of exotic bivalves from Brittany to Rome in a mere four days. It was taking us a lot longer than that to hike across the Morvan. How long did it take a Christmas tree from Planchez to reach Paris? A matter of hours, Philippe said proudly. I stifled the temptation to express concern for the way the magnificent forest of the Druids had become a trashed tree plantation. At least it was still a forest of some kind.

Like magic, the car skidded to a halt. The next moment, the hostel loomed dark and quiet before us. We hit our bunks and awoke before dawn to the barking of dogs. "I'm not sure why," I said, rubbing my eyes, "but this time I dreamed of pearls and gladiators and François Mitterrand."

IT'S SOCRATES, SHERLOCK

After many embraces and handshakes and promises to meet up with the project kids again at the Cité des Néfliers, of whom we had grown unexpectedly fond, we hiked away from l'Huis Prunelle heading for Anost, saluted the caged Madonna and the fountain-head of the Cure River, and picked up the Bibracte-to-Alésia Gallic trail that Vercingétorix had used to escape from Caesar in 52 BC. Morning sun brushed the tips of the fir trees. The air smelled of lemon and spices. We had many miles to hike today, but I looked forward to experiencing firsthand a slice of Gallo-Roman history.

Nowadays the Gauls' ancient road goes by the name Route Forestière des Potrons. It looks much like any other logging road, attractive in parts where mature trees grow, scruffy in others. There are no monuments on it to Vercingétorix or Caesar, and the signage is minimal. To appreciate it, you need to come equipped with a sense of history, a good map, and a love of forestry cycles.

We knew from reading that in the ancient world, the woods were solid beech at altitudes of over 700 meters—about 2,200 feet above sea level. Mixed beech and oak and ash grew at lower levels. But for the last century, Douglas fir has taken over. *Les Doog-lass*, as the Burgundians call them, grow like proverbial weeds. They're handsome trees in a random, natural setting. Commercial timber plantations of tightly packed, precision-aligned Douglas firs are lightless and sinister, however, like the insides of abandoned industrial plants, or freeway underpasses.

We climbed Mont Martin with great anticipation, hoping to find some trace of Vercingétorix, and came instead upon stacks of freshly felled firs. Some had trunks as thick as wine barrels and appeared to be centuries old. Stripped of their branches, they looked like beached whales. I sat atop one, waiting for Alison and enlightenment. To kill time, I counted the tree's growth rings and suddenly felt very old.

Impossible, I muttered. I recounted, unable to believe I was older than the tree by five years. No wonder the species had won out. To grow this large, a beech needs twice as long—a century or more. The thought of living to be a hundred filled me with dread. It meant I wasn't even halfway there. When Dante wrote in *The Inferno* of being lost in a deep dark forest "in the middle of our life's journey" he was talking about being thirty or thirty-five years old, the age of a mid-life crisis back in the early 1300s. We weren't even halfway across Burgundy, either, I reflected, though our hike wasn't Dantesque, not in the sense of seeing the tortures of the damned and learning what the fear of God really meant.

The poet had evolved during his journey, had come out a better man—having placed his enemies somewhere within the circles of Hell. Was I evolving or still meandering in Limbo?

Alison waved at me from a hundred yards away. It was a warning wave, I could tell. Earlier, we'd both heard the whine of motocross bikes. Now I understood. Her signal meant she would capture the bikers with her camera. I tempered my rage by remembering the kids from the Cité des Néfliers. No, I told myself, I would not want *their* heads lopped off by piano wire.

Moments later, four motorcycles flew by, spraying gravel and dirt. One popped a wheelie, making his mount rear up on its back wheel, like the boy on the Quad in Vézelay. Weren't they talented at channeling their testosterone? All four riders wore expensive leather body suits and shiny, multi-colored helmets with corporate logos writ large, the heraldry of our day.

Silence returned and a mile south, in what appeared to be the middle of nowhere, and probably was, we came upon a wild boar park. It resembled the deer park of the day before yesterday, except that here we saw no animals, only their tracks and traces—polished tree trunks and trenches dug with tusks. An arrow pointed down a logging road to something called Maquis Socrate. We recognized the name from Mitterrand's Résistance museum in Saint Brisson.

At a crossing of unpaved logging roads beyond the back of beyond, stood a rudimentary memorial to the two thousand fighters once based here. There were no barracks or physical reminders of Maquis Socrate. I wondered if any of the Résistants were still alive.

With our surveyor's map we navigated unmarked forest paths, re-crossed the Bibracte-to-Alésia Gallic trail, and picked up the GR-13 secular trekking route on a picturesque hillside cloaked in native deciduous beeches, their branches about to bud. Another fountainhead gave rise to a rivulet called the Chênelet. It grew as we followed it downhill, merging with other creeks to form an entrancing stream.

Across the valley south of us, a hillside appeared to have been painted with green letters spelling "NAUDET." The word meant nothing to either of us. As we pondered the mysterious message, a young Frenchman carrying a bridle came along, whistling.

"Naudet?" he laughed. "You're not the first to ask. It's the last name of a tree-farmer from Anost, the village around that bend in the road." He pointed. "Look carefully and you'll see the letters aren't painted. They're formed by two species of fir tree. One type provides the background, the other the letters." And reflect a large ego, I was about to add.

With our eyes fixed on NAUDET, we tramped a mile or more into Anost thinking of Benito Mussolini and his self-aggrandizing, propagandistic use of trees. Back in the 1930s in the Italian Apennines, Mussolini's followers felled pines to spell out D-U-X, Latin for *Duce*, Fearless Leader. Fearless Mussolini may have been, but not eternal. Italian *Resistenza* fighters strung the dictator up by his heels in Milan in 1945 and filled him with eight hundred rounds of lead. However, DUX was still legible on the Apennine hillside, the trees maintained by Fascist zealots.

Some things die hard in Old Europe, I mused. Fascism is one of them. Smoking is another. Despite anti-smoking campaigns and laws, the rules are bent and broken in many clever ways. The key to our hotel room in Anost was hidden in a bluegray cloud of tobacco fumes. It hung behind the counter of the Sherlock Holmes Pub on the sloping main street of the village. The lanky young Gauloise-puffing bartender did not look remotely like Holmes or Watson. As he handed us the key, he told us the owners of the hotel, bar, pizzeria, restaurant, and B&B, and much else in Anost, had imported the Sherlock Holmes Pub from England.

That the town's first family would be admirers of Sherlock Holmes seemed elementary. Like almost everyone else in

Anost old enough to remember World War Two, they were grateful to *les Anglo-Saxons* in the guise of the RAF and USAF, the angels of the skies who'd parachuted supplies to the Résistance.

Our room appeared to have been furnished in the 1890s. It was unusually large and comfortable by French standards. Outside on the main drag, tractors pulling wagonloads of manure thundered past the hotel. It was the season for mucking out the stables. Apparently the cows had been busy.

After several days in the wilderness, pocketsized Anost felt like a real town, with a church and cemetery, two mini-markets, a post office, restaurants and lodging, and a movie theater open twice weekly. Every stone in the tilting streets offered a view over tiled roofs to the surrounding forested hills and NAUDET.

We stocked up on chocolate, candy, fruit, band-aids, and bottles of water at the grocery before contemplating a visit to the church. Part of the landmark edifice went back to the 12th century, said our *Topo Guide*. But there was good reason to suspect something older lay underneath. As we poked around the aisles, we spotted two life-size effigies of a knight in armor, clutching a sword, and his consort in a long, straight dress. A sign identified them as Girart de Roussillon and his noble wife, Berthe, the founders of Vézelay.

What were they doing here? Girart and Berthe died in the late 800s AD, the sign reminded visitors. That meant the church, or part of it, was over 1,100 years old.

The news was disconcerting. It should not have come as a surprise. Had I done my math correctly, I would've realized Girart was a century too young to have died with Roland at Roncevaux in 778 AD, as *The Song of Roland* purports. It meant that the bone in my backpack could not belong to Vézelay's noble founder. Girart's mortal coil never made it north of Anost.

"The bone?" Alison asked with a crocodilian smile.

"The good news is we're hiking on the trail they used, the real pilgrim's trail, not the one those zealots in Vézelay concocted for tourist-pilgrims," I countered.

"That's unfair," Alison said. "They told us all trails were pilgrimage routes. The important thing is to set out and get there, wherever you're going. This route may be more historically valid than theirs, that's all. Everyone knows pilgrims have been passing through Anost for over a thousand years."

"Everyone? Really? Shall we phone my brother in Las Vegas and ask him if he knows that?"

Anost, world famous? Before becoming a martyr village and center for the French Résistance, Anost was known in France from the mid-1500s to late 1800s as the capital of the Morvan's *galvachers* and *flotteurs de bois*. They were, respectively, lumberjacks with oxteams that dragged trees from the forests down riverbeds or flumes to lakes, and the raftsmen who lashed the logs together and floated them to Paris. There were thousands of them and they supplied the capital with its burning wood for about four hundred years. Like the modern timber multinationals currently cleaning out Siberia and the Amazon, however, the Morvan's loggers also chopped themselves out of business. The environmental damage they wreaked must have been spectacular. A by-product of their hack-and-drag logging technique was the legion of colorful, Paul Bunyan characters who had lived in Anost.

That was why we wanted to visit the Maison des Galvachers museum. It stands behind the monument to the Maquis Socrate and is the town's main attraction. With dusk approaching, we hurried to enter the building just as a group of seniors was stepping out. One of the party broke away, introduced herself as Michelle Desmoulin, the mayor of Anost, and apologized that the museum was closed. We asked if she had any literature to give us on the timbermen of Anost and the Maquis Socrate.

"Better," she said; "I happen to have a live *maquisard* you can meet. He fought with the Résistance up there." She introduced us to a handsome, upright, blue-eyed octogenarian gentleman named Robert Ducreux.

Here was Doctor Watson, by Jove, complete with gray fedora. The more I studied Ducreux, the more I thought not of Watson but of Jean Gabin playing Simenon's Inspector Maigret, or Burt Lancaster in *From Here to Eternity*. How Hollywood failed to import a man as handsome and dignified as Robert Ducreux after the war, I do not know.

IN THE END, WE CREATED EUROPE

During the Great War of 1914–1918, about a fifth of the male inhabitants of Anost died under arms. One of them was Robert Ducreux's father. When in 1940 the Nazis occupied France, the young Ducreux, like thousands of others, was faced with the prospect of collaborating, being deported to a forced-labor camp in Germany, or joining the Résistance. Many French families were torn apart at the time, with one son buckling, another standing firm.

"It was war," Ducreux told us. "You had to do it." He downplayed his courage.

We asked about Maquis Socrate, the secret camp in the hills. "Socrates" was the codename for Georges Leyton, a National Forestry Officer. Leyton headed to the hills northwest of Anost in February 1944. His right-hand man was also a Forestry Officer, Marel Gey, who knew every path through the woods. With the help of sympathetic locals, the members of Maquis Socrate set up a camp several miles away from the nearest road. Back then, only a handful of paved roads crossed the Morvan.

"The monument you saw in the woods is where the Nazis parked their trucks when they came looking for us," Ducreux explained with a wry smile. "We could see them, but they couldn't see us. They never found the camp."

Only a few now remember where the Résistance camp stood. "We should preserve it," the mayor commented, bustling around. "It's a *lieu de mémoire*—a place of historic significance."

Ducreux said softly, "There's nothing left."

We talked for what seemed a very long time, and were joined by Ducreux's wife, Solange. She remembered how the Nazis had swept into farmhouses, like the one where she'd lived with her parents. The Nazis stole supplies, slaughtered animals, and bundled off the bloody meat in the bedsheets, she said, adding insult to injury. They also murdered and tortured anyone suspected of aiding the maquisards. They were not alone in their work. A special branch of the Vichy-sponsored French paramilitary Milice, called *Gardes Mobiles de Réserve* or GMR, worked closely with the Gestapo. They tracked down deserters, *réfractaires* who refused to collaborate, and maquisards. It was the French GMR that ambushed the *maquisard* Marel Gey, tortured and killed him. "He didn't talk," Ducreux said grimly. "He didn't lead them to our camp."

For Ducreux and his wife, every street in the village, and every turn in each forest road, still had a memory attached. There, in the field of wildflowers above town, the Nazis had shot François Basdevant, a seventeen-year-old, and his friend André Feffer, eighteen. The boys had been sent to Anost on "holiday" to escape battle zones in the north.

In the farmhouse across the way, a sixteen-year-old girl named Huguette Pahin was killed. "From the terrace of your hotel—the Sherlock Holmes Pub nowadays—they took potshots," said the mayor. "Huguette was looking out of the window of her parents' farm. . . ."

Ducreux explained the modus operandi of fellow Résistants at Maquis Socrate. Attacks on Nazi convoys, infrastructure, and trains could only be executed far from inhabited areas, he said, or reprisals would be immediate and devastating. So the maquisards were often on the move, at night. They walked for miles in the woods, down hunters' paths and dirt roads not marked on maps. Recruitment was tricky. Candidates were somehow directed by word of mouth to Résistants working undercover in cities, towns, and villages. These operatives were known as *Indicateurs*, because they indicated the route the vetted recruits would take to find their way to the Maquis. Later, in colloquial French the term *Indicateur* came to mean stool pigeon or police informant. Each maquisard did nightwatch several times a week. They worked in pairs, posted along a perimeter two kilometers around the camp.

"That was the most dangerous work," Ducreux recalled. "You were exhausted, hungry, sleepy, but you had to stay alert. You were carrying a heavy machine gun and waiting for the Nazi trucks to drive up. We wrapped ourselves in old parachutes to keep warm." He paused, becoming thoughtful. "The Allied planes flew low sometimes. When they'd heard one of our farmhouses or villages had been attacked, they'd tip their wings in salute." He paused again, his eyes glistening. "We were very glad to have America on our side in 1914 and 1940," Ducreux added quietly. "I'm honored to meet the children of Americans whose fathers fought in the Pacific."

We weren't sure where he got the idea of the Pacific, but didn't have the heart to correct him. My father had fought in Italy, Alison's in the Atlantic. It didn't matter. As Ducreux said, it was war, and, I suppose, our fathers, like him, had felt they'd had to sign up. I couldn't help wondering what young German tourists felt when they saw war and Résistance monuments in each and every French village, testimonials to the barbarity of their Nazi forebears.

"It's a point we're debating," the mayor answered. "Some think we should remove 'Allemands' and put in 'Nazis,' because it wasn't the Germans but the Nazis who committed atrocities."

"We hold no grudge," Ducreux said. "A few years ago my wife and I traveled around Germany and found the people very hospitable. Those days are over. We created Europe out of that hateful war."

I had one last question. What about François Mitterrand? Was he a collaborationist spy who reinvented himself, or a real freedom fighter? Ducreux looked askance. He tipped his fedora back and said, *En politique, y'a à boire et à manger.* Literally, it meant "in politics, there's food and drink to be had." I took it to mean that every politician has his snout in the trough, and his actions are determined by pork-barrel considerations and power. "Mitterrand got going the wrong way, then he saw the way the wind was blowing," Ducreux continued. "He changed course in time. And he married an authentic Résistante, Danielle, *une vraie maquisarde.* She was in Cluny."

Whether Mitterrand's marriage to a bona fide Burgundian Résistance figure had been driven by love and revelation, or was another calculated move on the part of the wily Sphinx, history will probably never know. Similarly, the mystery of François Mitterrand's lifelong loyalty to war villains such as René Bousquet, the notorious Milice officer and war criminal who for decades escaped arrest, is sure to remain unanswered. Too much still rides on Mitterrand's legacy. Too many active French politicians, bureaucrats, and political commentators made their careers in the Sphinx's shadow. What's even more mysterious is, despite the many damaging revelations about his past, Mitterrand remains a hero to millions of Frenchmen, including current French president François Hollande.

LET IT COME DOWN

Everyone knows Henri Contet was born in 1904 and wrote the songs that Edith Piaf and Yves Montand crooned. Well, a few music buffs know this obscure fact, which we learned that evening. Contet lived in a humble two-story house facing the church and butcher shop of Anost.

Another Anost resident who was authentically famous is composer Francis Poulenc. His wet-nurse came from here and, perhaps in search of the milk and honey of youth, he returned each summer in his sunset years. A plaque on a village house also states that Poulenc's music was "inspired by the wild woods" of the Morvan. That sounded accurate in a paradoxical way. "Wild" hereabouts means tamed by millennia of civilization and logging.

Poulenc was a fallen Catholic, uncomfortable with his faith. It's said he rediscovered God at the shrine of the Black Virgin of Rocamadour and bolstered his faith while here in Anost. Was it the wild woods, the rain, or the antiquity of the site that restored him to the church? Perhaps the presence of pious Girart and Berthe in the parish church, or the rare pilgrim passing under his windows had some effect? More probably the rapprochement arose from Poulenc's proximity to finitude, and the creeping realization shared by many imperfect creatures that the end is nigh and fertilizing the forest doesn't sound like a promising career move. Better a starry sky and shepherds than a compost heap.

Anost's current celebrity inhabitant is the Falstaffian innkeeper René Fortin. He and his wife Catherine appear to own everything in town, including the hotel we were lodging in, and the restaurant we were about to dine in. A sign outside the establishment informed impatient clients that René "is alive and well and resting, a true *Morvandiau*." We had not yet seen René in the flesh but somehow felt we knew him.

A dozen local boozers propped up the bar in a blue-gray Gauloise fog. On a wooden table sat a gift. The barman wore a tuxedo and bowtie. Had we stumbled into a party? A golden-handshake dinner or village fête, with locals in fancy dress? Some of the group looked crusty, like lumberjacks; others were clearly white-collar workers on vacation.

A pair of large human Cheshire Cats smiled at us as we entered. Conversation stopped to allow the locals to observe us. We threaded past, holding our breath. Once the merrymakers determined we were out of earshot, the party resumed. We took the farthest possible table, next to a window, in a vain attempt to avoid the smoke. The bartender was also our waiter.

"That's quite a Gauloise barbecue you've got going in there," I said.

"No nonsmoking section yet, darling," he chirped. "This isn't Paris."

A large diamond stud in his left earlobe sparkled, suggesting the contrary. Lithe and stylish, he swerved between the tables and seemed to have mistaken La Galvache for a Parisian nightclub. I asked if the robust couple in the entrance were the celebrated Mr. and Mrs. René Fortin.

"How did you guess?" he quipped. "Monsieur Fortin does look a little like Sherlock Holmes, doesn't he?"

There couldn't have been a greater contrast between our bouncy, ironic waiter and the restaurant's clientele and owners. The décor, comfortingly provincial, circa 1970, with wall sconces and white tablecloths, matched the sumptuous, creamy food.

"Either they're local bureaucrats or lumber merchants," I ventured, nodding toward the group in the bar. "It's a retirement party."

"Maybe one is Monsieur Naudet," Alison speculated. "It's definitely a birthday party."

They finished their volatile aperitifs, moved from the bar into the dining room and switched to bottles of vintage Vosne-Romanée from a big-name vineyard in Burgundy's Côte d'Or. No expense was being spared. Eventually, the birthday boy stood, opened a card and, much to our surprise, declaimed a poem by Charles Baudelaire.

Old Paris is gone . . . he quoted. *No human heart changes half as fast as a city's face.* . . .

It was as if a truck driver in South Dakota had suddenly quoted Walt Whitman. Garrison Keillor would've felt right at home.

So, the birthday boy was from Paris, or had worked there and retired to the Morvan? I could see they would keep us guessing.

Our waiter grimaced when asked for bottled mineral water. He brought out a pitcher of Anost's best, from a local spring. "I can't speak for the rest of what we offer, but the water is good," he quipped. Then he noted that there used to be too much of a good thing—Anost averaged 1,500 millimeters of rain a year, making it one of France's wettest spots. "It used to rain every day, but now it's only every two or three days, hardly any rain at all." Precipitation was down fifty percent over the last decade, he claimed. "We risk becoming normal, like everywhere else, a desert, practically."

OF LOGS AND TURQUOISE UNDIES

Today was going to be a very long and challenging day. We'd reserved a room at a place called Crot Morin, near Mont Beuvray, site of Bibracte, the "Lost City" of the Gauls. I estimated we'd be hiking for about ten hours.

An hour south of Anost near Bussy, Alison spotted a wood pile worthy of the Guggenheim or Whitney—a work of land art. She paused to photograph the meticulously stacked logs and kindling. No sooner had she raised her camera than out of a farmhouse popped a squint-eyed lumberjack. He cradled his jaw and wondered aloud why anyone in his right mind would want to immortalize the stuff he'd cut and would soon burn.

We took the opportunity to get the lowdown from him on the forestry situation. We'd heard an official version at the Morvan's park headquarters and had read widely about environmental issues in newspapers and guidebooks. Here was the vox populi.

Douglas firs "ripen" on average in a mere thirty years, said the lumberjack, and therefore have replaced other commercial timber species, not to mention native trees. Three other types of European fir, and some broadleaf forests, have survived against the odds. The *Office National des Fôrets* manages French forests private and communal nationwide, and auctions off lots to be "harvested" by the big timber companies. Few smalltime operators are left. The majors come in with state-of-the-art equipment, the same kind used in Siberia and the Amazon: towering machines designed to clamp, saw, lift, trim, and stack trees with admirable speed. Outsized trailer trucks with built-in cranes pick up the logs stacked at "platforms." The nature of the equipment explains why clear-cutting has replaced traditional select-cutting. Gone are the little old lumberjacks with their little old chainsaws, tractors, and local lumbermills.

That was excellent for free trade, I remarked, but as we'd heard from Morvan park officers, the heavy machinery reconfigured forest roads and lands, simultaneously causing soil compaction and erosion. The streams were clogged with silt, which was hard on everything from crayfish to trout and vacationing swimmers, and probably didn't do much for the quality of our Paris drinking water, either.

I had to wonder whether the Paul Bunyan-style chop, drag, and float had been any less damaging. The lumberjack shrugged. "It'd be hard to imagine anything worse than what's going on now," he said cheerfully. "I'd call it a disaster."

We walked on toward the hamlet of Athez, pronounced Ah-thay, which sounded comfortingly like *athée*, meaning "atheist."

At the top of the next forest ridge, cloaked by mossy trees and boulders, we stopped for a picnic. We'd bought baguettes from the bakery in Anost and, for a change, Alison had picked out an unusual filling: pig tongues in aspic. The tongues were braised in seasonings, split open, and conserved in aspic—and looked like dead slugs or the pickled organs of saints.

"Tongues of fire," I said, puzzled by Alison's choice. "I've seen these displayed in reliquaries in better churches in Rome," I added, "and have always wondered what they tasted like." Alison rolled her eyes. I braced myself, but neither a tongue nor eye lashing was forthcoming.

Perched on rocks in the thin shade of a beech tree, we were about to taste the tongues when the air was rent. "Another Mirage?" I asked, looking up. No, it was not a fighter aircraft but rather Alison's high-tech hiking pants. They had burst open, splitting down the seams, as spectacular an event as it was unexpected: Alison runs to raw bone and muscle. Her turquoise underwear seemed to scream from under the shredded pants.

"I must've put on weight," she said, twisting and turning and trying to figure out what to do. She did not have spare pants with her. My extras were far too big.

"At least we're not likely to run into crowds out here," she said. No sooner had the words left her lips than a pair of hikers appeared.

"Don't stand up," I whispered.

The young men huffed and puffed, held up their hands in salute, and without stopping said *bonjour!* It's not a French habit, we'd learned, to stop for a chat unless forced. It's not manly. Vercingétorix never indulged in chit-chat with strangers.

Once they'd disappeared, we feasted on the heavenly pig tongues, which were at least as tender, and considerably tastier, than beef tongue. I couldn't help staring at Alison's turquoise undies.

"Kmart," she said, "in Santa Rosa, near the hospital. Remember?"

How could I forget? She'd bought them on a visit to California, and had chosen the brightest colors and snazziest designs, largely because her niece had told her to stop wearing "granny undies."

"What would Jessica say now?" Alison laughed.

I thought of the Kmart outlet and how the prim woman at the check-out stand had averted her eyes from the undies, and asked us if we would please scan in our purchases. "We're instructing clients on how to do self-check out," the woman had said. "The procedure is very easy."

We followed her instructions, all three of us aware that her job was to put herself and coworkers out of a job, and that her smile and restrained gestures were being captured on video.

Upon our boulder with our pig-tongue sandwiches in hand, I thought now about the frightened courtesy of the Kmart check-out woman and the plucky brusqueness of her French counterparts—proud, prickly workers protected by unions, the kind that fought for such things as debilitating obligatory retirement benefits, enervating health care, and those subversive paid vacations and other unnecessary things we'd wisely eliminated back home. We were worlds apart, France and America, despite globalization. But how much longer would the throwbacks here in Europe wedded to the "welfare state" be able to hold out? There was nothing like a global financial crisis and recession to put them out of their misery.

PAST PERFECT

Another Roman road—this time the one from Autun to Orléans—appeared near the village of Roussillon-en-Morvan. We hadn't planned to hike through it to get to our B&B at Crot Morin. Intersecting the village on the straightaway was another long-distance hiking route, the "GR Tour du Morvan." That was the trail the tortoise-woman of Cure was following.

Somehow, despite our peerless map-reading skills, we got turned around not once but twice, and wound up on the umbrella-swirled terrace of a café on Roussillon's main square. Alison sat down quickly, hiding her torn pants. Around us, weathered houses and a many-times rebuilt manor propped each other up.

A serendipitous realization struck as we sipped our espressos. About 1,200 years ago, Roussillon-en-Morvan had been home to none other than Girart de Roussillon, the by now familiar pious founder of Vézelay, the Christian knight who somehow, despite being born in the wrong century, got drafted by the author of *Song of Roland* to die in the Pyrenees alongside the fearless Roland and the Peers of France, not to mention Charlemagne, who would have been a bicentenarian, with a long white beard But unlike Roland, Charlemagne did not die at Roncevaux, and there was plenty of documentation about his life. French history was confusing enough when it was told straight. When its own chroniclers scrambled things for political purposes, it was impossible to follow.

For once, the innkeeper who served us was friendly, and he gladly confirmed these little-known facts of misinformation as he filled us with a second round of strong coffee. "Girart de Roussillon would not have been born yet," he noted. "You must never look for linear logic in legend."

Another over-educated provincial, the innkeeper also confirmed our suspicions that he was a *néo-rural*, a reformed Parisian, slightly better versed in *The Song of Roland* than your average countryman. He and his partner had moved to the village recently, hoping to take advantage of the Morvan's natural beauty and live a semi-retired lifestyle.

"We wanted out of the big city," he continued, "and we thought we'd have plenty of time to take walks, but we're far too busy." He was out of breath as he said these words and mopped his brow. A voice from within the restaurant summoned him. He dashed away, never to be seen again, not by us, anyway.

Another customer shading herself from the unexpected sun also admitted to being a recently recycled refugee from urban civilization. She too was busier than expected, forced daily to drive long distances. "In the countryside everything is spread out," she said, as if that could be a revelation. "There are a lot of things you don't think of when you decide to leave the city."

With these wise words in mind, and coffee in our bloodstreams, we figured out what had befallen us. Because of lack of caffeine, we'd strayed down the wrong GR route—the tortoise route. Now we were off our maps, though not completely lost.

"It's that-a-way," Alison said, pointing south with one hand while holding her pants together with the other.

"Right," I agreed with moderate skepticism. "I mean left." I switched on my digital recorder, played Donkey Hotey for us, and limped along, braying with the kind of laughter which can only be induced by physical exhaustion.

A PAIN IN THE BACK

At a hotel-restaurant called Auberge de la Canche on the main modern highway to Autun, we stopped to ask directions for the third time. Alison stayed outside, hiding her torn pants and turquoise undies. I said, "I'm afraid we're lost," and the waiter retorted, "You're not lost, you're here. You're found!"

Throaty laughter rose from the tables around us in the restaurant's old-fashioned dining room. It was the kind of place where French hunters gather to drink amphoras of wine and devour wild boar with Vercingétorix sauce. "Next time you'll come here on purpose, not by mistake," added the waiter. The laughter rose again, as if from a tin can.

Why did I get the impression he'd recited these lines before?

After more good-natured banter, I once again asked the young man to show us how to get back onto our map. "Better get another map," he quipped. "We're not on this one."

Finally he and his father, brother, sister, and several diners took turns telling us to cross the highway, making sure we weren't run over because "the cars make shepherd's pie out of hikers around here." On the far side of the highway, we would find another, better, more beautiful hiking trail than the one we'd originally meant to take.

"Which is why you're not lost," he said. "You're lucky. You've strayed onto the right path. It follows the Canche River Gorge, the most beautiful river in France!"

Only somewhat skeptical, we crossed the highway and walked on the shoulder for about a hundred yards, Alison crabbing to hide her underwear. The cars were not many, but they hurtled by us like Gallic chariots bent on playing Coliseum Chicken. The waiter, his family, and several diners stood outside to watch. Either they wanted to make sure we found the trailhead safely, or hoped to see shepherd's pie.

This was our day for serendipitous discoveries. The trail coiled down into the gorge, crossed the foaming white waters of the Canche, and followed the creek's east bank. The scenery was as lovely as its Cure counterpart but more dramatic, a kind of mini-Yosemite. The presence of a small power plant and a large steel pipe creeping like a caterpillar across the mountainside didn't subtract from the spot's beauty, possibly because it reminded me of the abandoned Gold Rush mining works of my beloved Sierra Nevada mountains. Our friends from the restaurant appeared to have spoken the truth.

Once beyond the jumbo pipe, the trail paralleled the creek, crossing back and forth. Striated mossy cliffs were cut by cascades. Lichen-frosted boulders and bearded trees rose up, and the mesmerizing chant of water rushing over stone, wood, and sand led us deeper into the canyon. The trouble was, the trail petered out after a mile and a half. Unused to hikers' boots, the hillside gave underfoot as we tried to scramble up it, and over I went, with a clack of the knee and a click of the back.

"Nothing serious," I lied, picking myself up. "I can get an artificial knee at the B&B." I had promised myself to keep blisters, heat, pebbles in shoes, aching knees, and other impediments to Enlightenment out of mind and off the page. But, as I hauled myself along, silently singing *I think I can I think I can I think I can*, I knew this was the beginning of my very own martyrdom in D minor.

LIMP ALONG, LITTLE DOGIES

By dint of clawing, we made it up to the curlicue paved road atop the gorge and headed in what we hoped was the right direction. Neither one of us had a compass. If we were fortunate enough to run into anyone, we could ask for La Croisette, Le Haut Folin or Mont Beuvray—and triangulate from these points of reference to our B&B. Not that we were likely to run into anyone, which suited Alison fine, since her pants had torn open another six inches, exposing her long, shapely thighs.

"We've been walking how long now?" I asked rhetorically, through gritted teeth. "About six days? And have you noticed anything?"

"Several hundred things," Alison said. "You're limping and wincing, for one."

"Not that. I mean, two things in particular have dawned on me today. First of all, we haven't seen a single other pilgrim. Not a one. I thought I'd be flashing my scallop shell like a badge. Second, the people no longer run away from us when we enter villages. They seem friendlier or, put it this way, less unfriendly."

"You're no longer thrusting your water bottles at them or begging for food," Alison said. "But I agree. I think we've crossed into the Saône-et-Loire."

She was referring to the administrative *département* of southernmost Burgundy, which runs south from Anost to Mâcon, and happens to be one of the country's largest and least populated districts. Funnily, the Saône-et-Loire corresponds to the medieval region called Le Charolais, land of the big white cows we'd seen everywhere. Le Charolais also corresponds almost exactly to the territory of the ancient Aedui tribe of Gaul. According to Caesar, the citadel of Bibracte, the "Lost City" atop Mont Beuvray, was among the Aedui's most important fortified strongholds. As the arrow flies, it was probably fifteen miles south of where we stood. But for modern pilgrims such as we on the secular and serpentine GR route, Bibracte still lay south a day and a half of tortuous trekking.

ONE NIGHT A TRAVELER

Disinformation is the specialty of many governments, including our very own. We wondered which—French or Nazi—had been responsible for the signs pointing to mirages with place-names such as "Maquis Maurice"—an elusive Résistance encampment— and "Bois du Roi"—of which there seemed to be two, separated by several miles, two ridges, and a valley. Perhaps the signage was Maurice's joke? The Maurice of the Maquis Maurice? Was this a wartime leftover designed to misdirect the occupiers?

We hiked past a solitary sequoia looking very much out of place at La Croisette, an empty, shuttered mountain refuge at a crossroads. The hamlet of Crot Morin and therefore our *chambre d'hôtes* was sign-posted by the wayside as being somewhere down a curving paved road. "Paved" was the key word. We preferred not to take the road, given the state of our joints and vertebrae, and the danger posed by road warriors. Asphalt seems particularly rude after ten miles on springy dirt trails, especially if you've twisted your knee and thrown out your back as I had in the Gorges de la Canche. I could barely walk.

The sun was starting to dip. We put our confidence in a well-worn farm road. It seemed scenic and old and in the Roman style, with the occasional pile of mossy slabs that had probably been paving stones. Pastures and woodland on steep hillsides surrounded us, distracting me from growing discomfort. At the bottom of the valley we shuffled into Crot Morin and immediately sensed great antiquity. The rutted road, stone houses and

woodland setting seemed straight out of *The Conquest of Gaul*—
not that Caesar indulged in descriptive travel writing. To the west
rose the Morvan's highest granite peak, Haut Folin. Other forested
mountains with rounded, mammary silhouettes were arrayed
south-by-southwest and formed a bowl. Long lost Bibracte, where
Caesar dictated the book we'd been reading, was out there somewhere. I blinked into the twilight. Why had I thought of "mammary silhouettes"? Simple: Bibractis the Beaver Goddess seemed
to be stretched out naked on the ridge, belly and breasts to the
orange western sky.

If any living humans were in Crot Morin, they'd scattered at our
approach. The same disinformation officers who'd been at work
earlier hiding Maquis Maurice had apparently passed through,
removing signs as they went. We walked down the leafy valley in
thickening darkness and were glad to spot a pair of hikers coming
from the opposite direction.

"Hail good fellows well met," I said as loud as I could, in
English. The couple seemed about our age and similarly hot and
sweaty, torn around the pants and hobbled by worn joints. I thrust
out my hand and asked if they knew where the B&B was.

"We were about to ask you the same thing," the man said, a
wry expression on his tired, lean, but handsome face.

We introduced ourselves, finished shaking hands with Georges
and Bernadette, and unanimously decided that one of us should
be delegated to knock on a villager's door. Alison indicated her
shredded pants, so Bernadette volunteered. A woman would be
less threatening to fearful locals.

The tactic worked. A puzzled antique farmer appeared, lifted
his stained cap, and thrust an index finger out of his cottage
before slamming the door.

Once pointed in the right direction, we found the Gîte des
Fleurs—La Rivière, our flop for the night. The property looked
like the French answer to a Swiss chalet. As the name suggested,

it was a B&B in a cut-flower nursery and sat near a riverbank. The river proved to be small but lively. As you might expect of nurserymen, the B&B's garden was orderly. The house squeaked with cleanliness, and the young lady who greeted us spoke in a timid soprano. We left our boots in a mud room, and Alison snuck upstairs to change her pants before anyone spotted the Kmart underwear.

Our hosts Olivier and Florence, Crot Morin natives, were polite but retiring in the extreme. Unlike other residents, innkeepers are not allowed to run away at the sight of strangers. With some coaxing, they acknowledged that they'd been childhood sweethearts—the girl and boy next door—and were carrying on the family businesses. Talking didn't come easy to either. I guessed they didn't want to pry, and were weary of telling their life story to musty travelers. When the opportunity presented itself, Olivier disappeared and Florence went off to baste the roast, leaving their house guests to get to know each other. Dinner would be served at 7:30 P.M. sharp.

As we poked around the garden, we were joined by another forty-something guest named Denis, who identified himself as a Parisian, not necessarily a descendent of Vercingétorix or Caesar, and a musician by profession. Denis was on his own, wandering the Morvan without any particular itinerary and no maps, a thoughtful, wistful man. Georges and Bernadette described themselves as agricultural engineers, and were proud to hail from a small town in northern Burgundy. They'd worked in Asia and Africa, and were avid trekkers, despite Bernadette's debilitating physical handicaps caused by a car crash. She had no strength at all in one arm and shoulder, and had a delicate back.

"You travel the world and then discover your own backyard is as beautiful as Nepal or Ethiopia," Georges said, sighing with pleasure.

"And just as full of magic," Bernadette added.

We spoke briefly about Bibracte and Caesar and the layered history of the area, and how it attracted a mixed bag of bona fide historians and strange, New Age, often extreme rightwing Druid worshipers. All three hikers were readers of Astérix comic books and were game to say "Vercingétorix" into my digital recorder. "But I would never go to an Astérix movie," Georges hastened to add. "The comic books are intelligent, irreverent, with a sense of humor: the authors were a Ukrainian-Pole and an Italian, and anything but neo-fascist. The movies are populist garbage."

"You have to be quick on your feet to see a good French movie," remarked Denis with irony. "The average run is two weeks. You can view populist garbage movies and Hollywood blockbusters at your leisure. They run and run."

We limped in to dinner and soon were deep in conversation—about pessimism, *passéisme* and demagogic, dumbed-down populism, America, Caesar, Iraq and Afghanistan, coffee and tea rituals, Époisse cheese, and the gilded horse-head sculptures that once had marked horse-meat butcher shops in Paris. Words whisked us crosscountry as we enjoyed roast pork, salad, and homemade pie. Rarely had the ancient Roman saying seemed more appropriate: "Around the dinner table you never grow old." Time had somehow lodged in aspic, like our pig-tongue picnic earlier that day.

There are moments in life when the urgency of an exchange seems extreme, when you feel you have much to say and no time to say it, for the spell will be broken and you may never meet the person again. One-night stands, summer romances, and, apparently, unexpected encounters at isolated French B&Bs share a similar intensity.

From Georges we received a concise history of Burgundy's sublime, smelly Époisse, a cheese with an orangish crust, its ancient origins, decline, and recent rebirth. He had just published a reference book on the subject.

Bernadette told us that in Ethiopia the shells of coffee beans are not wasted. Locals boil them with milk and salt to make a potent elixir. Japan had its tea ceremony, said Georges, but the coffee ritual in Ethiopian homes has four stages and lasts half an hour.

It seemed odd to be talking of Ethiopia and Nepal as we savored homemade rabbit terrine and drank delicious Burgundy reds from vineyards in the nearby Côte Chalonnaise. So Denis told us about traditional French vocal music and then dissected the byzantine mechanisms by which French composers, singers, and songwriters gain access to grants. Funding is getting scarcer, he noted. French government support for the arts had peaked under François Mitterrand. The former president may have had a checkered past, but he'd done much for French culture. A series of blows had been delivered recently by the European Union's strictures on subsidies. And of course there were globalization and dwindling royalties because of piracy and the Internet. Denis admitted that his next move might be out of his music studio, currently located in a reconverted foundry where once upon a time horse-head sculptures were electro-plated with gold.

I couldn't help thinking how horses and buggies had given way to cars, and horse-meat to hamburgers. The Dutchman at the Chalet du Montal who'd spent his career collecting and distributing royalty payments to authors and artists had retired at the right time. Past certainties were gone, as dead as Vercingétorix and Caesar. Perhaps they'd never been certainties at all.

I waited for a lull in the conversation. "Do you think our walk is a pointless meander?" I asked. "When you go out and hike, what do you think about? Why do you do it?"

Denis shifted in his seat and poured himself another glass of wine. He looked uncomfortable. "It's late," he said. "I'll be leaving before breakfast." We shook hands and said good-bye, not ships but pilgrims passing in the night.

When he'd gone, Bernadette and Georges said that they felt happy when they hiked, that it kept them in tune with nature and the universe, and helped them keep fit. "I'd never say it was pointless," Bernadette confided. "You can find a spiritual dimension in your life in a million different ways. Some people meditate or pray. We hike. Whatever works. . . ."

TALKING THE WALK

That night Alison plumped the pillows and read aloud from *The Conquest of Gaul*. We'd reached a crucial point in the book, and it coincided eerily with our geographical position. The Gallic tribes involved in the rebellion against Caesar, Alison reminded me, were required to send hostages to Vercingétorix. Hostage-taking was common throughout the ancient world.

The whole of the cavalry, numbering 15,000, was ordered to concentrate immediately at Bibracte . . . Alison read aloud, carefully enunciating. She paused to point at the skylight and the hills just south of us, to drive home the fact that we were there, meaning here. *If Caesar saw the cavalry in difficulties anywhere . . . he moved up some of the infantry . . . dislodged some of the enemy, and chased them with heavy loss to a river where Vercingétorix's infantry was posted. . . .*

"A river," I asked, "this river, you think?"

Alison's eyes grew wider. "Maybe," she whispered.

As I lay in bed, listening to Caesar's words and the sound of the creek beyond our open skylight, I couldn't help speculating. Many of the bloody events described in the book had taken place in the mountains and valleys around us, perhaps in Crot Morin itself, on this spot. The house might be built on a battlefield, or a Gallic sacred site where the Druids would propitiate the god's wrath by rendering another life in its place, a favorite pastime.

"We'd better get some sleep," I said. "Leave the gore for tomorrow, and remind me to tell you about that bust of Caesar I made when I was a teenager."

Alison switched off the light. But we both tossed and turned through the night. When we awoke at dawn, Alison said she'd dreamed of Roman soldiers and heard them marching in the garden. I'd dreamed of Vercingétorix, Mitterrand, and Nazi torturers, and had relived again my nightmare argument with Miss Nelson, my old Latin teacher, about Cicero and Sissero, and wheny, weedy, wiki, her gooey southern accent spoiling the pronunciation and, decades later, still filling me with disgust.

Stretching luxuriously before getting out of bed, I was relieved to hear birds, cows, and babbling water. The cold air blew in, scented by fresh flowers from the nursery next door. I glanced out at the brook behind the B&B. It was not flowing with human blood, and Miss Nelson was nowhere to be seen.

Before we could make it downstairs to breakfast, the soulful Denis had left, missing the café au lait served in big bowls, and Florence's hot, butter-lashed homemade bread and trio of jams—tangy green tomato, rich banana-and-rhubarb, and tart white gooseberry.

Given my aching back and knee, it was a good thing we didn't have nearly as far to walk today, our plan being to get as close to Bibracte as we could, and hike there early the following morning. On Georges's and Bernadette's recommendation, we changed trails and followed "GR Tour du Morvan"—the tortoise's trail—planning to stop at the village of Glux-en-Glenne. Georges said they'd had lunch the day before at a café there run by a Dutchman. If we walked that way, there would be no need to ask Florence to prepare a picnic, which meant we would save carrying several pounds, and might avoid having to eat another baguette-and-ham sandwich. I'd lost plenty of weight for the time being. My pants were baggy and kept slipping down. We deserved a good, solid lunch.

Our new route curled through the valley and across the creek, skirting the Bois du Roi. It turned out to be a dense forest the Burgundian dukes handed over to the kings of France in 1477. That seemed far too recent to be interesting. Why search for relics only five hundred years old?

My neck had begun to ache almost as badly as my knee, and I now knew why. Ever since Fontaines Salées, I'd been scouring the trails for neolithic statuettes, shards, arrowheads, coins, bones, and other tokens of the past. Thinking back to various inner monologues and outward conversations, I wondered what the strip malls of Los Angeles, Salt Lake City, and Santa Rosa, California, would look like in two thousand years. Would pilgrims and wanderers scuff the tufted tarmac looking for traces of Arbie's and KFC? Would the surveyor's maps of the future show sections of "ancient Interstate 5" and the automobile cemeteries known in those bygone days as "junk yards"?

I stooped to examine a rock that looked like a neolithic tool, but decided it wasn't *neo* anything, just lithic.

We skirted several farmhouses in scenic spots where the Hounds of the Baskervilles bayed and leaped, restrained by chains. Rural slums the world round resemble each other. Requisite components are chained dogs, farm vehicles rusting in fields, broken children's toys, half-burned slash piles, screaming babies, tired mothers and unshaved fathers glowering from behind screen doors. I was glad hunting season had ended, and that there was no NRA in France.

The trail climbed steadily, curving around a bowl as it entered Glux-en-Glenne. How on earth were we to pronounce the name? Did Parisians and locals fight over the silent "x," and did anyone bother pronouncing the double consonant? But there was no one to ask. The site and views were splendid, and as quiet as Caesar's grave. Actually, we knew well that Caesar had been murdered and buried in Rome, Vercingétorix too. Six years after the fall of Bibracte and Alésia, Caesar had dragged Vercingétorix in chains to the Eternal City and paraded him before roaring crowds. He'd had the valiant Gaul strangled to death in the dread Mamertine Prison, the same dungeon where Saint Peter was imprisoned a century later, or so it's claimed. Violence unto the violent: a pithy motto true to this day.

Caesar and Vercingétorix may not have fallen here, but we knew from our readings that the green fields of Glux-en-Glenne were fertilized by the bones of countless lesser Romans and Celts. The Bibracte-to-Alésia trail runs through Glux, as does the Roman road-cum-pilgrim's route. The village's proximity to Bibracte has won Glux a large barrel of pork, in the form of the Centre Archéologique Européen. At this ultra-modern archeological research center, in a handsome, minimalist structure built during Mitterrand's presidency, teams of European Union archeologists analyze the thousands of objects unearthed at Bibracte each year.

We hadn't really expected to find anything for lunch. It wasn't done in the Morvan. So we weren't surprised when the Petite Auberge, the lunch spot run by one of the region's twenty thousand Dutchmen, was closed. "But Georges and Bernadette," I started to say.

"Remember the tortoise," quoth Alison.

"All this hiking makes me hungry," I said, trying to overcome my disappointment. "I wonder how many calories we burned charging up that hill like Roman infantrymen." I reached for my talking pedometer-cum-calorie meter. It had gone silent this morning. I'd last heard it at the rural slum several miles back. I performed a fruitless strip search on myself. "The pedometer will be a find for future archeologists," I announced.

"What a shame," Alison said coyly. She couldn't hide her pleasure. "Would you like to wear mine? It doesn't talk but may actually be more accurate."

I shook my head. Alison had hated the talking pedometer from the minute she heard it. One fewer gadget to think about,

I consoled myself. Who needed to know how many miles, minutes, seconds, and calories were accumulating or burning off? I wanted to walk the walk, not talk the talk, or hear a machine talk the walk, either. If I could live without e-mail and my laptop, I could do without the pedometer. "And another thing," I said, experiencing a small epiphany: "I've noticed that my eyes hurt less even though I'm spending more time in daylight."

Alison smiled, sincere now. "You haven't complained of a caffeine headache in a couple of days, either."

I was glad she'd used the word "complain." It put my flawless character in perspective. What she didn't know was, my twisted knee had swollen into something resembling a Red Delicious, and my backbone crackled like one of the many electrified cattle fences we'd passed. I hadn't *complained*. The boon from this pain was, one form of discomfort had driven out the other. Instead of eye pain, I had knee pain and backache. Stoicism was the best way forward.

Though we'd entered only a handful of churches and lit one candle so far, the pilgrimage appeared to be paying off in unexpected ways. For one thing, I was feeling distinctly less anticlerical, having discovered the delights of resting in dark, quiet churches, and our readings of Caesar reminded me of why the Roman Empire had slowly collapsed and gradually been replaced by a system of Christian governance at least marginally less brutal. Now that I was on the road to enlightenment and self-knowledge, I wondered if self-mastery would follow.

TIPTOE THROUGH THE TULIPS

Because we'd changed our route, our B&B at a hamlet called Anverse turned out to be closer than anticipated, only about a mile and a half west of Glux-en-Glenne. As we approached it, a wolfhound stood in the middle of the one-lane road. West of the wolfhound lay the only chance we might have of finding lunch.

"Nice boy," I said. The dog's large, baleful eyes followed us. He seemed less dangerous than the smaller, snippety mutt that raced out, teeth bared. It was a familiar village welcoming committee. I held up my digital recorder thinking, this may be the last entry before it's chewed up with my hand. The police inspectors will hear us as we're torn limb from limb.

Alison spoke gently to the dogs. For a moment, she seemed to have gained the powers of Saint Francis. The beasts backed off, fell silent, and watched us pass. "They sense fear," she said, sounding oracular. This was not news to me, an American mongrel raised among the vicious mutts of San Francisco's Haight-Ashbury district. I held my tongue and marched on.

A few houses west, we stopped to watch a vintage tractor piloted by a curmudgeonly farmer. They huffed and puffed in unison, churning up the soil in a sloping kitchen garden. When the pair neared the road, I waved. The farmer turned off the engine and sat there staring at us grumpily without saying anything. "We're looking for the B&B," I explained, stating the obvious. He jerked his thumb at a sign. It was a big sign and you'd have to be blind to miss it. I am only par-blind, but I was also tired and distracted by hunger. "So sorry," I said, unable to keep the irony out of my voice. "You must get people talking at you all the time out here. At least once a month, huh? By the way, how old is that tractor?"

"Built in 1953," he blurted, leaning forward. "American." He paused to grin. "No electronics. Always works." He restarted the engine and held up his hand in salute. A plume of diesel smoke rose above him.

The view of Mont Beuvray from the road to our B&B, propitiously named "Aux Sources de l'Yonne," was about as good as views get, and I felt happy despite the farmer's predictable rebuff. The B&B was in a restored farmhouse. It felt like a piece of Holland lifted from flat tulip fields and forced with gardening gum boots into hilly, Celtic soil. It was flanked by a mini-campground.

Many Dutchmen reportedly love trailers, campers, and tents, and are famous in France for hauling with them everything needed for a holiday or an entire lifetime abroad, including food, furniture, and plumbing. Cynics and disgruntled French merchants ascribe this to a penchant for parsimony, but I'm convinced it's atavistic and goes back to the days of the nomadic Frankish-Germanic-Scandinavian tribes that swept in by wagon and settled the swamplands we now refer to as the Low Countries. I shared my epiphany with Alison.

"For goodness sakes," she said. "Can't you stop with your pet theories? The Dutch are cheap, that's all, and it drives the French crazy, because the French are misers too and hate it when the Dutch outdo them."

As usual, she was correct. But two rebuffs within ten minutes was too much for me. I sulked silently as we neared the farmhouse.

Several hues of hydrangea and tulip brightened the terraced back yard, with its above-ground swimming pool and knotty pine trailer. There we found our hosts, Josje and Hauke Lageweg. They were surrounded by blond children, blond parents, and blond in-laws, all with names I promptly forgot and in any case would not have been able to pronounce. We were hours earlier than the normal check-in time for a B&B. Alison and I went out of our way to apologize, alternating between French and English, both of which the Dutch couple spoke fluently. I wondered aloud if we might break bread with them, given the dearth, not to say non-existence, of walkable options when it came to food, which we did not possess in our own right.

"You mean you'd like some lunch?" asked Josje. Her manner was straightforward, brusque, even, but I sympathized. It was unusually hot. She had her in-laws to coddle, and her kids were home on Easter break. Who needed pilgrims showing up at lunchtime?

Graciously the family included us in their frugal repast. The plate of diminutive ham and cheese sandwiches and glasses of milk whisked us back to the Netherlands. Josje, it turned out, is a professional guide and often works at Bibracte, the region's main tourist attraction. She also confirmed what we'd heard earlier about the demographic appeal of the Morvan, one key to understanding the Dutch "invasion" of recent years. The other key is, or was, the price: compared to northern Europe, property in Burgundy had long been cheap. Naturally, the arrival of tens of thousands of Dutch, Swiss, Belgians, Danes, and British has driven up values. But for people like the Lagewegs, who bought their rundown farm in the 1990s, the ticket seemed ridiculously low.

Wisely, the family chose one of the more scenic spots to plant their bulbs, with views in every direction across hills and valleys. "No, I haven't found any valuable coins or statues," Josje remarked unbidden. The name of the B&B, she added, also unprompted, comes from the springs that give rise to the Yonne River, the single biggest tributary to the Seine. We were standing on the Atlantic-Mediterranean watershed, she noted. On the north side of the hill the water formed the Yonne and Seine and flowed into the Atlantic. On the south side, and on the adjoining Mont Beuvray across the valley, the water flowed into the Saône and joined the Rhône, rolling into the Mediterranean. It was, of course, a sacred spot.

"Of course," we agreed.

"The spring is up there," noted Josje, pointing with the accuracy of the professional tour guide. "Did you see the dogs? They won't bite. Turn left and go up to the top of the mountain."

We got the message. Happily, we were glad to vacate the premises and eager to add to our collection of marshy mountaintop meadows—and continue our reading of Caesar. So we pocketed our copy of *The Conquest of Gaul*, borrowed a pair of books on local history, and backtracked, weightless, to the wolfhound and mutt.

THITHER, YONNE, AND RUBICON

Wildflowers and what looked like blooming yellow watercress filled a field at the crest. Someone had turned off the Yonne's cascade, or perhaps all French rivers started this way—with a trickle.

The hill was steeper and higher than we'd imagined. Its name turned out to be Mont Prenéley and at 855 meters it was the Morvan's second-highest peak after Haut Folin. That made it several heads taller than Mont Beuvray, which seemed within our grasp but was still five miles away as the crow flies.

We found a shady spot and stretched out near the puddle that would soon be the mighty Yonne River.

"Though it doesn't look like one, this is the source of a major river, correct?" Alison nodded in answer. "This is also a sacred spot on the Mediterranean-Atlantic watershed, is it not? It's on a mountaintop higher than Mont Beuvray, which is right over there. Doesn't it stand to reason there'd be a lost city here, too?"

"Maybe they haven't found it yet," Alison remarked, riffling the pages of the history book she'd picked up. "That's why it's lost."

A walking, talking Google, within minutes she'd analyzed key pages, and had a concise report on Mont Prenéley and the Yonne's spring to share with me.

During archeological digs, three ancient temples had been unearthed here, Alison summarized, and many votive offerings had been found—everything from bronze ears to pins and buckles. The buckles were the famous safety pin-shaped "fibulae" used to fasten tunics and togas. At this and similar fountainheads in the Morvan, female natives would make pilgrimages to scoop up virginal water and sprinkle their breasts, praying for abundant milk. The odd thing was, this milk ritual had continued into the 20th century.

Alison raised an eyebrow. "Apparently the men would sprinkle priests with springwater to ensure good weather for crops."

I was tempted to make a remark about sprinkling for penile enhancement but said, instead, "That's a neat role-reversal. The

Pagans probably got tired of being splashed with holy water, so they took revenge by sprinkling the priest once in a while."

"You remember the church in Anost?"

"Who could forget Girart and Berthe de Roussillon, and my dud bone?"

"This book says there used to be a wooden statue of a Virgin in Anost. When you opened it up you found a smaller statue of Christ inside. Pregnant women would make a pilgrimage carrying a diaper, to ensure easy childbirth." The statue had been removed from Anost and now reposed in the regional history museum in Autun, four days' walk down the road.

From where we lay under the scented fir trees, the three temples were nowhere to be seen. I wondered if they, too, had been dismantled and packed off to a regional history museum. The book didn't specify whether they were pre-Gallic, Gallic, Roman, or paleo-Christian temples. It was common to build your god's shrine atop whatever was already there. Prehistoric fertility goddesses hidden in their sacred spots had morphed into lithe water nymphs—or Venus cupped by a marble scallop shell—ensconced in Pagan temples later transformed into churches. Likewise the "idols" of Paganism had given way to what the French called *Bonnes Dames*—the Virgins and Madonnas and saints of Catholicism. During the French Revolution, the Virgin Mary morphed into Marianne, symbol to this day of the Republic. Now we had movie stars and athletes and CEOs to idolize, and tele-evangelists, Viagra and plastic surgery instead of springwater and priests— and for unregenerate materialists there were shopping malls as temples of consumerism.

"Shall we see what Caesar has to say?" Alison asked rhetorically. She flipped to Book VI and read about *The Customs and Institutions of the Gauls.* I closed my eyes and fell backwards in time.

As a nation the Gauls are extremely superstitious . . . wrote Julius Caesar. He gave as an example the case of when people seriously ill or faced with the prospect of battle offered human sacrifice, employing Druids, the priest class. They believed the best way to save a man's life was to *propitiate the god's wrath by rendering another life in its place.*

"Didn't you read that last night?"

"I'm just checking to see if you were awake."

"Who could sleep with all those dead warriors underneath us? What was all that stuff you read to me about colossal images made of wickerwork?"

Alison found the entry and finished it. The limbs of these huge "burning men" made of wicker would routinely be filled with living men and *set on fire, and the victims burned to death.*

"Very civilized," I remarked.

"It gets better." Alison now declaimed in the style of Caesar. *Husbands have power of life and death over their wives. . . . When a high-born head of a family dies . . . if the circumstances of his death are suspicious, they examine his widow under torture, as we examine slaves; if her guilt is established, she is consigned to the flames and put to death with the most cruel torments . . .* Alison paused to editorialize. "I'm not sure I would've liked living back then."

"Not sure?"

"Oh, here's how the servants were rewarded for their services." *. . . [S]laves and retainers known to have been beloved by their masters were burned with them. . . .* "And here's something very modern," she added. "Talk about freedom of the press." *The magistrates suppress what they think it advisable to keep secret, and publish only what they deem it expedient for the people to know. . . .*

"The more things change," I sighed, "the more they sound like modern warfare and corporate communications, albeit with fewer burnings." I stood up and stretched. "Let's explore the mountaintop. Maybe we'll find a temple."

"Don't you want to hear about heroic cannibalism? The Druids and their god of darkness, Dis? We haven't even gotten to the part about the customs and institutions of the Germans, who make the Gauls sound like pacifists."

BOEUF BOURGUIGNON À LA DUTCH

Whoever had found the buried temples of Mont Prenéley had done a good job covering up afterwards. We walked several miles through enchanting forests on a leafy, stone-flanked road that followed terraced contours. We had no doubts that the contours were abandoned, overgrown fields and not Gallic fortifications. No doubt at all. Sort of. En route we saw no creatures mythical, dead or living, save for the giant wolfhound and mongrel that awaited us on our return. They didn't bother to bark this time.

After our lunch of miniature sandwiches, I was ready to eat anything, as long as it wasn't the Gallic specialty of human flesh roasted in a wickerwork statue. As we stepped into our B&B, we could smell something wafting from the kitchen—a slow-cooked stew, perhaps. It was either *coq au vin* or . . . "How did you guess?" Hauke asked. He'd been slaving for at least half an hour to make the *boeuf bourguignon*, which generally requires half a day to cook, but not in Holland, apparently.

The immediate family, extended relations, and the two of us filled a long wooden table. The milk flowed, the stew disappeared amid talk of tulips, and before we knew it we had slept through the night and were back at the table for breakfast at dawn. This time, Josje was in charge. She whisked yeasty, fresh-baked bread to the assembled, famished masses. It looked suspiciously like other loaves we'd seen of late at other B&Bs.

"It comes out of a machine," she admitted. "You put in the ingredients, flip a switch, and out it comes." The nearest bakery was too far, she explained. It had become a familiar refrain. "I think everyone is getting a bread machine these days," she concluded. "It's maybe going to put the last bakeries out of business. I don't like that. I'm not sure what to do about it."

As we devoured the bread, another overnight guest appeared. She hadn't eaten dinner with us. She, too, would be at Bibracte and the Museum of Celtic Civilization later today, she remarked, but was driving, not hiking there. "I'm going to curate a new museum near Clermont-Ferrand," she explained, "and am traveling around the country visiting museums with similar themes, to learn what to do and what not to do."

The future museum was to be dedicated to Gallo-Roman pottery, meaning earthenware from the 2nd century BC to the Merovingian period—around 500 AD. "Wasn't Vercingétorix from Clermont-Ferrand?" I asked. The city's name sounded familiar. "That's where Michelin tires come from."

"Precisely," said the curator. "Everyone thinks Vercingétorix was from Bibracte, but he was actually an Arverni chieftain. The tribe gave its name to the Auvergne region of southern-central France. The museum is at the site of Gergovia not far from the Michelin tire plant. You've heard of Gergovia?"

Had we ever. Vercingétorix had defeated the Romans at Gergovia, Caesar's worst setback in the conquest of Gaul. "How nice to have a museum in a place where the Gauls were victorious," I remarked, sure the Michelin guidebooks would do everything in their power to promote the venture.

The timid curator told us about the tons of foundation stones and shards found at Gergovia, and seemed excited about bringing to light another chapter of the distant past. With bad-news Alésia and Bibracte, this new victory site would be an essential part of a trinity of Gallic antiquity.

As we prepared to say farewell, the term *passéisme* came to mind. Was the new museum yet another manifestation of the French obsession with the past, or a legitimate scientific endeavor whose aim was to use the past as a tool to understand the present—and the future? "You haven't found any effigies of Janus, have you?"

The curator paused to think before shaking her head. "Why do you ask?"

"A silly pet theory of mine—about looking backwards and forwards at the same time."

As I wrestled on my boots, I reflected on why, over the years, I'd come to think of France as imbued with a "Janus culture," a nation whose world-view, like the ancient god of thresholds, managed at the same time to look back and ahead. For us, there was no looking back today. It was B-Day—Bibracte Day.

SPRING FORWARD

Full of fresh yeast and good cheer, we set off between the breast-shaped mounts of Prenéley and Beuvray. It was a mild, breezy morning. As we walked under the shivering beeches, their leaves unfolded like puppy's ears. The soil exhaled earthy, floral scents— of must, moss, honey, and mulch.

"The first real day of spring," Alison sighed.

It was indeed, not on the calendar but in the air and earth. We could see spring unfolding, and feel it underfoot, the gentle but forceful arrival of new life, of sap rising and slumber stirring to wakefulness.

At a crossroads in the highway below Mont Beuvray, a pair of French hikers sat at the requisite crucifix and appeared to be struggling with their boots and blisters. Seemingly delighted for the opportunity to play Florence Nightingale, Alison asked if they needed band-aids, disinfectants, boot laces or anything else. "I'm carrying everything and have plenty to spare," she offered. The couple stared blankly at her with that peculiarly Gallic mixture of bafflement, distrust, and disdain. Their expressions seemed to proclaim "oh god, a foreign do-gooder."

"No," the man grunted. "We don't need anything." His partner merely stared, like a stunned goose unable to quack.

"You're very welcome," I said. "Nice talking to you, and have a swell day."

Our plan—my plan, foisted on Alison—was to cut east at the base of the mountain and follow the ancient Gallic trail to the Museum of Celtic Civilization, take a quick look, and then head to the summit, a sacred place not only to Bibractis but also to me, for my own, obscure reasons. Alison agreed to the plan, though she voiced skepticism about visiting the museum again. We'd spent hours examining its displays back in 2004, on assignment, and had come away underwhelmed.

"You'll see," I protested; "now that we've been reading Caesar and hiking across Gaul, you'll enjoy it this time around."

OF SNOW-BUNNIES AND SMELTERS

The museum of Celtic Civilization is nearly invisible from the outside, a long, low layercake of stone, metal, and glass hidden below a beech grove. We slipped by the crowds, checked our packs, and found the museum café. It was closed. Why open a café for Easter, with all those people to serve? That would involve far too much work.

A clutch of seniors watched a video on a flat-screen TV. We marvelled at the special effects. Snow rabbits bounded and mammoths roamed over the wind-blown, frosty steppes that surrounded Mont Beuvray in the year 18,000 BC. This was climate change with bells on. The next sequences showed thriving Bibracte before Caesar, the happy sound of hammers ringing out against metal. The late-Iron Age site looked startlingly like modern Vézelay, a handsome, fortified hilltown of the La Tène culture bustling with cheerful workers and merchants—the ideal Gallic Oppidum. Next in the show came the abandonment of Bibracte in favor of Augustus Caesar's new city, Autun. Then images flickered past from the early Christian era and the building of the 7th-century Saint Martin chapel atop the sacred hill, followed eight centuries later by a convent. Trees gradually crowded in and all trace of ancient Bibracte was lost . . . until the 19th century, when a wine merchant-turned-archeologist named Jacques-Gabriel Bulliot became convinced that phantom Bibracte lay atop Mont Beuvray.

"Better than you remembered, wasn't it?" I asked hopefully. Alison demurred.

A map showing the territory of the Aedui tribe confirmed that it corresponds to the contemporary Morvan plus the Saône-et-Loire *département*, stretching from a village named Prégilbert to Mâcon. Alison remembered a thought she'd had and turned on me. "Did you plan our walk knowing we'd be crossing Aedui lands the whole time?"

"No," I lied.

Had she said Aedui Land? It sounded good, like the name of an amusement park.

More videos, maps, and charts—and long lists of the sixty or so tribes associated with the area—told the tale of the mysterious Celts' arrival and movement around what's now Switzerland, Germany, Italy, and France, displacing the older residents, members of the so-called Halstatt Civilization, about which we'd read when in Marigny-l'Eglise. Over the centuries, the many different Celtic nations built Oppida hillforts across Europe, many similar in design. Having enslaved the locals, these tribes proceeded to slaughter and enslave each other, forming alliances with Rome or Germanic tribes when convenient. It did sound civilized and modern.

Flanking the documentation, rows of display cases held reconstituted artifacts or copies of reconstituted artifacts. It was very exciting material if you were an archeologist. Apparently the

Aedui were hot-headed bigshots, with many subject peoples beneath their callused heels. The word "Aedui" means "men of fire" in ancient Celtic, a fine complement to Bibractis, the Beaver Goddess's water element. Aedui warriors kept serfs, whom the skeptical Caesar compared in his notes to Roman slaves, because of the miserable conditions in which they lived, their chattel status, and the ease with which they were dispatched, meaning tortured and killed.

Pulses and grains, hares and domesticated pigs, plus sheep and goats, were what the Aedui raised or hunted, ate, and—in the form of woolen cloth and salted meat—exported to Rome, along with raw tin, silver, gold, and lead and skilfully made metalwork. The names of nearby villages Villapourcain and Préporché to this day recall the Aedui's love for things porcine, one panel explained.

"But in the Astérix comic books," I noted, unable to hide my consternation, "they're always roasting wild boar, not domestic pig, and drinking beer instead of wine."

"There's no wine in Brittany," Alison said, "and that's where Astérix is from."

"Surely that's a minor detail."

At the time of Caesar's assault on Bibracte, the tribe's chief was Dumnorix, a man perhaps five feet tall, but fearless and adept, like his warrior brethren, at separating heads from shoulders using a finely crafted short sword. We admired the wax Dumnorix dummy on display—it came complete with dangling shorn enemy head—and then moved swiftly through other display areas, pausing to inspect an ancient fibula similar to the one we'd seen in the archeological museum at Saint-Père-sous-Vézelay, the pride of our guide, Astérix. Might our word "fib" be derived from fibula, I couldn't help wondering. It meant something straight that is twisted into a new shape.

"That just about does it for the museum," I remarked, stopping for one last glance at some broken earthenware. "Are we glad Caesar won?"

LOST & FOUND

Puzzlement accompanied us as we exited. The only surviving records of Bibracte were written by the bad guys—i.e., the victorious Romans. Much about the fabled site is speculation, from its age and extent to the origin of its name and the reasons for its demise. Also, there was plenty of room for skepticism about the Celts, their ethnicity, and the soundness of claims to a pan-European Celtic "civilization," as opposed to, say, groupings of ever-warring, semi-nomadic tribes of mixed and mysterious origin.

While thousands of objects have reportedly been found atop Mont Beuvray, the museum's collections appear to contain primarily documents and broken castoffs often unearthed at sites other than Bibracte. Had the Louvre or the museum of antiquities in Saint-Germain-en-Laye claimed the important finds, we wondered?

We'd heard rumors that about half the towering old beeches atop Mont Beuvray would soon be cut. They got in the way of archeology, it was said. No coherent image of the lost city's urbanism could be formed while the ruins were cloaked by vegetation, claimed researchers. The inhabitants had been farmers, metalworkers, and merchants—or so it was thought. To build their Oppidum and encircle it with a double ring of timber-reinforced walls, they deforested the hilltop, because they needed about five hundred acres of mature woodland for building material. Unsurprisingly, Bibracte now appears to have covered almost exactly five hundred acres.

Population estimates have been revised upwards to about twenty thousand people at the time of Caesar. Modern-day Autun—founded by Augustus, not Julius Caesar—has seventeen thousand inhabitants. In other words, Bibracte was a very large city by ancient standards, and was probably Romanized long before Caesar arrived. One of the main activities was metallurgy. The soil still shows clear traces of contamination from heavy metals. To fuel their forges and foundries, the Gauls needed wood—wood and water. The springs were not merely used for sacrificial reasons, but for industry. It appears the site may have been abandoned in the 1st century AD because nearby resources became scarce, and industry uneconomical. They chopped themselves out of work, and polluted their environment.

OF FIBULAE AND FRANKS

Ever curious and open to knowledge, we signed on to take a guided tour. As we waited for the tour group to show up, I asked Alison if she'd seen this, and she asked me if I'd seen or heard that. This was our second visit to the site, after all, and we were nearly as baffled as before. Didn't it seem odd there was no mention anywhere that heroic Vercingétorix mutilated, tortured, and killed those who refused to go along with him in his war against Rome? And what of the ritual human barbecues organized by those masters of wickerwork, the Druids, who also handled cremations and the *Fahrenheit 451*-style destruction of written records?

Funny, where in the displays was the part about heroic cannibalism? As I recalled, Vercingétorix's fellow Arverni chieftain, Critognatus, had harangued the besieged at Alésia suggesting they do as their ancestors had and "keep themselves alive by eating the flesh of those who were too old or too young to fight." Or so claimed Julius Caesar. We probably just didn't spot that citation among the display cases and waxworks.

Surely somewhere there had been a discussion of the ritual hostage-taking, slavery, institutionalized wife-torture, and murder presented as "justice" which we'd read about in Caesar? We must've missed that, too.

It struck me as strange that the monstruous violence, cruelty, and military prowess of the Swiss-Celtic Helvetii and Germanic invaders was not mentioned either. It was this ferocity that, according to Caesar, had prompted the terrified Aedui—who were, after all, "friends of Rome"—to call upon Caesar for help. They did call Caesar in to help, didn't they? Perhaps not. Who knows? You wouldn't guess it from the museum displays. Caesar was the consummate villain.

Both of us wandered away feeling that the Bibracte museum of Celtic Civilization is none other than a Celtic curlicue of subtle propaganda, a golden fibula twisted with considerable artistry. The Celts were not only a great, ancient civilization predating Rome. They were also ethnically, culturally, and linguistically linked in a coherent, civilized manner from northern Italy via the heartland of France to Spain, Portugal, and the Low Countries—all core European Union members.

Somehow, in the museum's extravaganza of rubble and rust, videos, maps, and wax dummies, the Celts of Britain and Ireland got short shrift, shorter even than Dumnorix, the shrimp local chieftain. These two English-speaking countries didn't rate a mention, despite the reality that they were and still are the keepers of the Celtic flame. Even in Caesar's day, that was known. To quote our tattered copy of *The Conquest of Gaul* I now pulled from Alison's pack and leafed through to refresh my memory, "The Druidic doctrine is believed to have been found existing in Britain and thence imported into Gaul," wrote Caesar. "[E]ven today those who want to make a profound study of it generally go to Britain for the purpose."

Not, apparently, if they're French and have a political agenda. For instance, a desire to build the European Union atop a solid Franco-German base, thereby marginalizing the rival, recalcitrant, perfidious United Kingdom. Never mind that the Anglos and their outsized American offspring had saved Franco-Celtic France from the Germanic hordes just as Caesar had, more than once.

History hemorrhages with ornate fibulae—history refashioned, bent, and gilded to elevate and mythologize the past, or comfort the troubled present. The subtlety in this case seemed remark-able, potentially on a par with the zigzags and loop-de-loops of France's postwar rehabilitation of its role in the Occupation, and the necessary, even benign role supposedly played by Vichy. Was this an elaborate exercise in sanitizing dirty Franco-German laundry? It had François Mitterrand written all over it.

RUBBLE, RUBBLE, TOIL & TROUBLE

How to destroy the Gallic magic of Mont Beuvray more efficiently than Caesar or Saint Martin, that scourge of Paganism? Simple: cut down the trees and let the sun shine in. Expose buried foun-dations. Excavate sacred springs. Faithfully reconstruct ruins, re-erect city walls, and turn Bibracte into a Celtic theme park. Scientifically, of course.

Such were a few of the unfriendly thoughts that accompanied us as we hiked up the steep, coiling road toward the main city gate of Gaul's landlocked Atlantis, following an official tour guide and her flock. Fifty-something years old, with dyed reddish hair, dry and wry of humor and voice, between puffs on her cigarette our guide seamlessly recited the site's history, pausing at strategic points to go over information we'd read or seen in videos. The same information was repeated on large all-weather panels by the roadside, with drawings and architectural renderings, plus selected quotes from *The Conquest of Gaul* in French and Latin.

There were several dozen of us in the group. We trailed along, everyone unabashedly enchanted, enjoying the scattered sun and shady glades of strangely twisted old trees—beeches whose lower branches had once been plaited to create boundary hedges, said the guide. Some looked like bentwood chairs, others like leafy couches. Though we'd been here before, I felt I was seeing Bibracte with virginal eyes, new eyes set in the orbits of a new man. For one thing, having shed fifty pounds since our last visit, the hike up seemed a breeze, despite my bad knee and back. My pulse raced as we passed through the reconstructed city walls. The guide stopped to read out Caesar's description of the impressive technique used to build the so-called *murus gallicus*, a rampart of timber, stone, iron rods, and soil Caesar called "indestructible" by fire, sapping, undermining, or bombardment with a catapult. It was Caesar's step-by-step notes that had made it possible for archeologists to identify the wall's remains, and recreate a city gate that looked astonishingly like a vertical beaver's dam. Did anyone else pick up on the irony in the guide's voice? That the un-take-able wall had been taken? The ultimate uselessness of even a double rampart, the Maginot Line of its day?

"Ladies and gentlemen, if you look beyond my shoulder you'll see Autun," intoned the guide perfunctorily. She explained that Autun was about thirty kilometers south as the crow flies, at a lower altitude and therefore closer than Bibracte to vineyards and the Saône River, which flowed into the Rhône that rushed to the Mediterranean—"a direct link to Rome." Rome. Again. I squinted. Anyone with normal vision would've seen the great walled city of Augustus Caesar spreading on the horizon away and below, and presumably would also have understood the topographical and geopolitical logic of resettling there, away from isolated, windy Bibracte. "The oldest and biggest forum in Gaul was here," said the guide, waving her arms. "Recent excavations prove it." This surprising fact had troubled some historians, because it meant Bibracte was thoroughly Romanized before Julius Caesar, making him slightly less a villain who had invaded and conquered. The discovery of an early Roman heritage reinforced accumulating evidence that the Gauls had borrowed much from more advanced Mediterranean cultures in the preceding centuries, through trade and exploration.

With a wave of her cigarette, our guide segued straight into my thoughts with the latest speculations on the mysterious uses of an almond-shaped pool of hewn stone. It sat in what had been the main street of the Iron Age settlement, a pool only a Greek, Etruscan, or Roman could've designed and built, apparently, given its geometric perfection. "Fertility rites," she explained. "The shape is that of a vulva."

Whoah, wasn't that the favorite shape often assigned to Mary Magdalene? Several visitors tittered and made lurid quips. Someone asked about something they'd read on the Internet— that a Druidic seminary had been here, an institution of higher learning with forty thousand Druid cadets, supposedly destroyed in the 4th century AD by mobs of Christian fanatics. The guide exuded skepticism and nicotine, and said she had no knowledge of the claim, thinking it unlikely any school in the ancient world could possibly have housed anywhere near that number of students. "There's a lot of unverified nonsense on the Web," she snorted, and most of the group joined in laughing and grumbling about the unreliability of the Internet as a resource.

Feeling disconnected, Alison and I drifted away under the sheltering trees, leaving the guide and the dusty archeological digs behind. We'd heard plenty enough about mass drunkenness and the selling of Gallic slaves for wine, the thousands of amphorae and fibulae and car keys found, and knew that only twenty percent of the sprawling site had been dug up so far. God only knew how many more tons of ancient treasure and garbage lay hidden under the vegetation. Vegetation that would soon disappear.

The trees, the trees, I thought, glancing up through their contorted boughs and oval leaves, stopping to touch a thick, scarred gray trunk. Soon most of you will be gone. For science.

Taking off our packs, we sat in the hallowed beech grove atop the mountain and did damage control on ourselves and each other. I had no blisters, despite the walking, and neither did Alison. I unlaced my boots, took off my toxic socks, and soaked my feet in one of Bibractis's springs, the one nearest Saint Martin's rebuilt chapel—a fraud from the 1800s, but what did it matter? The scourge of Paganism had spun the Druids' sacred tree around on this spot, had he? And now the archeologists were going to chop the trees down. The algae were warm and squishy between my toes. Mosquitoes were soon upon us.

What was it about this spot, I wondered, feeling lightheaded? The timelessness? The welling water and droning insects? The scent of the warm beech leaves and mulching beechnuts from last fall? Or was it that I knew questers had been coming here, worshipping someone or something, pleading, weeping, rejoicing, sacrificing, and hoping against hope that finitude wasn't inevitable? Three or four thousand years' worth of hopes, if the place was as old as Fontaines Salées. I closed my eyes and felt happy. Deeply, unspeakably happy.

THE ORIGINAL SEE-FOREVER VIEW

The megalomaniacal President François Mitterrand may have had a few flaws, but he also had good taste. He'd bought the rounded crown of Mont Beuvray, and as we walked past the sylvan site where he'd hoped to be buried, we couldn't help admiring his chutzpah. On a sloping lawn in a clearing stood a *table d'orientation*, a table marked with the cardinal points, distances, and a hand-painted panorama. Last time we'd experienced this view from this site, I'd been unaware that I had hepatitis. I had had feverish visions, convinced I was seeing the Pyrenees and that I had to hike over them. It was here that I'd made my vow to change my life and walk across the country. Now I could verify that what I'd actually seen were gentle mountains on the Morvan's southern edge. There were corkscrew roads and church spires, but no snowy Pyrenees peaks or gloomy Spanish abbey where Charlemagne and Roland battled the Moors.

"I was delirious," I said. "I was a mess."

"But you were right to make this happen," Alison murmured.

Up to now, we'd been following the GR-13 crosscountry hiking route, a section of the trans-European E-4 trail to Spain—one of the many official Ways of Saint James. From here, the trail continued south by southwest. Our maverick way lay instead to the southeast on another trail, GR-131. It ran through Saint-Léger-sous-Beuvray and Autun, then east to the great vineyards of the Côte d'Or and Côte Chalonnaise, before dipping south and reaching Cluny. Though Autun and Cluny had long been pilgrimage sites on the ancient Roman road from Mâcon to Paris, somehow they'd fallen off the main branch of the modern Saint James itinerary. We didn't care. Like Frank Sinatra, we were doing this walk my way—our way, since Alison had finally given the venture her blessing.

"Only another two months to go," I quipped. "Ready?"

Alison signalled us on. We crossed a trail marking Bibracte's imaginary southern ramparts, climbed down through a fir forest into pastures, and doubled back north on a fibula-shaped detour to a narrow river valley. Here the ancient Gallic-Roman road paralleled a clear, tuneful stream. So enchanting was the setting that we floated for about four miles in an Iron Age dream and only returned to earth on the edge of sleepy Saint-Léger-sous-Beuvray. A milk-white calf on wobbly legs stared at us, attempting a moo.

"You've taken the wrong road," said Lucie, the elder of two pre-teen farm girls, when we asked her where to find the Hôtel du Morvan. She marched up carrying an old bottle of Cremant de Bourgogne, the region's answer to champagne. It contained milk. Leaning on the wooden paddock as she spoke, she told us the calf's name was Alexandre, and suggested we turn around and take the main road into the village. "Alexandre's mother died while giving birth," remarked Julie, the other girl. She turned the bottle upside down and slipped it into the calf's mouth. "He thinks we're his mothers."

Another bottle of Cremant de Bourgogne, this one chilled and swarming with bubbles, stood on the worn bar of the Hôtel du Morvan. With mud on our boots and our backpacks slung to one side, we watched the proprietor fill two fluted glasses with the bubbly and carry them across the old-fashioned café, which doubled as a lobby, to a pair of guests in the equally old fashioned dining room. "Old-fashioned" seemed to apply to everything. It was precisely 7:15 P.M., aperitif time for most Frenchmen. For us, it was time for showers and a change into slightly less gamy attire.

Lovingly restored with limited means, Hôtel du Morvan turned out to be another study in time travel—not all the way to Bibracte, but far enough. A late-1800s vacationer would feel at home climbing the winding wooden staircase and making the waxed-plank floor creak. A wooden armoire and desk filled our room. Its single, wide window overlooked the weathered village's triangular-shaped main square.

"Narcoleptic."

"I can barely stay awake."

"I meant the village."

Luckily, like many of the inns along our route, the dining room had recently been declared nonsmoking. The affable, dark-haired owner, Éric Mazière, looked like a well-fed Roman patrician, more Seneca than Julius Caesar. As he and his wife Laurette led us through potted palms to our white-draped table, he told us they'd had to fight to enforce the anti-cigarette rule. No sooner had we settled in than Éric accosted a brittle female and asked her to extinguish her Gauloise or smoke outside. Contorting from a nicotine fit, the woman let fly a quiver of barbs about puritanical prohibitionism and Draconian joylessness. Éric countered with black lungs, cancer from passive-smoking, and respect for fellow diners. Eventually the puffing grasshopper hopped angrily outside. Meanwhile, the bar area, still not off-limits to smokers, filled with acrid plumes, demonstrating how locals would vote if asked.

As it transpired, a Gallo-Roman food specialist from the Bibracte museum had helped Éric and Laurette create a menu featuring the delicacies eaten around the time of Caesar—nothing was known of what Vercingétorix preferred. These delicacies sounded like the forefathers of several French classics. "Bring on the ancients," I said, hungry enough to eat a sandal, even though shoe leather wasn't on the Gallo-Roman menu. We savored the plump *helixes*, alias escargots. They were served with "macerated cabbage." We decided that snails and sauerkraut weren't bad, especially if you were a hedgehog or hungry centurion, or had hiked about ten hours as we had. The tender, slow-cooked stew made with beef, lamb, and pork tasted a lot like Alsatian *baekkeoffe* of the kind we'd had near Strasbourg, another Roman city. The fresh goat's cheese sprinkled with minced chives was straight out of the manuals of the Latin writer Columella, having graced tables descended from Rome for at least the last two thousand years. For good reason: it was delicious. Ditto the walnut cake. If the recipe isn't broken, don't fix it.

I couldn't resist asking the mild-mannered Éric where he came from. His round, benevolent face beamed. "Rome?" he laughed, shaking his jowls. "No, try the outskirts of Paris. Life was just too crazy there." He shrugged when I asked if he and Laurette had integrated with the locals. "Takes about seven years, we figure. They're private and conservative. We've got another two years to go."

VINTAGE RALLIES AND CARBON FOOTPRINTS

Dawn drizzle highlighted the slumping tile roofs and winding streets of soulful Saint-Léger-sous-Beuvray, one of those once-upon-a-time places. Gallic, Roman, and medieval pilgrim roads had traversed its main square, and still did, though they were now covered with asphalt. In the mid and late 1800s, Second Empire and Belle Époque vacationers had come for the clean air and gone with the wind. End of story?

We bought supplies at the local grocery, counted the names of dead soldiers on the war memorial, and stood in silence in the many-times rebuilt church, gazing at a remarkable cross. It was sculpted with grapevine and tree-of-life motifs, and spoke of earlier times of faith, ignorance, and poverty. Incongruously, the rumble of powerful engines shook the stained-glass windows.

We'd seen posters advertising the crosscountry vintage car rally that was to pass through the village en route to Mont Beuvray. Up the Gallo-Roman highway roared the antique Maseratis, slaloming amid Ferraris, Triumphs, Austin-Martins, and Morgans, the leather belts over their hoods rattling. I wondered how many chickens had been run over so far. Local boozers in the main square swilled wine from a shared bottle and shouted at the drivers. We were about to dart across the road when I sighted a 1966 Mustang convertible. It was white inside and out. Mine had been black on black. Otherwise the cars were identical. I recognized the chirping of the tires—early Mustangs were overpowered, the body weight badly distributed. They didn't hold the road. For a moment my skin prickled. I was a teenager again, sun-bleached and mindless, life an open road. But that was a willing misrepresentation. If memory served, fog was more abundant than sunshine in the San Francisco of my youth, the minds I'd known had been sharp, often brilliant, and traffic had long clogged the Golden Gate and Bay Bridge, and most of the scenic roads on the coast. California Dreaming was precisely that, even in the 1960s and '70s, a time now shrouded in the rosy fog of nostalgia.

"You used to collect cars like these, didn't you?" Alison asked. "Can you explain to me what the attraction is?" I know she didn't mean to sound judgmental. As someone who suffers car sickness, and prefers nature to the automobile, she was quite simply baffled by the sight of grown men and women playing with toy cars.

I shook my head. I couldn't explain it. Not any more. The utter vapidness of the exercise made me smile. Some people dance, I said to myself, others drive on the deck of the Titanic. Granted, walking across France was a pretty silly, selfish thing to do too, but at least it was quiet and pollution-free. "Some people grow sideways," I said, lost in my thoughts, "like those trees back on Mont Beuvray."

Ghosts in platform shoes and bell-bottoms walked with me past a herd of cows gorging on dandelions, under a grove of blossoming apple trees, and sang 1970s tunes in my ears. Perhaps that's why we lost our way and turned due south down a dirt road. It was marked Voie Celte—the Celtic Way, not the Roman Way— and appeared, from the signage, to lead to a town called Arroux.

"Arroux? Isn't that where Caesar's army fought the Helvetii?" Alison asked. She paused to take out *The Conquest of Gaul.* "Six Roman legions," she announced, reading a footnote, pleased to have remembered. "That makes about 30,000 men, against 370,000 Helvetii—including the supply train and families. In the Arroux River Valley. The massacre took place near here."

You had to marvel. Some people enjoy car rallies; others spot trains, or trace out ancient roads, tacking up improbable signs along the way. This road apparently ran from Bibracte to the battleground where the contemporary town of Toulon-sur-Arroux stands. It indicated that the locals were either serious about history or obsessed with the Celts and Romans. "Enough with the *passéisme,*" I said. "It's past time for a picnic."

OLD CHESTNUTS, BUM STEERS, AND MONKEY MEAT

Alison brushed the sappy fir bark off her pants and pointed southeast. "I say it's that-a-way." We'd wolfed our sandwiches under cover of my windbreaker, sitting on Alison's poncho, spread imperfectly over a freshly sawn log. The glorious Celtic Way had somehow turned into a trashed logging road whose muddy ruts shimmered with spring rain. One particularly tall pile of trunks in a clearing proved marginally less wet, perhaps because the sap was waterproof.

"Okay," I said, skeptical but no longer starving, "that-a-way."

Logging had destroyed signage and added extra roads. From our survey map I could see things were going to be complicated. We were aiming for an isolated farmhouse B&B, Ferme de la Chassagne, and there was no direct way to it once you strayed from the GR-131, which we'd managed to do. An hour and several miles later, we were stung to attention by bees swarming from hives in the woods. "This path must lead somewhere," I said with the obtuseness of panic, running while batting away belligerent bees. "I mean, the beekeeper comes from somewhere, right?"

"To paraphrase Philippe back in Marigny l'Eglise," Alison joked, "everything comes from somewhere, something can't spring from nothing."

I was about to ask her how she knew what Philippe had said, if she'd been in the kitchen, but we both stopped dead, despite the bees still pursuing us. Even Mr. Magoo couldn't avoid seeing the majestic trunk and boughs rising before us. "Saint Martin's tree," I said, only half joking. Still leafless, an old chestnut even bigger than those at Château de Bazoches towered over spindly firs, its roots twined around crumbling stone walls. Caesar's chariot had probably grazed them in passing. California has its redwoods, I reflected, spreading my arms in a futile attempt to embrace this great-grandfather tree. Italy and Greece have their olives. But France has the most astonishing chestnuts known to man—or bee. I swatted a drone that was attempting to sting me through my rain gear. Unsure why, I'd felt an instantaneous and deep kinship with this giant tree, and leaned my head against its damp, rough bark. How much had this chestnut seen, I wondered aloud, feeling myself fall into a well of timelessness. What would it say if it could speak?

"You've become a tree-hugger," Alison laughed. "Like those Earth-Firsters! we met in the redwoods. Next you'll be living on a platform up in the branches, and worshipping Pan."

"It could be worse," I said, stung by the reference to my mother and the recollection of our time spent with a group of earnest Earth-Firsters!, who were battling to save old-growth redwoods in the Headwaters Reserve of Humboldt County, California. At the time, I'd admired their courage but thought them extremist crazies. Now I was beginning to understand their desperate conviction, though I'd still never condone spiking trees or other forms of lethal sabotage. Piano wire wouldn't stop the motocross set any more than steel spikes would stop Georgia-Pacific or Weyerhauser from cutting down trees. The battle had to be fought elsewhere, in courtrooms, on the streets, in schools, and in the hearts and minds of consumers lining up at the big-box stores.

Lost but not hopeless, we lingered under the chestnut before hiking west on a looping, mossy trail, past a hidden millpond and up a hill to clustered stone houses, one freshly and expensively restored. If I was reading my map correctly, the village was named Boudédé. The usual dogs barked. Smoke curled from a single chimney. We shouted.

"Yes, you're in Boudédé," said the short but handsome man who strode into his yard, scratching his stubbly cheeks as he peered suspiciously at us. "How did you get here? From the main road?"

We couldn't explain which way we'd come, other than to indicate the beehives and giant chestnut.

"There's an even bigger tree," he said, pointing west with a throw-away gesture. He looked and moved like James Dean in *Rebel Without a Cause*. "They're registered landmarks," Dean added, made even more suspicious by my stares. I realized he thought we were militant environmentalists. "No one can cut them down," he added. The trees were at least five hundred years old, the lookalike claimed. But that was nothing. Five hundred years? Boudédé and Bibracte were ancient beyond words, he said, swelling like Astérix in Saint-Père-sous-Vézelay.

I asked if he were descended from the ancient Gauls and could pronounce Vercingétorix. "I'm collecting words," I explained, playing dumb.

The man seemed skeptical but eventually agreed to speak into my recorder. "I'm descended from Dumnorix," he wanted us to know, splaying his legs like a gunslinger. "Vercingétorix was Arverni, not Aedui, he wasn't from here at all."

Dumnorix-Dean struggled with our map and soon gave up trying to pinpoint where we were in Boudédé, which seemed to be spread all over the valley and hills. He waved at the thick, wet forests, instructing us to return to the chestnut, cut right at the beehives, and head south by southeast. "You might have to climb over a few fences, but you'll get to the farm eventually," he chuckled. "Watch out for the bulls. Look underneath."

"Look underneath?" Alison asked as we hiked east. "What does he mean?"

Some historians claim the Gauls invented the art of weaving live beech branches into impenetrable hedges or "living fences," as they're sometimes called. Whoever first grew them, the hedgerows of Burgundy are formidable barriers. We followed Dumnorix-Dean's directions, crossing hill, dale, and fence to a boulder-strewn Druid's site ringed by pastures. "Now what?" I asked, glancing from the hedge to the mud that reached to my knees. The herd of large white bovines at the top of the dandelion-spangled pasture had spotted us. "What do you see underneath?"

Alison paled. More than mere teats dangled. A bull!

Doubling back, we circled the valley clockwise on a dirt road. An hour later, we tramped filthy into a farmyard muddier and filthier than any other I'd seen. "Help!" I cried, hoping this slum wasn't our B&B. "Au secours! Where are we?"

"You're Americans?" asked the grizzled man who teetered out toward us moments later. "I haven't seen Americans in fifty years! Okay, okay!" He pronounced the word *oh-keye*.

Before we could speak, the man shushed his howling dog, shuffled around a rusting Citroën, shook our hands, and latched on to Alison's right upper arm. Oblivious to our queries and clear state of tired disorientation, he was going to tell us about the war and the Americans and how they'd driven out the Germans, he said, peppering his words with *oh-keye, oh-keye*. He had been nineteen years old then, he explained. Now he was over eighty. And he remembered everything. Everything.

Mr. Okay spoke in a fluty tenor, doggedly hanging on to Alison. She blanched. The geezer's calloused free hand felt its way over her body, as if milking a cow. He was groping her. The dog barked and leaped, restrained by a slender chain. "Oh, we liked the *corn-ed boeuf*, we liked it *okay*," he sang now in an accent so thick we could hardly understand.

Corn-ed boeuf? The penny dropped. He meant canned corned beef—SPAM—army rations.

"It was good, *oh-keye*, and we were hungry, we called it monkey meat, and in their kits the soldiers also got other things. . . ." He winked and smacked his lips. "Monkey meat and two condoms right in there with the *corn-ed boeuf*! Just in case. And do you know how many Americans had nice little 'wives' while they were here?" He grinned, showing his dentures. "And then they left, they went back to America to their real wives."

Alison eventually extricated herself by saying she wanted to take a photo. I stepped closer, not sure how to calm things down. The farmer was, I realized, the archetypal dirty old man, a lecher, but far too old and fragile to belt in the chops. "The priest," he said, when he learned we were on the pilgrimage route, "the priest has seventeen *communes* on his beat, and you know how many women he has? I'll tell you, he has three. A priest! And three girl-friends! He has to service all three, I swear he does, and does a good job of it, too. And here I am, a widower, with no woman at all."

We managed to extract enough information between the salacious stories to confirm we were within half a mile of our B&B in yet another part of Boudédé. Apparently the hamlet spread for miles. To keep him off Alison, I got the farmer to talk into my digital recorder. *Corn-ed boeuf,* he said several times, laughing. "We called it *le singe,* monkey meat, and it came in tin cans. . . ."

As Alison and I backed out of the farmyard, the man shuffled after us, telling us how he'd been saved by the Virgin Mary twice, in car crashes, and if we invoked her we'd be all right wherever we went, as long as we were believers. "Making love is a form of prayer," he called out through cupped hands, sounding like a character from a film by Fellini. I turned as we hiked up a twisting paved road between massive boulders. The codger was still grinning and waving.

"What do you think he did during the war?"

"Chased skirts," I said, "and ate monkey meat."

OLD MACDONALD HAD A FERME

The fireplace at Ferme de la Chassagne was big enough to roast an ox in, or enough monkeys to fill several cases of army rations. For the time being, logs crackled to the ticking of a grandfather clock and the warbling voice of a vintage crooner. Was it Edith Piaf or Barbra? A painted wooden rooster stared out from among knick-knacks on heavy wooden furniture. The air smelled of burning oak, beeswax, stew, and coffee.

We were too muddy for the armchairs, so despite exhaustion we stood warming our backs by the hearth, gazing at the vast room's thick ceiling beams, stone walls, and gleaming flagstone floors. Our hostess, Françoise Gorlier, bustled in with steaming mugs and homemade cookies.

"Back in a few minutes," she chirped, in turn adjusting her checkered apron, eyeglasses, and pink rubber gloves. "Time to milk the goats," she added. I did a double take. They weren't gloves. Her forearms and hands were bright pink from hard work and cold.

After bathing, napping, and changing into our best wrinkled evening attire, I was composed enough to recognize that our nicely furnished bedroom under the peaked roof could easily swallow an entire Paris apartment such as our own. Broad uprights and crossbeams held aloft a cathedral ceiling. Sunshine poured through skylights, illuminating a desk, overstuffed armchairs, and our giant bed. I could get used to this. Maybe we should stay a few days and regain our strength?

Before joining Alison in the farmyard, I stood at a south-facing window with a surveyor's map spread open before me. Theoretically at the far end of the river valley below was Toulon-sur-Arroux, the resting place of the valiant Helvetii. Two Celtic roads from Arroux mounted toward Bibracte, edging Boudédé.

So far, our journey seemed to be a hike not to Santiago de Compostela but backwards in time and place to ancient Gaul and Rome. All roads led to Rome as usual in Europe, forming a funnel to convey wine and blood to the Eternal City, the blood of Christ, the blood of slaves and captured warriors. Wine and blood metaphorically flowed on the countless rutted roads of the Empire. Had Rome really disappeared, or had it simply mutated and evolved?

Mallards quacked and ganders honked as I stepped outside onto the porch. Jutting from the foundations was a boulder. A mortar had been scooped from it, god knows when. Françoise saw me staring at the mortar. "Neolithic," she said, appearing beside me. "At least that's what one archeologist thinks. The house is only from the 1600s." Apparently, the area was pocked with marks from antiquity. "Later this evening, my husband will show you some aerial photos if you like," she said. "You can see walls and roads and the foundations of Roman villas scattered around."

Cows and calves mooed, horses neighed, donkeys brayed, porkers oinked, and sheep and goats bah-ed and bleated, trying to get Françoise's attention. Clearly they adored their mistress. Her pet animals seemed to be everywhere, in pastures, courtyards, and pens, all of them tidy and proper. A tune started up in my head. *Here a cluck, there a cluck, everywhere a cluck cluck.* I sang it under my breath as Françoise told me how she and Jacques and their then-teenage children had found the semi-ruined farm and spent the last decade rebuilding everything. She'd been a hospital administrator, the daughter of farmers. He was a maintenance engineer in charge of buildings and roads on Mont Beuvray, and also came from farm roots. Neither had had hands-on experience raising animals. "Our parents dreamed of educating their children; I dreamed of recreating my grandmother's farm," she said, smiling. For a moment she seemed the incarnation of Ma Kettle.

In their own way, the Gorliers had traveled back in time—to the subsistence farms of their youth, before big agribusiness had reconfigured the world. For them it really was a dream come true, with dreamy views, honeyed flowers and tree-ripened fruit, a vegetable garden, clean air, and 24/7 responsibilities, meaning never a day off. Jacques still worked fulltime. They both had pensions to look forward to a few years down the road. In the meantime, his paycheck and the B&B kept the dream afloat. The farm was self-sufficient, Françoise explained. The family and guests like us consumed everything it produced.

We talked statistics while walking toward Françoise's next farmyard task. Everyone knew, she said, that France received around $15 billion per annum from the European Union's Common Agricultural Program. That was twenty percent of Europe's total farm subsidy. But eighty percent of France's share went to twenty percent of France's farms, all of them giant agribusiness concerns. Since the end of World War Two, these factory farms had transformed France into the world's second-biggest farm-products exporter, after the United States. And it was precisely the big farms that were resisting environmentally friendly practices. They got government money to buy chemical fertilizers, pesticides, and farm machinery, and used it to tear up hedgerows and build facilities for battery chickens and other animals raised using intensive breeding methods. Françoise shrugged. It was a shrug from which hung many a tale.

We found Alison across the farmyard, talking to three adults and a child while rubbing her left shin. "It looks like a petting zoo for children," Alison laughed. "I hope I don't get a big yellow bruise."

Françoise frowned. "Was it a cow?"

"Albert the billy goat butted her," said a thirty-something man, offering his hand for a shake. He and his wife owned the neighboring farm, and were real live Burgundian locals, he said. "We're more Vercingétorix than Caesar," he said when asked about his roots.

"You look more like a Saracen than a Gaul," said their friend, a plump, middle-aged Parisian wearing camouflage safari gear. The boy with him was five or six years old and had a cappuccino complexion under a wavy Afro mop. He smirked and bridled. Straw had gotten stuck in his hair. The contrast was striking. I wondered if he had any idea what Saracens and Gauls were.

We teased the group about France's ancestor-worshippers, from Mitterrand to Dumnorix-Dean, and superficially compared our various genetic heritages, concluding that we were all the hodgepodge children of Rome, Gaul, and the Near East. I smiled inwardly. It seemed too complicated to anatomize my extended family, spread across several states. One sister and one brother had married African-Americans, with five offspring to their credit. Another brother's five children were Mexican-Americans. These cappuccino nieces and nephews of mine had added Asian, Latino, and African units to the primarily Scottish, French, and Italian bloodlines that had filled our veins for the last two centuries or so. They in turn had had children. I'd lost count of my great-nephews and great-nieces, only two so far from a Caucasian union. "We are the world," I hummed, using one earworm to drive out another. "E-i-e-i-o."

FROM FARMYARD TO TABLE

"You were there when the calf was born?" The woman's tone merged urgency, disbelief, and guilt. "And the cream? From the calf's mother?" By now she'd finished her portion of utterly unkosher, creamy veal-and-mushroom stew. She gulped. "But the animals, they're like pets, they're so . . . cute."

Jolly and roistering until now, the table fell silent.

Françoise was unflappable. "That's what happens on farms," she said. "You don't raise livestock for the fun of it."

Jacques, her husband, a stocky, boisterous man well past fifty, confirmed that everything on the table came from the farm—the orange-yellow freshly churned butter, the goose pâté we'd had for starters, everything. Even the mushrooms came from the woods. "Okay, we didn't make the wine," he laughed, pouring liberally from an old-fashioned demijohn and looking like a modern-day Bacchus. "It comes from a friend's winery in Mercurey. He makes it without sulfur, so it's practically organic. Drink to your heart's content!"

Our fellow diners took Jacques at his word. As the Mercurey refilled the ten wine glasses ranged around the big, square table, I could see the moment of you-killed-the-calf crisis passing. All six paying guests and four family members sighed almost simultaneously. Yes, the dream farm-life had its unpalatable flipside, populated by slaughterhouses and butcher knives. But even the sensitive, inquisitive Belgian lady with qualms about veal-in-mother's milk allowed Françoise to serve her a second time. It was quite simply the most succulent homemade veal-and-mushroom stew that I or anyone else at the B&B had ever eaten. We took turns saying so, some of us with crocodile tears. The goose pâté had been excellent, too, and it struck me as odd that no one wondered if Françoise had played Mother Goose before wringing the bird's neck. Patently there was a hierarchy in our affections. As the conversation ranged wider—from Brussels and Santiago, Gaul, and Rome to the inevitable America, Afghanistan, and Iraq—I felt a twitch of heartburn, wishing we wouldn't always be taken for ambassadors of our country's democratically elected administrations. Françoise's fresh goat cheese came to the rescue. It was tangy heaven on earth. The delicate apple tart untainted by corn syrup and artificial anything had a buttery shortbread crust as flaky as snow, the fruit filling still firm. I refused not to enjoy them.

Later that night, back at the window overlooking the valley where Caesar's 30,000 had slaughtered and enslaved 370,000 Helvetii, I reflected on what the Belgian woman's personable husband had said after dinner, out of earshot of other guests. "It must be terrible for you," he'd remarked thoughtfully. "Not only did that man in Washington wreak havoc in the Middle East. He also undid the goodwill your country built up for decades, and the sympathy we felt after September 11th."

FAITH WILL SET YOU FREE

The crucifix stood perhaps forty feet high, its shaft and crossbeam fashioned from blocks of gray granite. Wind whistled past, blowing so loud I could hear nothing else, not the toy cars and trucks and trains in the valley far below, not even the tolling of Autun's immense cathedral bells. Swinging in majestic Gothic towers, they were no more than a mile away as the swallow flies. The view from the monumental cross reached southeast over lowlands and a range of hills to the vineyards of the Sâone River Valley. But it was the phrase sculpted on the base of the monument that commanded my attention. Chiseled in Latin and French, it meant "Their faith set them free." The words had been composed in 1944 by Monseigneur Lebrun, bishop of Autun, a thanksgiving for the city's liberation by French and Allied troops. Autun came out practically unscathed. The cornerstone had been laid a year later, in September 1945, when Monseigneur Piguet, bishop of Clermont, had returned from the death camp of Dachau.

Leaning into the wind, I flashed back to our morning departure from Ferme de la Chassagne, the giant chestnut at the fork in the wheel-worn road, and the many ancient sites we'd tramped through on the way. Alison had spotted the pilings of a ruined Roman bridge under the rushing waters of the Arroux River, and from there onward the centurions had marched with us into Laizy, a place so old the fortresslike medieval pilgrim's church and its fine 1400s canvasses seemed recent. The climb uphill through lemony firs from Laizy to where we now stood—accomplished, for me, in considerable pain from swollen ankle and knee—had been steeper than any so far. A small roadside crucifix in the middle of the forest, lost among symmetrical timber stands, had felt like it had been placed there for our benefit. A robin had peeped and fluttered from branch to crucifix as the chainsaws roared, drawing nearer. Loggers on powerful Quads had sped by us, the vehicles' wide, knobbled tires throwing up mud and rocks.

It wasn't just the physical workout and the weathering. It was above all the encounters, the streaming thoughts, the kaleido-scope of sights and smells and sounds along the way that simul-taneously sapped and filled us with energy.

Françoise Gorlier's breakfast—a fabulous feast of homemade jams, fresh-baked brioche, and fresh cottage cheese—was a long time ago. We'd covered ten roller-coaster miles. So while Alison methodically framed and shot the granite crucifix and the walled Emerald City below, I wolfed my pâté sandwiches. As hunger ebbed, the ambiguousness of the bishop's sculpted motto came back to me. *Credentes liberati sunt.* Faith will set you free. Or, literally, the faithful are free. Free, with a little help from their friends. Meaning, among others, the Résistance fighters who were more often than not Communists, atheists, and anti-clerical republicans and whose faith in a manmade utopia was certainly not that of the church. I clicked back mentally to the photos we'd seen in the Résistance Museum at Saint-Brisson, and the words of Robert Ducreux, the Résistant we'd met in Anost. He'd been here in Autun on those mid-September days of death and glory. Freedom? Had the bishop meant the freedom of the souls of those who'd died on battlefields and in concentration camps? Released from their mortal coils, had they flown heavenward—if nowhere else, in his mind? Perhaps it was enough to have faith while living, to live free in spirit. What a blessing that would be, more comforting even than atheism. Comforting until you asked yourself how God could allow Dachau, why a perfect God would want to play with his creatures, tempt and tease and punish or reward them, and set them at each other's throats. How human God was, after all.

I stared at the tall stone cross, and thought of all the crosses we'd seen so far. It was a symbol, a powerful symbol, one I'd always cringed at when passing. Literalism was the problem, I now recognized, the thought coming not with a flash of lightning or a clashing of cymbals, but rather with a quiet revelation. Literal belief was what deadened belief systems. Did anyone literally believe there were winged angels, glowing saints, and an all-powerful creature shaped like a man watching from above?

TOP: Dirt road and clouds, Allier. BOTTOM: Sign with cockleshell, pilgrimage route, Allier.

TOP: Rochegude Chapel, Allier.

MIDDLE: Granite bridge on pilgrimage route, Aubrac.

BOTTOM: Boulders in pine forest on pilgrimage route, Allier.

TOP: Sainte-Foy Abbey, Conques, Aveyron.
MIDDLE: Merovingian-era stone caskets, Conques, Aveyron.
BOTTOM: Wooden cross on boulder with stones and cockleshell, Conques, Aveyron.

TOP: Granite boulders, Aubrac. MIDDLE: Cow looking from behind stone wall, Aubrac. BOTTOM: Cross in stone wall on pilgrimage route.

TOP: Trimmed hedges, Lot. MIDDLE: Dog looking out from behind metal gate. BOTTOM: Stone cross wired to chestnut tree, Gers.

TOP: Morning glories against a garden wall, Espalais, Tarn-et-Garonne. MIDDLE: Golfech nuclear power station, Pommevic, Tarn-et-Garonne. BOTTOM: *Gendarme Flageolet* policeman puppet figure and David's walking sticks by fair tent, Bearn.

TOP: Fence and ties, rural abstraction, Bearn.
MIDDLE: Cross and graffiti in mist, near Neuebout, Lot.
BOTTOM: Music bandstand and pruned trees, Condom, Gers.

Knotted church bell cord, Saint-Jean-le-Vieux, Bearn.

Sadly, I knew the answer was yes. Patently there were many, starting with members of my own family, people I loved and respected but could no longer have a civil conversation with, so bent were they on proselytizing. But, at the same time, I had to wonder whether I'd been too literal in the opposite way all these years, whether my wayward life of gluttony and materialism had led me into a back street leading to the side door of—what? Perception? Tolerance?

MOATS IN YOUR EYE

The time had come to leave the hilltop and hike downhill into Autun. My legs were trembling from fatigue, and Alison shivered in the relentless, cold wind. As the trail passed behind the granite cross, one sweep of the eye took in placid pastureland, the cathedral's lacy spires, and a ring of tall, forbidding walls conceived to keep enemies out and taxpayers in. Autun was a prototypical gated community.

An hour later, we got off the ridge trail and into the outskirts of the upper part of town. I paused to glance up and catch my breath. The Virgin Mary teetered atop a medieval spire within the city walls. She glanced down at us as we walked along what had once been the moat. The ramparts lay between us. They were mostly medieval, built atop Augustus Caesar's bulwark, which was balanced atop earlier, cyclopean foundations, Druid rocks, petrified dinosaur bones, and primeval rocks spewed to the crust of the earth in the beginning of time. Poking out of the disintegrating ochre limestone blocks were wall flowers blooming sweetly, vying with garlands of ivy and tangled wild plum.

A practical jokester had apparently pulled up the drawbridge or blocked up the city gates. We wandered half a mile down the yellow brick moat, trying to get into Oz, and at last found the cobbled, curving way into upper Autun's main square. In its center soared

173

the spiky Gothic spires of Saint Lazare cathedral, a cross between a startled albino porcupine and knights in limestone armor, their lances pointed skyward.

"Viollet-le-Duc strikes again," said Alison.

Before contemplating a visit to Saint Lazare, we set ourselves down at an outdoor café and, as the chill wind blew, tanked up on coffee. I felt dizzy. Or was it giddy? By now we'd covered something approaching thirteen miles, almost entirely on steep, slippery terrain, buffeted by cold gusts. Even Alison looked wan. She barely had the strength to give me a blow-by-blow account of the Old and New Testaments as they related to the sculptures depicting stories told above the cathedral's southern doors. The doors and a tilting stairway faced our table, but the distance was such that all I could discern were worn lumps of stone.

Lumps of great beauty and art-historical significance, I learned. But before entering the portals, first we crossed the street and treated ourselves to the staggering, petrified displays at the Musée Rolin, a museum which turned out to be the headquarters of an association called the Société Eduenne. The setting was a rambling medieval-Renaissance townhouse cluttered with sarcophaguses and statuary. There was a startling three-horned bull and an extraordinary high-relief of Eve that might've been Art Déco but had actually struggled out of formlessness nine hundred years ago. Not to mention the Russian-doll Virgin with Christ hidden in her belly—the one that once reposed in the church of Anost, and was used in fertility and birthing rites. I stared at it long and with squinted eyes, trying to imagine the milk-and-diaper fertility rituals of old. But I was too tired to concentrate.

There were so many layers, so much to recall. And what, precisely, was the Société Eduenne, named for the Aedui tribe? How could its members possibly keep alive the Druidic flame of their ancient forebears, the mysterious Aedui, who'd been forced to relocate to Autun from Bibracte nearly two thousand years ago?

Had everyone gone mad? The Druids were monsters, the Aedui pantheistic cannibals. It was too strange to be fictional.

We staggered back to the cathedral, and Alison positioned us directly under the main tympanum, so that we could better appreciate the sculptures. "Help," I whispered, looking up now at the Bible chiseled in the tympanum's worn stones. My eyes glazed over. Among the stylized sculpted flock of faithful, Alison spotted a pilgrim figure. This was the repository of Saint Lazare's relics, after all, a pilgrimage site that long rivalled Vézelay and even Compostela. She described the stone pilgrim to me until I almost saw him with my mind's eye, since my physical ones had given up trying. "Enough," I begged her. "Give me Kmart and a parking lot."

Foolhardy in my exhaustion, I sought refuge from the wind and the cathedral's external wonders by holing up inside the nave, where I thought I could nap long enough to stay vertical until we got to our B&B. The sensation was that of stepping into a refrigerator large enough to swallow a small city. Columns soared from darkness toward filtered, ethereal light. Colors danced through the airborne stained glass, a fandango of human tableaux spinning with dust motes. At floor level, the sparkling motes waltzed with the vapor billowing from our wind-burned mouths. Live lilies and very old incense scented the air. A lone senior woman bustled in the gloom, removing burned candle stubs and dusting down silver-encrusted crucifixes, chalices, and other mysterious implements. Alison asked her if the canon of the cathedral was receiving visitors, and before we could say Jack Robinson or begin to admire the sculpted capitals in the Lapidary Room upstairs, a quiet middle-aged man appeared from the shadows and offered us his hand.

"Jacques," he said softly. I staggered back at this apparition, staring at the floppy hat he clutched in his left hand.

"Up from Spain, are you?" I blurted. Jacques seemed perplexed. I was about to explain that I'd mistaken him for a saint, but thought better of it.

"You asked to see Chanoin Grivot," he explained, in English. "My name is Jacques Vaud."

OF CANONS AND LOST HEADS

We barely had time to exchange pleasantries with Jacques as we crossed from the cathedral and spiraled up a massive stone staircase to the canon's residence, which is ensconced in a medieval townhouse. We sensed in our go-between a soulful, quiet, quizzical man, a believer whose melancholy face had been weathered by great storms. Chanoin Grivot instead appeared to be his opposite. Somehow I'd been expecting a big gun, but Denis Grivot, the celebrated canon of Autun's Saint Lazare cathedral, proved to be more bon vivant than church militant. Even with a slight stoop attributable to his eighty-seven years, sixty of them spent running this extraordinary place of worship, Grivot appeared to stand about six-foot-eight. That made him a good foot taller than anyone else in the room.

"They haven't figured out how to get rid of me," Grivot joked in a breathy tenor, folding himself into an Empire chair at a polished Empire table and inviting us to do likewise. "In 1948, I found the head of Christ that'd been broken off and stolen from the tympanum," he said, unprompted. "I was a mere vicar at the time, a young man. . . ."

Grivot recounted his tale with the tones of a bard used to embroidering his personal mythology. He paused to adjust his glasses, twisting around in exasperation, looking for something.

How plump, clean-shaven, and soft he seemed, at eighty-seven still a boy. "Lucette, leave the door open for Joseph," he ordered, "and bring in something for these poor travelers to nibble and sip." But it was more a plea than a command, and his housekeeper Lucette knew it. She pulled luxuriously on her Gauloise, cracked a dry smile, and answered the canon as she blew out a cloud of bluish smoke.

"Joseph is perfectly capable of scratching when he wants to come in," Lucette said to the canon, shaking our hands silently. Nicotine exuded from her pores.

"Potato chips?" pouted Grivot. "Haven't we anything more appropriate?"

"Though he would be loath to admit it, Chanoine Grivot enjoys junk food," Lucette said in a husky smoker's contralto.

"Only because it's all we ever have."

How long had Lucette been taking care of Denis Grivot? Decades? They made quite a pair. Their antics were framed by a suitably ecclesiastical setting: bookshelves and leather-bound volumes. On one wavy wall of the cavernous apartment, a plastic Virgin with tiny electric lights twinkled. "Sent by friends in China," Lucette said, catching my eye.

Grivot picked up his tale where he'd left it. Lucette disappeared and reappeared with a bottle of white wine from Rully, a wine-making village on the nearby Côte Chalonnaise.

"Finally! Now don't let's argue, Lucette; pour, please, and be liberal." He paused and turned to us. "She delights in forbidding me everything I crave. I was nursed on wine, my father was a grapegrower at Rully with nine children, I being the last. My mother received a medal for exemplary child-rearing. Where was I?"

Jacques Vaud glanced across the table. He winked at me. "How much did the head of Christ weigh, Chanoine?"

"Ah, yes, 20.75 kilos," said the canon. "It was stashed away in the Musée Rolin and when I saw it I said, 'That's the head! Sculpted like the rest of the tympanum by Gislebertus in 1130!!' And without further ado I climbed up and snatched it, hid it under my vestments and rushed to the cathedral. There I mounted a ladder nine meters high, climbing with the sculpture in my hands, to see if it was indeed the pilfered head of Christ. The ladder shook. I almost fell. The weight was tremendous. Do I save the head or my life, I asked myself, as I teetered. Oh, I have sinned, Lord almighty!"

Luckily for Grivot and the world, the ladder did not collapse. He saved his life and the 45-pound stone head too. It was restored to its rightful place atop Christ's shoulders in the tympanum. Some months later, Grivot confessed his act of theft to the museum's director, at the time a fellow priest. "Oh, he was vexed indeed," Grivot said now, chortling, gulping his wine, his fingers plucking up chips and popping them into his large, soft mouth. "So many of the cathedral's treasures were stolen or sold off before and during the Revolution. Eve too was removed and then found—behind the walls of a pharmacy. Imagine that! Eve! I'm still looking for Adam," he said, puffing from excitement and raising his eyebrows at Lucette. "I'm getting closer. We'll find Adam soon enough."

Joseph the cat wandered in, rubbing himself on our legs. The sun began to set, its rays slanting across the study, until they fell on the blinking plastic Virgin from China. Somehow the bottle of Rully had evaporated and Lucette declined to get another—too much was bad for the canon, she said, quietly triumphant.

Just as I was about to slip into the land of dreamy dreams, I heard Alison asking Grivot provocatively whether he thought the act of pilgrimage was egotistical. It seemed, after all, self-indulgent, an apparently pointless meander. Grivot stopped fishing for potato chips, taken aback.

"Egotistical? Pilgrimage? No. Never. Heavens, no. Why? It is one way to know thyself, and, through that inward knowledge, to know God."

"You walk with yourself," Jacques Vaud said softly, "but that does not mean you walk selfishly. Serendipity plays a part. You never know what you'll discover. I walked and rode on horseback once down the pilgrimage trail. . . ."

We didn't have time to ponder Jacques's words or ask for details. Grivot interrupted. He was eager to hear his own voice again. Excitedly, he recounted how during the Occupation he'd ridden a bicycle from Brest on the Atlantic coast all the way back to Autun, his own personal pilgrimage, and how he'd covered the Saint James route many times by car. "Alas, I've never had time to walk more than a few short sections," he added. I asked if he'd noticed a surge in pilgrims in recent years. He faced Lucette and lifted one eyebrow into a circumflex, pointing a long, plump finger at the bottle. "We don't get many pilgrims here," he said. "There used to be a regular pilgrimage from Chalon-sur-Saône to Autun."

Chalon was a river port on the Saône and had been used as a beachhead by Caesar's invading Romans. Once Gaul was within the Empire's orbit, Rome had shipped wine up the Rhône to the Saône. From Mâcon and Chalon the Roman colonists had converted the Gauls into "the slaves of Bacchus." Eventually the church had taken over from the Gallo-Roman governors. Chalon and Autun had become important religious sites, with cathedrals and relics. The Roman roads had evolved into pilgrimage routes. But over time, the mainlines to Rome and Compostela had veered west, bypassing sleepy Autun just as the autoroute and TGV high-speed train line now bypassed it.

"We no longer have relics," Grivot remarked with disgust. "In 2002, thieves stole the Grail of Saint Nazaire. One day they stole the skull of Saint Philibert from the abbey in Tournus, a little further south on the Saône River. The very next day they came here and stole our relics. They stole the relics of Mary Magdalene from Vézelay, too. For some sort of cultish black magic ritual, I suppose. Sooner or later I'll catch the ringleader," Grivot said, rising up in his chair, his right arm shaking. "You know what I'll do? I'll cut off his head and put it in the place of the relics he stole!"

"Chanoine, don't excite yourself," Lucette reprimanded. "His blood pressure gets very high."

"Hah!" the canon yelped. "What the malefactors don't know is they probably got a fake anyway! Serves them right! Yes, indeed, there was a mixup centuries ago. In 1120, the bishop of Autun, Étienne de Bagé, ordered the skull of Saint Lazare to be moved here from the original cathedral across the street, but he wound up with the cranium of a rather nasty fellow from Marseille also named Lazare!"

"Oh, my," Lucette exclaimed.

"Do people really believe in the power of relics nowadays?" I couldn't help asking.

"Do they?" Grivot paused, but not for long. "Perhaps. They certainly did once upon a time," he said.

"Someone stole them," Jacques noted. "Someone still believes in their powers."

"Surely it's not the relics that count," Lucette insisted, "it's the intention of those who come to revere them, to pray and hope. So whether it's Lazare or Nazaire or any other relic, it doesn't matter. Relics aren't needed, only spiritual intentions and faith."

"Naturally," Jacques agreed. "Of course you're right."

Grivot shrugged and batted at invisible gnats. "There are a hundred fingers of Saint John out there," he said, pursing his lips. "Hundreds of them."

I felt myself drifting as Grivot explained the church's reticence regarding relics. As the sun set and the study filled with Lucette's acrid smoke, canon Grivot told us in minute detail of his sixty years of studying the cathedral and the history of Autun, of the dozens of books he'd written, and of his role in carrying on the cathedral school and choir. I felt Alison's fingers pinching my thigh under the table and bestirred myself.

It was dark by the time Jacques walked us back down the snail-shell staircase of the canon's residence and led us to the cathedral. Even the cold wind couldn't revive me. Before we entered, Alison pointed up at the head of Christ and the pilgrim figure she'd spotted earlier. "You see a pilgrim?" Jacques asked. "Are you sure?" On cue, floodlights flickered to life, illuminating the cathedral's exterior. After a moment of silent scrutiny, Jacques turned to Alison, his face beaming. "And to think, all these years I've lived here, and I never noticed the pilgrim."

I couldn't help wondering how much the pilgrim figure on the tympanum weighed, and how long it would be before my head rested on a feather pillow. Jacques Vaud began a polite postmortem of the canon's tales. But I could take no more. I was beyond replete.

LOOKING WITHOUT SEEING

Was it Picasso who said "I don't seek, I find"? But surely the Bible commanded "Seek and thou shalt find"? Who was right? Both, perhaps. Or neither.

Such were my thoughts at dawn as I recalled Jacques Vaud's delight at discovering the pilgrim figure on the tympanum, a thing of beauty he'd looked at a thousand times—looked at without seeing. Until, serendipitously, observant Alison with fresh eyes, the accidental pilgrim, had come along and recognized a fellow traveler, this one carved in stone.

Lying in bed at the B&B, I struggled to keep my eyes open in dawn's semidarkness. The other lessons provided by our encounter with Jacques and Grivot appeared to be several. First, don't plan everything in life, because not everything is in your control; and second, sometimes when you let go, you grow in unexpected ways and meet extraordinary people. Just let go and drift, see where life takes you. Specialization? Certainly. An excellent thing. Grivot was an object lesson in the strength of it—sixty years of his dedication had saved a school and produced thirty books that unraveled the mysteries of Autun. But specialization also meant sacrifice. Like Grivot, you missed the wide, wonderful world—you missed walking to Compostela, marrying, changing directions and careers and your views on history, life, faith.

Hadn't there been another lesson? The third and last lesson of the evening was the one that confirmed my nearly fifty years of observing those who thrive and grow ripe and wrinkled with the fullness of a long life. The lesson was simple. The bigger your ego, the longer you were likely to live.

A bird trilled on our windowsill. I opened my eyes again and glanced up at the cathedral ceiling of our room, wondering where we were. Eventually I realized we'd somehow made it to a B&B late last night, and were somewhere on the outskirts of town. The smell of coffee and croissants wafted up to our room. It was a gorgeous room. I'd been far too tired after our meeting with Canon Grivot and our unplanned dinner with Jacques Vaud and his wife to notice how grand our lodgings were.

During our ritual pre-breakfast stretching session, three swallows flew into our room, pirouetted around Alison's head, and darted back out. A good omen? I certainly hoped so.

As our host Peter poured coffee for us, he told us he was Danish and had been a clothing designer based in Amsterdam before reinventing himself as an innkeeper. His understated taste shone through in the minimalist décor done in shades of pale green, and also in the collections of silver, carafes, and glasswork arranged like so many Morandi still lifes. Some people painted. Others wrote poetry. Peter was an artful nester.

Alison abruptly left the table. She was suffering from Grivot's Revenge—one glass too many of Rully. Out for the count, she retreated to our room. We both needed a day off from being pilgrims.

Peter and I took our coffee mugs into the garden, where he showed me the foundations of what had probably been a Merovingian abbey. I wondered aloud what would happen if the archeologists decided to do a Bibracte to Peter's private paradise.

"Oh, dear," he said, blanching, "what a nightmare that would be."
I could see he regretted telling me his secret.

Talk of Bibracte led us down winding roads to Rome and the
Catholic Church, and, before we said farewell later that morning,
Peter had shared a peculiar, Danish perspective on Western European culture, social democracy, religion, and the meaning of the
loaded word "barbarian."

As the child of a Pagan Mediterranean mother and an atheistic American father of distant Scottish descent, I'd never really
thought much about Germanic and Scandinavian history and
myths and how they might lie at the root of both Protestantism
and modern social-democracy. I'd failed to consider how offen-
sive it might be to the gentle descendants of Vikings to have their
ancestors tarred with the brush of barbarianism. To Peter's mind,
the nomadic, unruly ancient tribal traditions of Nordic peoples
had gotten a bum rap. It was another case of the victor's version
of history. No one had the monopoly on cruelty and violence,
he said, acknowledging the live burials, ritual immolation, torture, and so on, practiced by his ancestors. "But we've moved on,
haven't we? We don't live in the past."

Astonishingly, Peter thought, the French were still stuck in
their Gallo-Roman mold. What he meant was, they were slaves
of linear logic, the Gallo-Roman laws and traditions that had
become Napoleonic and then modern French laws and traditions, the Cartesian world view of right and wrong, symmetry
and order, belonging and exclusion. This explained why the
French demanded assimilation to their culture—the submission
to Frenchness, the French language, French customs, the French
model, and the so-called republican values of Liberty, Equality,
and Fraternity. Mere integration wasn't enough. "If you don't
embrace them and abandon your own culture and values and
language, they hate you," Peter summed up. "We Nordic peoples
and the British and many North Americans who're the product

of a different tribal reality, and who rejected Rome's gods and Catholicism's single God in favor of democratic Protestantism, for us the model is tolerance and integration, not assimilation. Who's to say that they—the Romans and Gallo-Romans—weren't the real barbarians?"

Later, as I revisited Autun's ruined Roman amphitheater—a scallop shell of tiered stone scooped from the hillside, grass-grown and topped by budding horse chestnut trees—Peter's words came back to me, sounding particularly pertinent. Once, this amphitheater had been the biggest in Gaul, with seating for twelve thousand spectators. The spot was quiet and empty now, the artificial lake facing it uncluttered by the rowboats of summer. But I recalled one hot August day a few years back, when Alison and I had passed through Autun and stumbled upon chariot races being held in the amphitheater. There'd been clouds of dust, horses neighing and galloping, cardboard and plastic swords waving. Warriors in papier-maché helmets had clashed to the sound of tinny trumpets. Thousands of tourists and locals had cheered and shouted, as if they'd been at a football match, or the Coliseum, with lions and Christians on the bill. As with most French historical spectacles, the kitsch was palpable, with ham actors declaiming incomprehensibly, recreating not history but the 1960s sword-and-sandals movies they'd seen—*Ben Hur*, *Spartacus*, or *Hercules and the Mongol Maidens*.

Standing alone now amid the amphitheater's gray stones, I smiled inwardly at the fundamental tragicomedy of the French historical obsession. Were the French really French? There was no such thing. The Gauls had been violent interlopers from the east—Mongols before their time. They in turn were beaten and subsumed by the hodgepodge called Rome. As self-styled Gallo-Romans, they'd been admixed into oblivion by invading Germanic tribes, Saracens, Spaniards, Britons, and god knows what else. Yet French spinmeisters had spent the last two thousand years simultaneously elevating Vercingétorix and Charlemagne, paradoxically advertising themselves as the heirs and victims of Rome, while vilifying the Germans as invaders, and denouncing foreigners in general, Africans in particular nowadays. What would France do about India and China? Perhaps the time was nigh to put Vercingétorix and Caesar to rest, and move forward, not as Frenchmen, but rather as Europeans, arms open to the Brave New Globalized World?

Non, non, non came the resounding answer. It echoed as I explored another of Autun's soulful Gallo-Roman monuments, the so-called "Temple of Janus." Apparently, fractious local historians continue to argue whether the temple was dedicated to Janus or another deity; but the moment I laid eyes on it, I had no doubts. Pocked stone walls, holed by time and troubles, rose gape-eyed to the height of a giant tree, surrounded by the emerald floodplains of the town's northwestern suburbs. The Arroux River—the river that had once run red with Helvetii blood—curved between the temple and Autun's walls. The main Roman road also once ran by the Temple of Janus, linking Augusto Dunum—the fortified hilltop city of Augustus Caesar—to Chalon-sur-Saône, Beaune, and Mâcon, alias Cavillonum, Belenos, and Matisco, their ancient names. A roadway seemed an appropriate place to build a temple to Janus, the two-faced god. One pair of eyes looked back to the road already traveled, the other looked forward. Not to mention the mouths and noses and ears of Janus's bearded faces. He was a complicated fellow. Janus lived simultaneously in the past and the present. This struck me as absolutely appropriate. Forget the Druids or Hercules—King Louis XIVth's role-model. Forget Jupiter, Mercury, and Mars, the favorite gods of the Gauls. Janus was the god of Old Europe. Janus was contemporary France.

PART TWO

TRUE DRINK

ACROSS WINE COUNTRY
FROM BEAUNE TO MÂCON

For my flesh is true food, and my blood is true drink . . .
—*John 6:55*

BEAUNE APPÉTIT

"Jump!" I shouted, pulling Alison out of the way. The tourist train rolled silently up on us. The pilot sounded a tinny horn. Headlines flashed before my eyes:

> ***American Pilgrim Struck Dead by Plexiglas Elephant Train***
> ***Dateline:*** *Beaune, France, wine capital of Burgundy.*
>
> *Eyewitness reports say American photographer Alison Harris was struck and killed by a crowded tourist convey-ance one block from Beaune's Hôtel Dieu, also known as Les Hospices de Beaune. Harris, a longtime resident of France, was on a cross-country pilgrimage. She was said to have been tired and distracted. Her husband David Downie, also a pilgrim, though of an unorthodox kind, was present when the accident occurred. Downie confirmed that Harris had spent the previous day in the company of an 87-year-old clergyman in Autun and had "Possibly drunk too much white wine."*

What the imaginary dispatch failed to report was, in the hours before the conveyance appeared, we'd clicked our heels, checked into our hotel, showered, napped, and limped back onto the cobbled streets of Beaune. It felt like a Burgundian theme park, a model of prosperity and order.

Disciples of Bacchus founded ancient Belenos nearly two thou-sand years ago. Since then, Beaune has grown ramparts around its concentric rings of streets. The streets are studded with medieval churches, Renaissance townhouses, and other landmarks, the most celebrated of which is Les Hospices. A prototype hospice-hospital-cum-winery built in the 1400s, the building spreads around courtyards under gabled roofs topped with brilliant glazed tiles. This is the site of the annual November wine auction, during which actors and other celebrities promote Beaune and its wine for charity. It struck me as unusual that an institution long associated with the pain and suffering of the infirm should be given over to Hollywood-style glitz.

Walt Disney probably loved Beaune. It merges Mainstreet France and Fairytale Castle, but is in fact a real town, not a cardboard imitation. Beaune seemed all the more surprising to us now for its apparent lack of authenticity.

"Coffee," Alison yawned, beating me to the word. "I guess I didn't have enough this morning."

"Admit it," I yawned back, taking her by the arm and leading her across the street, once the elephant train had silently passed. "We overdid it yesterday, and need a rest before we start across wine country."

Alison modulated her voice. "Would you like to spend an extra day in Beaune?"

"In Beaune?" I glanced at the window-shoppers slurping the season's first ice cream cones and peering into the windows of fashion boutiques. Musicians played on street corners. Visitors lined up at the Hospices and a self-styled Museum of Wine nearby. It wasn't really a museum, but rather a wine-tasting center and wine shop in the Convent of the Cordeliers. Somewhere down a banner-draped street, a public-address system blared advertisements in French and English. In the window of a wine shop, a single fake bottle of Domaine de la Romanée-Conti wore a price tag equivalent to the average annual income of about five billion of the planet's inhabitants.

So, to answer Alison's question, clearly in our questing frame of mind, Beaune was wasted on us and we would not be spending an extra day here.

Caffeine soon dissipated our cloistered mood. Alison herded me to the medieval ramparts to get the blood flowing, and then into the cavernous church of Notre-Dame de Beaune to cool me off.

Every significant building in town seemed to be signposted with a date, like a vintage bottle of wine. Notre-Dame was no exception. It had been built from the 12th to 16th centuries. A contemporary banner strung over the door promised *Ravivez votre Mariage.* Instinctively we scrutinized each other. Did our marriage need reviving? Was this walk putting a Lazarus bounce back into our nineteen-year union? I could feel my left eyebrow rising. After hiking all day every day, there wasn't a great deal of zip left over to get a rise out of anyone. Perhaps the resuscitation would come later, on our return? Or would it, like so many aspects of our journey, manifest itself metaphorically?

Displayed inside the incense-scented Gothic church was a celebrated Black Virgin, so classified not by race, but because of the dark wood she was carved from, made even darker by staining from the oily fingers of the faithful. She wasn't nearly as renowned as her counterpart at Rocamadour in the southwest of France, the one that helped bring composer Francis Poulenc back to the faith. Beaune's Madonna was less primitive than the one in Rocamadour. The setting was also less dramatic. We stared at her and tried to filter out the voices of tourists and the camera flashes. Postcards and souvenirs beckoned from a stand.

A pious woman at the information desk directed us to a stained-glass window depicting Beaune's martyr, Saint Floscel. I asked her to spell and pronounce the name. "Floscel was very young when he died," she said acidly. I couldn't help thinking that her face looked distressingly like a baked Granny Smith. "We have Floscel's jawbone," she added. My eyes followed her sinewy finger to a reliquary.

"What special properties does the jawbone possess?" Alison inquired earnestly.

The woman said she wasn't aware of particular powers. "That's not what veneration is about," she added, her mouth disappearing and reappearing amid arid folds. "It's a question of culture and history and faith."

"Of course," Alison agreed.

"Of course," I echoed.

Yes, I thought with grim satisfaction, remembering Lucette and Canon Grivot's words. The relic-veneration business has evolved into the historico-cultural-enogastronomical tour business, turning places like Beaune into 21st-century pilgrimage sites. Easy to consume and navigate, they come with good signage, full-color postcards, wine-tasting tours in deconsecrated chapels, Plexiglas tourist trains, and sound-and-light extravaganzas.

BEAUNE VOYAGE

As we headed for the vineyards of the Côte de Beaune in morning sunlight, I couldn't help reprimanding myself. The weather was chilly, but that wasn't why Beaune left me cold. We'd had a fairly good time. We'd seen a martyr's jawbone and, later, in the Hospices, the preserved heart of the hospital's benefactor, François Brunet de Montforard. We'd been suitably impressed by the architecture. The ceiling of the former dormitory, built like an overturned wooden ship, boasted delicate, decorated ribbing and cross-timbers. We'd been genuinely moved and disturbed by the many-paneled polyptych in the museum. The painting had started life in the 1400s as an altarpiece, and its nine panels showing *The Last Judgment*, painted by Flemish master Roger van der Weyden, had stifled my irreverence. The nails and thorns and blood, the tortures undergone and the tears wept, were eerily contemporary and spoke all languages, uniting religions and creeds, including atheism.

On a lighter note, we'd slept in a comfortable room at l'Hôtel du Cêdre, and had enjoyed an extravagant meal consisting of snails and frogs' legs in buttery cream sauce, exquisite spring lamb, and ripe cheeses, accompanied by a bottle of vintage wine.

Beyond Beaune's ramparts and nondescript suburbs, we paused for a last look. "What a relief," Alison said.

"Are we misfits? People would kill to be doing what we're doing. What's wrong with us?"

"Maybe we're discovering what's right with us," Alison said cryptically.

Leafless, the vineyards of the Côte de Beaune spread before us. Again, I felt like a misfit. As we hiked into the terraced rows of Chardonnay and Pinot Noir grapes, the first words and images that sprang to mind were "cemetery" and "Normandy landings." For the first time in days, I felt in my red windbreaker for my misshapen cockleshell from Utah Beach. Perfectly aligned, the vines held up by cement posts looked to me like gnarled black Christs on white crosses marching to infinity—or finitude. Here and there, a pale grape bud struggled to open. Forget Disney and Nietzsche. What would Walt Whitman say? There wasn't a blade of grass to be seen, and not a single weed. Wasn't green the color of hope? Or did it represent faith or charity? I couldn't remember. I'd never really understood why any sentient human being needed to be instructed to be charitable, why charity didn't come naturally, without Saint Paul lecturing the Corinthians. Yes, I had read the Bible, not in church or Sunday school, but while studying Political Science at the University of California at Berkeley.

Despite herbicides, the hillsides would soon burst back to life, the grape leaves unfurling. Given the almost-zero church attendance in Burgundy, it was probably the only resurrection that mattered in wine country.

The familiar scallop shells and other signs marked our route, obviating the need for maps. According to the Council of Europe, our trail was an offshoot of the Way of Saint James. The local tourist board called it "la Route des Grands Crus." If the regional tourist board was to be trusted, we were about to follow "la Route des Moines," not Des Moines, Iowa, but rather the medieval monks of Cluny and other winemaking Burgundian abbeys. In their cowled brown habits, the monks had spread the art of transforming grapes, ostensibly to supply "true drink" ready for transubstantiation into Christ's blood. Clearly, the monks had excelled at their job of making sacramental wine. But they and their ways had come and gone. So too had the Wars of Religion, the divine-right kings of France supposedly descended from Caesar, Clovis, and Charlemagne, and the devastating Revolution of 1789. Only the vines and the drink made of their fermented fruit had survived, enriching Burgundy, perhaps to excess.

VIRGINS AND ROCK FARMS

Wild lilac, fruit trees, and wall flowers sprang from the sun-bleached vineyards edged by walls of golden stone. The walls were stained by bluish copper sulfate. They parceled the hillsides neatly. Working in one plot marked "Premier Cru—Les Vignes Franches" were three grape-growers. They finished rooting out an old vine and prepared to plant a new one. I couldn't help asking where the rootstock came from.

"America," said one of the growers. Middle-aged and gruff, the roadmap of burst capillaries on his cheeks spoke volumes about his devotion to his profession. "Phylloxera killed our vines over a hundred years ago. Every rootstock in France is grown from American vines." He paused to scrutinize us. "*Eh oui*, all good things come from America, starting with phylloxera."

Did I detect irony? Though his apparent goal was to make us uncomfortable, the strategy failed. I smiled back relentlessly. "How in the world did you guess we were American? What I meant to ask you was, is there some kind of wholesale nursery for grapevines in Burgundy, or do you buy direct from America?"

Abashed by reverse irony, the man waved the trunk of the old grapevine and told us there were several dozen specialized root-stock suppliers, most of them in Provence, but the biggest of all was in the Savoie region. Everyone in Burgundy got their vines from the Savoie.

We said goodbye and in less than an hour were hiking downhill into Pommard. It looked remarkably like a winegrowing village should, with low stone houses wrapped by balconies, and small, no-nonsense gardens. The wineries and warehouses stood out back. The air was scented by sulfur. We'd been breathing it in the vineyards, and my head was beginning to throb. Organic grape-growing did not appear to be popular hereabouts. "Tradition" was what the winegrowers clung to. Tradition meant the 1950s chemical-warfare style of horticulture.

I knew from having read it somewhere that Thomas Jefferson's wine supplier was a certain Monsieur Parent of Pommard. By now Parent would be at least the great, great, great-grandparent of anyone still running the family business. Beyond the ungainly church and fountain on the main square, a sign pointed to the Parent winery. We knocked and rang but no one answered, which was for the best. Coffee is what I needed, not wine. By the looks of it, no coffee would be available in Pommard. And it wasn't.

Borne along by a cool breeze, we blew into neighboring Volnay. A high-tech tractor stood by the roadside. Mounted on it was a large tank of clear chemicals. "Nice of them to do the weeding," I remarked, my throat parched and eyes stinging. Alison spluttered. Her lips had gone the bluish color of copper sulfate. Either she'd succumbed to the vineyard treatments, or she was cold and hungry.

As if by sympathetic magic, the noon siren blew in distant Beaune and was echoed by a bell tolling from the church belfry. My stomach growled, turning my thoughts to finding an uncontaminated spot for our picnic. Volnay's small square, shaded by clipped, leafless trees and set above a sea of chemically blasted vines, seemed a good place to enjoy our cheese sandwiches, apples, and water. The cold was intense. Alison's teeth chattered relentlessly. The sound of her splitting molar was audible to me several feet away.

"Ouch!" she yelped. Granted, the local baguette wasn't as tender as some, though it didn't seem tough enough to break a tooth. "That dentist," she muttered, trying to separate the shattered tooth from the lead filling.

After vain attempts at finding a villager or functioning telephone booth, we decided to hike as quickly as possible to Auxey-Duresses, the next village, and seek a dentist. To get there in a hurry, we'd have to walk on the highway. Otherwise, we could follow our trail to the ridge and expect to walk for several hours. Alison decided that a broken tooth wouldn't kill her, whereas a speeding truck, tractor, car, or tour bus might.

From nestled village and groomed vines we found ourselves in a Mediterranean microclimate atop the hill. Lilacs vied with contorted pines. The scent of wall flowers gradually replaced that of the pesticides, and the meandering trail curled unexpectedly to the feet of an imposing Madonna. Standing high on a pedestal above the vineyards, she wore robes of royal blue and white and didn't look much like Catherine Deneuve, whose effigy was long used as the model for Marianne. The sun was bright, glinting off the Virgin's white cloak. I couldn't be sure, but Notre-Dame des Vignes appeared to be weeping rusted tears. A plaque stated that she'd been erected here on September 17, 1871 to protect the vines: *Posuerunt me custodem in vineis*, Cant 1.5.

Relics and veneration were in vogue at the time, weapons in the fight against phylloxera, the vine-destroying aphid that changed the world. I repeated the thought to myself. "The aphid that changed the world." It sounded like the title of a SciFi flic.

Despite phylloxera's tick-like appearance when first born, the button-sized insect had struck like winged lightning. In a matter of decades, *Phylloxera Daktulosphaira vitifoliae* had crept and wriggled and flown across Europe from the contaminated American soil unwittingly shipped in the 1850s with plant samples from the East Coast to England. It crossed the Channel mysteriously, perhaps in produce shipments or by flying with its own little wings, to France, Italy, Spain, Germany, and Eastern Europe, devastating vineyards everywhere. Nine in ten European winegrowing areas were affected.

Modern treatments including pesticides and ultra-heat-treating of soil had failed to kill phylloxera, which still thrived. That explained the continuing need to use American rootstock. Nature has equipped the wild American vine with a flavor phylloxera abhors.

The view from the ridge of Burgundy's great rolling vineyards and the Saône Valley east of them filled me with the irrational desire to fly. Flight would've been the natural reaction of locals afflicted by phylloxera, whose female offspring in alternating generations sprouted wings and flew from vine to vine before going to ground, where they sapped the grapevine roots. I realized, standing at the Virgin's feet, that a brief history of phylloxera would have to include more than the pest's scientific identity card. It would beg a description of the insect's eating habits and of the collateral damage it had done. Did phylloxera prefer Pinot Noir and Chardonnay, the main grape varieties of Burgundy? Or did it, as many authorities seemed to think, have a proclivity for Syrah, Grenache, and the other vines of the Rhône Valley? Perhaps it found the Cabernets and Merlot of the Bordelais region even more attractive?

Nowhere had the question of varietal preference been answered definitively. With self-lacerating satisfaction, every winegrowing community in Europe seemed to proclaim itself the most devastated of all, its vines the pest's favorite. Only a handful of isolated, undistinguished areas with sandy or volcanic soil had been spared, and were therefore unable to join in the lament.

Naturally there was much more to phylloxera than biology. The wrecking of Europe's vineyards ruined economies and spurred mass population shifts, as bankrupt peasants, wine wholesalers, and retailers packed their corkscrews and tramped to the cities. Whole swaths of southwestern France were de-vined and replanted with truffle-bearing oak trees, for instance. That had given rise to an abundance of melanosporum fungi, alias black Périgord truffles, truffles that global warming and sudden drought were now destroying. Cattle took over vineyards in other areas, like the Charolais region of southern Burgundy, which we'd be crossing in a week or so. Everywhere vines grew, superstition triumphed and cast-iron Virgin Mary statues like this one appeared, heavenly guardians against the aphid. A pestilence-driven Catholic Revival spread on the insect's wings. Devotional pilgrimages to blue-and-white Madonnas perched among the vines had become obligatory, or so claimed the history books I'd read.

I looked up again. On the base of the rusty Virgin could be read the words "Forty-day indulgence for all who invoke the image of Mary."

"Hail," I said, removing my billed cap. "I'm not sure what the effect will be, since you're programmed to fight aphids, but if you're out there, Mary, please do something about my knees and eyes and my wife's tooth, and help bring peace to the world while you're at it."

Alison put her camera away. "It only works if you believe."

"Does it?"

"That's what's said. The leap of faith. Intentionality. It's like a placebo effect."

"Tell phylloxera."

As we trudged south on the ridge through musty boxwood, pine, and sweet-smelling wild plum, following yet another ancient, rutted road, I couldn't help wondering what the phylloxera pilgrims wore. Did they have heavy leather boots and woolen capes, three-cornered hats, breeches and gaiters? Did they carry long staffs to steady themselves and ward off wolves? I tried to imagine what it was like walking cross-country back then, in the 1800s, without good maps and signage, let alone cafés, hotels, and B&Bs. In open countryside, phylloxera pilgrims found their way forward from crossroads to crossroads, because each was marked by a crucifix visible from afar. Or they navigated from steeple to village steeple. There were no asphalted roads, a good thing. I now knew from experience that for a hiker's knees and feet, surfaces of asphalt, cement, and stone were tremendously tiring. Even with the cushioned, rubber-soled boots I was wearing, my knees and back had been killing me, ever since I'd slipped in the Gorges de la Canche. But I dared not complain. We had hundreds of miles to go.

"If Mary won't help, maybe Marianne will," I said. "Do you think Napoléon called a conclave or a revolutionary council meeting to work out how to transfer the Virgin Mary's powers to Marianne?"

"You're being sardonic."

"I'm joking," I said, "sort of."

It's a fact, contested by some, that Marianne is the secular reinterpretation of the Virgin Mary. But this was no joking matter for most French, who were either Catholic and therefore insulted by what amounted to blasphemy, or were Bonapartists and therefore insulted for having their symbol associated with Catholicism.

With this no-win series of thoughts in mind, I took notice of our path and the rocky, eroded bluffs underfoot. The origin of the term *côte* had suddenly become clear. It was the French bastardization of *costa*, "coast," which in Latin and Italian means both rib and coastline. The escarpments of the Côte de Beaune and the land at their base were like a ribbed coastline, an ideal terrain for grape-growing and little else. Out of the lunar wilderness sprouted patchy fields of bright green grain. We paused to run our eyes over the landscape and wonder why anyone was trying to grow wheat here. In answer, the familiar word sprang to mind.

"Subsidies," Alison said before I could.

"Rock farms. No yield. The government pays. It's a boondoggle for winemakers no longer able to compete."

"There goes the rest of my molar," she groaned, cradling her jaw and extracting a hunk of ivory.

I braced myself for the ache that would soon follow us and clobber her.

About an hour later, we each did a double-take while entering Auxey-Duresses. It looked surprisingly like Pommard and Volnay, and we worried for a moment that we'd returned on our tracks. But no: here was a café-restaurant called La Cremaillère on the main highway. An affable woman carrying a tray strode back and forth between the smoky dining room and the quiet bar area where we sat, sipping our espressos.

"A dentist?" she asked. She paused to shake her head. It was as if I'd asked to see a Martian. "You'll have to go back to Beaune," she said. "No dentists left around here." She handed us the telephone book and a cordless phone and, with a nod and grunt, expressed sympathy for Alison's bad luck. She also seemed to want to communicate to us the central tragedy of post-phylloxera village life, by defining the meaning of *désertification*. As she spoke the word, the title of that celebrated 1940s book on dessicated rural France sprang to mind, *Paris et le désert francais*.

It was Saturday, and by now afternoon. Unsurprisingly, half a dozen attempts failed to raise a dentist in the villages on our path. We thanked the waitress, paid up and stepped onto Auxey-Duresses' main street. "Back to Beaune?" I asked. Alison shook her head. "Onward!"

POLISH SNAILS AND LEAPING RATS

Meursault is easy to pronounce as long as you don't look at the way it's spelled. Happily, the chalky white town doesn't look the way the name sounds. Too robust and sprawling to be a village, its long, dusty main street led us into a vaguely triangular main square where a fountain splashed. Over one side of the square towered the town hall, which appeared to have been grafted onto a medieval tower, no doubt rebuilt by Viollet-le-Duc in the mid-1800s. Near it, soaring into the sky was the dunce-cap belfry of an outsized church, by the look of it, late do-it-yourself Gothic many times remodeled. Specialty food shops, a pharmacy, bakery, restaurants, and hotels completed the picture puzzle. Visitors animated the outdoor terrace of l'Hôtel du Centre, our overnight address. After unharnessing ourselves and dusting each other down, we sat in the sun and waited. And waited. Refreshments proved long in coming. We had enough time to dry our sweaty garments in the breeze and read up on local history.

Alison had unearthed a guidebook in the hotel lobby. She cleared her parched throat. The town hall had been erected in 1337, she informed me. The church was from the 1480s onward. But Meursault was older. The town straddles the pre-Gallic, Gallic, and Roman salt and tin roads from the Saône Valley to Bibracte. We were seated in the center of what had been an Aedui stronghold, upgraded to a Roman encampment during the Empire, and reconfigured in Late Antiquity by monks and feudal lords.

By the time the hotel's only waiter had hobbled over, taken our order, and returned with tepid beverages, Alison—apparently unfazed by toothache—had paced us through several thousand years of history. According to the menu propped up on our table, the hotel's owners were named Xavier and Martine Foret. Monsieur Foret slid his brush-over aside and brightened when we told him we were overnight guests and had also reserved dinner. Forty years of waiting tables, greeting, accounting, stepping, fetching, and smiling had clearly taken their toll. Like most proud Frenchmen, Foret's facial muscles were easily strained.

"You ask me why it is called Meursault?" Foret repeated my question at considerable volume. Either I was an idiot or ignorant, for everyone knew that Meursault was derived from a corruption of "rat" and "leap"—*muris saltus*. "In Latin, of course," he added.

"Of course," I said.

"The Rat's Leap—*le saut du rat*—is what we call the geological cleavage between the Côte de Beaune up there and the land of Meursault over here." He waved.

"Thank you for the clarification," I said. "I'll refrain from asking you for the etymology of Puligny-Montrachet. And I'll wrestle to the floor anyone who tells me that *murus altus* actually means 'high wall' in Latin, or points out that *saltus* also means forested slope or woodsy pastureland. And of course I'll also happily duel with those who tell me that there are several other variations on the theme of 'Meursault' in parts of the country with a wholly different geological configuration."

"Smart-alec," Alison said, as Foret retreated, scowling. "Just because you studied Latin."

I pointed to the guidebook. "Read that. Are we men, or parrots? Don't answer."

Our thirst slaked, we glanced at the clock on the belfry and realized there were nearly three hours to wait until dinner. Half that time disappeared between showers and naps, leaving us approximately ninety minutes to walk a few more miles. With vespers tolling, it seemed obvious where Alison would head first. I caught up with her among the pews. Candles flickered and sun streamed down through bull's-eye windows. I recalled the figure fifty-seven meters—about 180 feet—for the belfry's height. The nave was less uplifting, and seemed constituted by cellars joined together and held up by Gothic arches. The builders had perhaps learned their trade in the winery business.

Pleasantly tired, I leaned my forehead on the waxed rail of a wooden pew and tried to think great thoughts. My eyes would not stay shut, however. I'd noticed half a dozen family names written with a felt pen on signs propped on the pews around us, names such as Patriarche, DeSousa, Rossignol, Simonin, Gente, and Capella. They didn't sound much like Aedui names. More likely, their owners had come north from Rome and other winegrowing parts of the Empire those many centuries ago, when an amphora bought you a strong Gallic slave.

High walls of bleached limestone ran into the vineyards south of the church. As we explored them on our stroll, Alison reminded me that local grapegrowers had been unearthing pottery and burial monuments here for many years. Some of the vineyards we peered into seemed like walled gardens, the pale stones radiating the warmth of the afternoon sun. Several of the more prized white wines of the world came from here, but the fact seemed less daunting than I'd anticipated. Perhaps our morning's walk through so many prime vineyards had been a salutory reminder that we were, after all, talking about dirt, vines, and fermented fruit juice. "Bone white," I murmured, recalling a ditty I'd read in a wine encyclopedia once upon a time. "Bone as in Beaune, white as in white wine," I explained. "The best whites come from the Côte de Beaune. Dark as night. Nuit's delight. *Nuit* means night, right? So the best reds come from the Côte de Nuits. Something like that."

"Why do you bother to remember such things?"

In answer, I pushed open the door to the Hôtel du Centre's dining room and shrugged. "Words pester me, like phylloxera. I suppose you'd rather I memorized Nietzsche?"

This was not a gratuitous remark. The Nietzschean eternal return seemed less about spiraling repetitions of history than food. Nietzsche also said, "That which does not kill us makes us stronger." At table again, armed with clamps and slender two-pronged forks, we waited for the snails to arrive. "It does take a while to herd them from the kitchen," I quipped. The dining room was filled with cheerful, rotund, middle-aged Germans and Britons. They drank beer, cappuccino, and wine with seeming indifference to the order or pairing of drink and food, and several roared with beery laughter.

Fully fleshed and with a pinkish complexion, a young woman named Aurélie introduced herself, smiling wide around plump eyes as she served our escargots in the shell. They bobbed in butter, flecked with golden chunks of sautéed garlic. "Dozens," I said. "No wonder it took so long."

"Dozens and dozens," Aurélie teased. By her estimation, she served seven hundred snails each week. I paused before digging in. The escargot is the symbol of Burgundy, and worthy of respect. Seven hundred per week made 36,400 snails per year at the Hôtel du Centre, I calculated. Multiply that by the hundreds of restaurants in Burgundy—the tens of thousands in France—and you reached numbers even Google would have trouble turning into advertising revenue. What chance did a snail stand? Much footwork would be needed to survive. If you worked into the equation factors such as death and injury due to chemical poisoning and climate change—snails need constant moisture, and recent droughts were decimating them—the results weren't hard to guess.

"There aren't enough local snails to satisfy demand," Aurélie admitted, returning to our table with more bread. It proved a fine sponge for mopping up our garlicky snail butter.

Demand and limited supply explained why there were specialized snail farms in the Morvan, Aurélie added, and in the Jura region to the east, and elsewhere in France, too. Most of the farms were actually in Eastern Europe, she explained, and they were doing good business.

"It's like the plumbers," Aurélie said without irony. "The snails and frogs' legs come from Poland too."

The days of wild Burgundian snails were over. "Snail's pace" still seemed appropriate when describing local eating habits, exception made when a Dutchman was behind the stove. We waited another half hour for our main courses, knowing that in the kitchens at l'Hôtel du Centre the *coq au vin* and *boeuf bourguignon* simmered throughout the afternoon. That is what Aurélie claimed, in any case. "The trick is to use beef shanks," she whispered, motioning to her own sturdy legs once she'd set down our dishes. "The butcher saves them for us. Unquestionably, the best *boeuf bourguignon* is made with shanks, and cooks for three hours."

JANUS AND THE GLOBAL VINEYARD

The meteorological conditions as we packed our picnic and medical supplies, massaged joints, and sterilized Alison's broken tooth were sunny, breezy, and—according to the pharmacy's outdoor thermometer—11 degrees Centigrade. It was precisely 9:30 A.M., a Sunday morning. Our sense of time had quietly disappeared. Days and dates blurred, a further step, perhaps, toward Enlightenment? I wondered.

We scaled the Rat's Leap following a winegrower's path. On it, another vineyard had been de-vined and planted with wheat. The stalks shimmered emerald green, a hue travel writers see everywhere and in reality find almost nowhere. Halfway up the grade, a ruined chapel lay across our path. Adjacent to it slumped a 19th-century garden folly—a mock Romantic ruin. Now it was authentic. The chapel and folly sat atop a murky spring, possibly the fountainhead, I reflected, that had once fed Gallo-Roman Meursault. That would make sense. The view was spectacular. I couldn't help turning my head to look back over the town and Saône Valley, feeling like a modern-day Janus. If only we could all look backwards and forwards at one and the same time.

Friable limestone littered the shortest cut through the vines. As elsewhere, not a blade of grass or a single weed sullied the slopes. Our survey map showed the telltale straight dashes of a Roman road lying atop a series of false ridges. To dispel any lingering doubts, a symbol and the words "Roman encampment" marked the section directly ahead. Boxwood grew thick and slow to about eight feet, but hadn't obliterated the ancient roadway, or the piles of cracked limestone that had once encircled the military camp. We crossed GR-76 and followed the deeply rutted Roman road to a pile of boulders and cliff. Wind rattled the shrubbery. For a moment I felt my lumbar region tingle. Either my knees and back were about to lock up or the spirits of long-dead centurions were sending me messages.

"Gorgeous," I muttered, trying to bat away the unwelcome messengers of pain.

"It must've been utter misery," Alison said, startling me. "Imagine being stationed up here, fighting Gauls and brigands, with nothing but wild boars and bears in the woods, the wind whistling. In winter, the snow must have been waist-deep."

"You paint a pretty picture." I shivered despite the brilliant sunshine. We could see its rays above the musty, sweet-smelling boxwood. Misery was right. Why was it easy to recognize the misery of the past yet be par-blind to the awfulness of the present? How many tens of thousands of contemporary centurions were freezing or roasting in godforsaken places, wondering why they'd been sent into battle? "In retrospect," I started to say and then stopped short. My frontal lobe throbbed. "Janus," I murmured. "Maybe he's not such a bad guy after all."

Before Alison could respond, we heard the sound of a car approaching on an unseen road. Doors slammed. Dogs barked. "Shall we think about moving on?" she asked rhetorically. "This place gives me—"

"The creeps," I cut in.

We marched as if Julius Caesar himself were behind us, cracking the whip, and within an hour had emerged from the boxwood tangle and scrambled downhill into Gamay.

MONKING AROUND

The medieval château of Gamay rose in isolation among the vines. If you turned your head and plugged your ears, you wouldn't see or hear the RN6 Expressway running along the southern edge of what had once been a handsome valley. You could ignore visual and even audio blight. But what would you do if your red Burgundy wine was made not from Gamay grapes, but from Pinot Noir, and your village was called "Gamay," a name older than your grape variety? You would probably ask officials at the *Appellation d'Origine Contrôlée* bureau—the AOC—in Paris to loan you a neighboring AOC name. The village abutting Gamay is Saint Alban, and so, with a sleight of the paper-pusher's hand, the vineyards of Gamay produce Pinot Noir labelled Saint Alban AOC. It is good. Very good. But not before lunch.

Saint Alban looked startlingly like Pommard, Volnay, Auxey-Duresses and Meursault, not to mention Gamay, though Saint Alban's squat medieval church was decorated with an unusual *rocaille* consisting of artistically arranged, gnarled fieldstones. We hadn't encountered this type of décor elsewhere in Burgundy. In spirit it reminded me of the masterpieces of sculpted redwood sold along Highway One in California and in better beach motels.

Another feature of this charm village was a fountain with a sculpture of the Virgin and Baby Jesus, whose tiny fingers clutched an orb. A plaque informed thirsty passersby that the fountain's water had been supplied since Gallo-Roman times by an aqueduct the height of a man. Unfortunately only a dribble of water seeped out of the aqueduct, which explained the large "Unsafe for Drinking" sign. Like most of the villages we'd crossed since leaving Beaune, Saint Alban had no cafés, restaurants, hotels, grocery stores, or drinking fountains. We hiked on.

One of the more challenging moments so far faced us. The trail continued on the south side of the RN6 Expressway. There was no underpass or overpass. We waited for several minutes and then dashed between speeding cars and trucks. On the south side of the highway, a service station advertised unleaded 98 octane gasoline for 1.38 euros a liter. A quick calculation revealed that to be about $10.00 per gallon, a good reason to walk, leaving behind a balletic carbon footprint. We might as well get used to tiptoeing through life, I told myself. Living without cars or potable water looked like our common future, one already shared by about four billion worldwide.

The gas station was closed for lunch and the water spigots had no handles: they'd been removed to make sure no thirsty pilgrims got a drop for free. Cars swooshed by us at what I reckoned was close to 100 mph heading to lunch. Our throats were dry.

"Did you notice that our trail is now called la Route des Moines?" Alison croaked.

"I thought we'd been on the monk's road since Beaune? The GR76?" We took turns nursing the last drops from our water bottle. It didn't matter what the trail was called or numbered. One man's wine route is another's Grand Cru or Way of Saint James, and none offered water to the pilgrim.

We climbed switchbacks out of the valley, over a ridge and down the other side, pausing en route for a slender, dry picnic. The zigzag descent made me think of a feather freefalling, and that summoned a pair of related metaphors, the zigzags of life, and the apparently pointless meander we were on. The time for reinvention was long overdue. Like a falling feather, first I had to zigzag to earth. Granted, the metaphors were imperfect. Weren't they always? For some, the zigzag road to reinvention meant visits to a psychiatrist or a course of pharmaceuticals. For others, it might take the form of a zigzag pilgrimage, a seemingly pointless meander. Ours seemed to be about many things, few of them directly relating to Saint James, but maybe I wasn't looking in the right places. I counted the days we'd been walking, and wondered whether I'd progressed yet from the physicality of tired

muscles—the legs of the pilgrim's first week—into the second
week of the mind.

Chassagne-Montrachet lay below us, its steeple and winemakers' houses ranged on coiling streets. I laughed inwardly
thinking of the price of even a mediocre bottle of local wine, and
looked forward to mineral water, preferably sparkling. I glanced
around and was about to say something. But Alison had disappeared. She reappeared in time to steer me down an inauspicious
alleyway. "Look," she said excitedly. Folded onto the side of a
gate was a long plastic bag with a handwritten note attached to it.

Bien cuit SVP!

"Well cooked, please?"

"Bread," Alison said. "They deliver bread and hang it on the
gate. She wants it thoroughly baked."

"That's quaint. It means there's no bakery in town. Which probably means there's no café or anything else, and no water either."

"We can rest in the church."

"And drink the holy water?"

The church was locked. Everything in the village was bolted
shut. How could I have forgotten again? Time had disappeared. It
was Sunday. "Aren't churches open on Sunday, or is this another
exception française?" I asked.

"What I'd like to know is, are we really on a pilgrimage route?"

The village looked remarkably like Saint Alban, Gamay, Meursault, Auxey-Duresses, Volnay, and Pommard. I couldn't help
reversing the order this time to test my memory. The silence in
the streets vibrated. Then it exploded into a thumping, grinding,
howling techno beat. Alison's eyes met mine.

"A funfair," she trilled, her expression transfigured. She
bounded off, cameras swinging, before I could react or stop her.

Funfairs aren't much fun when there's no one around having
fun. The remarkable thing about this funfair was the total absence
of paying customers. The glum operators sat smoking cigarettes,

distractedly spinning their wheels of fortune. Techno rap blasted from a stack of loudspeakers, the notes physically striking our faces as we plugged our ears and walked by. I realized the rapper was singing in Italian. *Surreale* was the only word I could make out. We hurried through, unable to think and astonished not to find a single booth selling food or water. Though dying of thirst, we were glad to find our way back into the vineyards.

A POLE, MOUNT ROME, AND A CLEAN SLATE

Eva Fage spoke such flawless French that I would never have guessed she was a Pole. She had slipped under the Iron Curtain in 1960 as a teenager, and arrived unprepared for a new life in France. What gave her away was her relentlessly smiling, wide oval face, her sincere enthusiasm and love of life. Eva showed us around her modern tract home in the outskirts of Remigny, about an hour south on foot from Chassagne-Montrachet. It wasn't the B&B we'd expected, in part because we had no expectations, but also because every other *chambre d'hôtes* we'd seen was in an old stone farmhouse or vintage village building. "I didn't want *vieilles pierres*," Eva explained, using a term, "old stones," commonly employed by lovers of antique properties. She preferred modern creature comforts, she said.

While we drank coffee from outsized mugs and snacked on waffle-shaped cookies in the warm, glassed-in patio, Eva told us she'd recently retired after a career at the Kodak plant in nearby Chalon-sur-Saône. "Digital photography has changed everything," she admitted. A few years ago, the plant employed 12,000. It was being dismantled, providing former employees with "an opportunity to try something new," she said brightly. "I'm an unflagging optimist."

The slow-flowing Canal du Centre curved above and behind Eva's house. I glanced up at it from where we sat below, in the garden.

PARIS TO THE PYRENEES

Someone leaned on a ship's rail, sailing effortlessly through the sky.
That word, surreal, came back to me from the funfair. It seemed to
capture the essence of what we'd experienced since leaving Vézelay.

"But you're not driving, you're hiking," Eva said suddenly, clap-
ping her hands. "You'll miss so many wonderful things around
here. Please allow me to show you a few sights by car."

Disarmed by her enthusiasm, our pulses racing because of the
caffeine and sugar, we piled into her late-model compact and
drove west. The banks of the Canal du Centre looked different
from the perspective of a passenger seat. I was no longer used to
viewing scenery in motion. Walking was like still photography—
deep, slow, and meditative. Riding in a car was a movie.

In the time it would've taken us to walk a mile, we covered
twenty, rolling through a series of handsome canalside villages.
One was called Saint-Sernin du Plain, and had a tall belltower
built of granite slabs. That much I had time to notice. Beyond
it, we shot uphill, parked, and followed Eva on foot up a gravel
path to a hilltop amphitheater. "Mount Rome," she said; "it's my
favorite spot around here."

Rome again? If this were a novel, readers would rightly exclaim
"oh, sure."

We sat in silence, cupped by the amphitheater atop Mount
Rome, and watched the sky veil itself. I was deeply happy, and
couldn't help wondering about the Roman fortress that had given
the hill its name. But I was also too tired to scramble through the
fenced pastures to the summit. I closed my tired eyes and thought
of Rome, but instead of seeing the Coliseum or Circus Maximus
I saw motorscooters on busy streets, platters of grilled lamb, and
Caesar's clay nose being pinched by my adolescent fingers. The
same dream again. Alison shook my shoulder. I awoke and followed her back down the hill to Eva's car.

Santenay lay several miles below us. It's the southernmost
winegrowing village of the Côte de Beaune astride gentle hills

north of the Canal du Centre. The streets were dark by the time we arrived. Eva deposited us at a restaurant called L'Ouillette on the main square and said she'd come back and pick us up later. The place turned out to be the archetypal French country restaurant, where serious eaters take to their comfortable armchairs amid old buffets and armoirs, and devote hours to savoring rich, generously served classics of French cuisine.

Somewhere between the rib-eye steaks and the wheel-sized cheese platter, Eva Fage's earlier remarks about "the French character" welled up in my mind. While driving us to Mount Rome, she'd shared her thoughts with us. "Old-fashioned," "fuddy duddy," and *passéiste* were terms that seemed to apply not only to the restaurant, but much else we'd seen so far in Burgundy. Yet Eva had provocatively disagreed, defining the French approach to culture and history as *tabula rasa*—the Latin motto meaning "clean slate." It also meant blanket destruction or cancellation. Her theory was that the Romans had destroyed the Gauls' language, culture, institutions, and cities. Then, barbarians had wiped out the adopted Gallo-Romans' culture and institutions. The church eventually erased the last traces of Paganism, and French Revolutionaries had scrubbed out everything precious to the ancien régime, from the royalty to the clergy, from religious art and architecture to popular festivals and saints' days. France's was actually a tragic, dark history of rapine, wrack, and ruin.

The theory appeared at first glance to conflict with my own, which I'd begun to think of as the Janus Principle. But the more I reflected, the more the two theories appeared to be complementary. The *tabula* was never truly *rasa*, just as a re-usable CD or DVD bears traces of earlier "writing." The *tabula rasa* was more a palimpsest, a many-layered thing, written and rewritten. French society in each age was certainly racked by violent upheavals, but it was always divided almost equally between the preservers and destroyers, between those who liked dark, shady lanes and ruins to those who preferred highways and sunshine, from the Gauls to the Futurists. That included contemporary "neo-liberals" who wanted to throw out the Gallic baby with the global bath water, destroying French "protectionist" institutions in imitation of America and Britain. The innovators-versus-the-preservers was an ongoing struggle, a millennial wrestling match, and it was guaranteed to run and run.

After all, the French had the TGV, Mirage fighter jets, and extremely sophisticated high-tech devices of all kinds, plus some of the world's most advanced medical techniques and scientific equipment, not to mention more nuclear power plants and nuclear technology than any other country except the United States. *Passéisme* was only part of the picture. We forward-looking Americans had almost totally lost our sense of history and had systematically destroyed our past, excelling at high tech and actually building the futuristic cities the Europeans had imagined. Yet we had the worst trains in the Western world, rusting bridges and leaky dikes, an electoral system from the 1700s, and we still used Fahrenheit, inches, and ounces. No one would dare call Americans *passéistes*.

"It's complicated," I sighed to myself, too tired to work out the equation.

"What's complicated?" Alison's knife was poised over the pungent, creamy center of a 70-percent-fat Brillat-Savarin cheese, the most luscious, fatty, caloric, and delicious cheese known to man.

"France, the French, America, history, the things that drive us. It's all wonderfully complicated," I said. "Even the cheese platter. Look at it. There are dozens of cheeses. No wonder de Gaulle said it was impossible to govern a country with two hundred cheeses."

Before leaving the restaurant to meet Eva outside, I stopped by the restrooms, and felt Providence calling. The wallpaper above the urinal bore a scallop-shell motif. I stared at it for a long time. Whether it was an incitation to march onward all the way to

Compostela in Spain, or simply meant L'Ouillette was a site of gastronomic pilgrimage, I was unsure. Back at the B&B, Eva Fage confirmed that there wasn't a single fast-food restaurant within miles, and that, at least in the food department, Janus was still winning out over *tabula rasa*.

THE "WHERE'S MY STUFF" SOCIETY

The topics that kept us company the next day as we marched along the sluggish but beautiful tree-lined Canal du Centre were digital tabula rasa of everything that was analog, from Internet chat rooms and budding social media, to wiki-everything, bloggers, podcasters, even the delivery-tracking feature, the "where's my stuff" button on Amazon.com. The previous night, we'd slept like stones. While discoursing with Eva over breakfast on the topic of individual isolation and youth culture in the electronic age, we'd each drunk about a quart of coffee and orange juice and eaten thousands of calories. In her curiously optimistic way, Eva had lamented what she thought of as the spoiled, single-child family, and the neutered, sanitized, virtual-reality world offered by the digital age—an age of pixels and screens and earbuds and photo-cellphones and unlimited downloads of everything you ever wanted but probably didn't need. Where, she wondered, was the human contact, the faith, hope, and charity that once taught children the virtues of selflessness and altruism? Where in this electronic, self-satisfied orgy did anyone learn that virtue is its own reward, with no payback necessary?

A refugee from the Age of Ideology, someone who'd escaped an Orwellian, totalitarian world behind the Iron Curtain, Eva was a lover of risk-taking, unsubsidized, passionate, hands-on, idealistic outgoing personality types. The coldness of computers and the Web turned her off. That was why contemporary French society, it seemed to her, rewarded the wrong behavior patterns: passivity, fear, welfare-lust, world-weariness, cynicism, and navel-gazing or voyeurism. Though we weren't privy to her family situation, Eva appeared to have first-hand knowledge of the problem. We'd reluctantly agreed with much of what she said, but in doing so felt technophobic and middle-aged. Digital tabula rasa, I couldn't help thinking, would turn out to be like all the other attempts at wiping the slate clean—only a partial success. Something from the old analog world would persist. Not everyone would clamor for in-vitro fertilization, for instance, or downloaded pornography. Sex firsthand had an excellent chance of surviving well into the 21st century, as did food and wine and the quest for understanding. Our meandering could not be digitalized and, as the neo-Buddhist Philippe had pointed out way back at our B&B in Marigny, nothing was pointless.

A cruise boat glided by as we clicked our heels and rolled forward onto our toes, following the paved towpath flanking the canal. Nothing magical happened. Instead of waiting passively to be transported, we hit the merciless asphalt road again, and soon enough found ourselves in soleful Chagny, a small, homely town at the junction of the Canal du Centre and the slow-flowing Saône River. It was May Day. On every street corner, sellers of lilies-of-the-valley hawked their blooms.

Chagny's rust-belt industries had departed decades ago, leaving tourism, winemaking, and discount big-box outlets to pick up the slack. Leprous stucco flaked off the damp-looking houses. We were at the bottom of a valley, and the topography was reliably flat. We walked past a handful of fast-food joints and nicotine-scented parimutuel bars. Groups of youths sat astride motor scooters and smoked cigarettes, their cellphones chirping.

"Tabula rasa," I remarked, "the sooner the better."

The scarred façade of the church of Saint Éloi was cracked open and seemed on the verge of collapse. Inside, a lone organist played haunting music. The air was scented by lilies and sprays of other fragrant spring flowers. A cockleshell holy water font confirmed that we were on the medieval Saint James pilgrimage route, the once-important branch from Autun to Chalon-sur-Saône. We were now a mere 863 kilometers—about 540 miles—by freeways to the Pyrenees. On hiking trails it was much longer, another two months' walk. But the distance no longer seemed daunting.

In the middle of the square between the church and an abandoned funeral parlor stood what looked like a rusting dumpster. I circled it, holding an empty plastic bottle and bakery bag, brushing off croissant crumbs from my windbreaker and looking for an opening, so that I could throw away my garbage.

"It isn't for trash," a white-haired woman called out from her garden, facing the dumpster. "It looks like a trash bin, and everyone throws tomatoes at it, and everyone hates it, including me, because they moved the crucifix that used to stand here; but it's an artwork. We tried to get the authorities to take it away and put the cross back, but they won't."

Judging by the encrusted tomato seeds, gashes, and graffiti, the woman's report was accurate. On a plaque I read the artwork's title, "Octagon for Saint Éloi," a date, 1991, and the name of the artist. Richard Serra? There must be some mistake.

As it turns out, the artwork had been commissioned by François Mitterrand and his culture minister, Jack Lang, to commemorate the defunct steelworks of nearby Le Creusot. "Octagon for Saint Éloi" is solid steel, though not stainless. It weighs fifty-seven tons, and stands as tall as a roadside crucifix. Tabula rasa wasn't going to be easy. Maybe that's why successive governments had declined to remove it, despite the locals' loathing of art imposed from above by Paris.

With relief and another ten thousand clicks of our heels, we rejoined the canal, picnicked among the abandoned industrial plants, crossed a floodplain scattered with tract homes, and took the main asphalt road into sleepy Rully, where we'd reserved a room for the night. The villagers might well be trying to sleep after working in vineyards since dawn, I reflected. But the young men on roaring, spluttering dirt bikes circling the winemaking village's main square made napping impossible.

In most other ways, however, sleep had come to Rully as it has come to much of rural France. The butcher's shop, bakery, and grocery, not to mention the church, were shuttered. Had the newly built shopping malls and discount outlets of Chagny and Chalon-sur-Saône already put the town's stores out of business? The new religion of consumerism required a new forum, the mall. I said so to Alison with something like righteous wrath, as if I had lived the life of an ascetic, reclusive monk, and never shopped at Kmart or CostCo or bought digitally from Amazon.com.

"That's another interesting theory you have there," Alison remarked. "The problem with it is, today is May Day. It's a holiday, and it's also lunch time. So you might not be able to extrapolate about the death of rural France or the relationship of ancient Gaul to Rome and modern consumerism from this random sample."

My badly shaved, wind-burned cheeks hid a spreading blush. She did know how to take the stuffing out of me.

Slightly crumpled, I was pleased to see that our hotel was open and packed with customers, despite its unpronounceable name, Le Vendangerot. The word felt like saltwater taffy in my mouth.

The creaking stairs, groaning planks, and squeaking hinges suggested a pre-modern construction date. Our room tunneled back in time, through the linoleum of the 1950s to the wood and bevelled mirrors of some indefinable yesteryear. It was another objective correlative of France's layer-cake civilization, a palimpsest, not a tabula rasa, of décor. A robin perched on the windowsill and watched us through the fluttering lace curtains. We stretched out and, lulled by birdsong and motorcycle engines, woke up two hours later, refreshed and ready to explore.

HIGH PRIESTS OF THE AEDUI

The familiar blue-and-yellow scallop-shell signage led us back across Rully to the church. By some miracle, it was open now. Praying pilgrims were few. We had the sanctuary to ourselves. It reminded me of others like it, several hundred of them, churches rebuilt and enlarged during the 1800s' war against the twin foes of phylloxera and the secular materialism of the industrial age.

A sheet of paper gathering dust on a worm-eaten table provided local statistics. In 1966, there were 541 parishes and 527 priests, average age 51, in the Saône-et-Loire *département*, claimed the compiler of the statistics. In 1987, the figures were 541 parishes and 388 priests, average age 64. By 2006, the 541 parishes had been folded into 50, presided over by 213 priests, average age 72.

A faded newspaper clipping on the same table reported the words of Monseigneur Rolland Minnerath, who welcomed the new cardinal, Benoit Rivière, wishing him a "happy and vigorous, energetic apostolic ministry in Aeduan country."

"Aeduan country?" Alison asked, reading the sentence aloud. "Do they mean the Saône-et-Loire and the Aedui tribe?"

I couldn't help smiling. "The Gauls are alive and among us, like Jesus at Easter. The territory of the Aedui extended to Mâcon. Why be surprised that local clergymen still evoke the memory of a cannibalistic Pagan tribe crushed by Caesar two thousand years ago? And remember, Julius Caesar was declared 'divine' by the Senate. Augustus Caesar was later considered divine partly because he supposedly foretold and possibly was himself the Messiah. Remember Vergil's little story about a child who will be born and usher in the Golden Age? Who led Dante through the Inferno? Vergil did! Vergil wasn't punished in the worst part of Hell. He was in Limbo, along with many of the great classical figures, and the innocent, unborn babies. Because he foretold the coming of Christ in the guise of Augustus."

Alison blinked and sighed, waiting for me to run out of breath. "So where is Augustus in the Divine Comedy? In Limbo with Vergil, or in a hotter part of Hell?"

"That's complicated," I said. "The worst part of Hell was frozen, not flaming."

"You really should have become a professor or a politician, or maybe a lawyer."

"Nonsense," I objected. "I'm a fabulist by profession, and it's a noble profession. Let me finish my thought train before you derail me again. What is the fatal flaw—in the eyes of the French clergy—the flaw in our divine, putatively Christ-like ancient Romans, who were just coincidentally the inventors of the Pontifex Maximus—the Pontiff? I'll tell you what. They weren't Gallic! It's downright shocking. Even the Catholic priests here are infected by nationalistic neo-Druidism."

Alison shrugged. She glanced around the church, probably looking for a taper to light. It was too hot and dusty for talk of Druidical French Catholics and the Imperial Cult. True, this was also a fairly old hat whose brim I'd worried before. There is nothing particularly new or controversial about Augustus the *divi filius*—the son of a god—one of his many titles. To some he was also apparently the "anointed one," and that made him a messiah of sorts or perhaps, god knows, The Messiah. That's what the word "messiah" means: anointed. With what? Olive oil or spicy unguents? Had Augustus been born in Gaul, perhaps the locals would've smeared him with rendered beaver fat.

I now recalled with delicious mirth that pundits in the Augustan Age reportedly recognized Augustus as a divine being by affiliation with Julius Caesar, but also because he was born by the mysterious impregnation of his mother—not by the Holy Ghost, who hadn't put in an appearance yet, but rather by a god who had taken the form of a snake. Which was more outlandish? At least the snake had reproductive organs. Before Christ had uttered more than a baby's squeal, the authentic living Augustus was viewed as a wondrous being whose destiny it was to bring on the Golden Age and share the "good news" of a savior to the foundering Republic. What the good news was remains an open question, though Christian interpretations might lead one to surmise that Augustus was the horn-blower, the trailblazer, for Christ. At least some followers of the early Catholic Church, who were just as nutty as the Vatican's current occupants, thought Augustus may have delivered the message of the coming of the Lord before its time—their time.

While we were at it, I couldn't help remembering that the word "gospel" simply means glad tidings, good news—the news borne in this case by the unwitting if divinely inspired son of a snake and a Roman matron. How did today's aged Burgundian priesthood, not to mention the cardinal of Aedui Land and his diminishing flock, square these myths or tales or whatever they were with what sounded like a rather unorthodox veneration of Druidism and the Celts?

"Have you finished your ruminations?" Alison asked, watching me as I paced around the apse cradling my jaw, as if tethered to a satellite cell phone. "Didn't Saint Martin supposedly convert the Aedui to Christianity on Mount Beuvray about, what, seventeen hundred years ago? What if the churchmen down here are referring to the Aedui converts, not the headhunter Celts?"

This seemed a distinct possibility, I had to admit. "It's a strange way of describing the region in any case," I said, only slightly chastened. "They have ancient Gaul on the brain!"

"They may not be the only ones."

TURRETS SYNDROME
Our Golden Age afternoon in Aedui Land promised much good news—and gorgeous views of the village and countryside. Rully

climbs from valley floor to gentle hillside, and from there up a steep, craggy escarpment. Reached by a paved road, the village's turreted château looked as if it'd been shipped over from Anaheim. The soil of surrounding vineyards was a russet hue, which also would have pleased Walt Disney, no doubt. "This seems familiar," Alison said. She was right. We'd visited Rully some years earlier, on a whirlwind driving tour through wine country. At the time, the owner, Countess Brigitte de Ternay, had welcomed us into the second of two walled courtyards. No one else had turned up for the guided tour. Clearing her throat and killing time, she'd said the château had been re-roofed with its original 800-year-old stones. She'd gone on to confide that the property had been in her family's hands since the roof first went on, around the year 1200. Stuccoing would be the next costly project, she added. We assumed the shutters would get a coat of paint in a future generation. Years later, on this, our second visit, the shutters were still waiting, broken and flapping like elephant ears in the spring breeze.

Genteel penury afflicts many Burgundian lords whose fortunes were made before Louis XVI and Marie Antoinette were deprived of their heads. I recalled now how the proud but affable countess had showed us around the crumbling château, revealing a secret nutcracker built into the kitchen's 500-year-old table. She'd also shown us a soldier dummy made of leather. Its task in the bad old days was to spook potential attackers. Both heirlooms had been jealously guarded and saved, tokens of *passéisme* incarnate.

However, since it was May Day, the château was closed to visitors. We circled it before scrambling up a rocky trail to a deeply cleft cliff, drinking in the scent of warm boxwood as we went. A natural spring lay hidden in the woods, and proved to be a remarkable mosquito hatchery, like Saint Martin's spring at Bibracte; so while my instinct was to search in the spring's waters for statuettes and votive offerings, the winged protectors of the site drove us away.

"I sense that you're about to come up with a theory linking mosquitoes and Druids or water nymphs," Alison said. "Have you had any revelations yet, or are we still in the pointless meandering phase?"

"*Pointless meandering* . . . you were eavesdropping in Marigny when I was talking to the first Philippe, weren't you? You already gave yourself away back in Boudédé, at that big old chestnut tree, when you slipped up and revealed your perfidy as a spy."

She smiled like a guilty crocodile. "I happen to have very sensitive hearing, and you and Philippe were speaking loudly."

"That's what I'd call a fib, or a lie, and if you heard the whole conversation, you also know the corollary. There is no such thing as *pointlessness*. I like that, by the way. The more churches I go into, the more Druids and Virgins we meet, the more I find Buddhism attractive."

Alison nodded. "That's okay, that's perfectly valid. Once upon a time you scoffed at Buddhists the way you scoffed at Catholics. You're becoming more tolerant, though you probably don't realize it yet."

I shrugged and allowed Alison to help me up the cliff. She saw the handholds better than I could, and was stronger and fitter anyway.

Druids, Caesar, and Vercingétorix seem like Johnny-come-latelies when you find yourself in a paleolithic or neolithic cliff dwelling like the one atop Rully's limestone escarpment. From one of the caverns came a roar. We recoiled, earnestly terrified, searching for an escape route. A moment later, two kids wearing teddy-bear backpacks scurried out of a cave, snarling and growling. We rebounded in time to surprise them. They loved Alison's pantomimed fainting act. Once the delighted young warriors had galloped off to where their parents were standing, we picked our way into the mouth of the musty cavern.

"Are those paleolithic drawings?" I asked, overwhelmed by the darkness.

"I love you," Alison said slowly. "I love sex."

"I beg your pardon? I'm glad you're still passionate, but. . . ."

"That's what the graffiti says." She pointed to a niche encrusted with candlewax.

"Druids or Satanic rites?" I wondered aloud.

"Devilish lovemaking," Alison said. It was probably the third time she'd punned in our three decades together, and I found it disconcerting.

We emerged, blinking into the sunlight. The view took in the 800-year-old château of Rully and its vineyards, and the vast sweep of the Saône River Valley. I could've gazed at it forever, except that I was eager to walk on the neolithic footpath atop the escarpment.

We knew it was a pre-Gallic, neolithic trail because it led to a spot on our map marked with a star and the words "site néo-lithique." Somehow I still wasn't readily able to tell the difference between a neolithic path, a Gallic path, and a Roman path, though a paved Roman road was easy to identify. After a few thousand years, antiquity becomes a blur of rubble and numbers. But the essence of ancientness lingers in certain places, creating a kind of electromagnetic field, or so it seemed to me in my questing frame of mind. We climbed another mile or so, buzzing with feelings of magic.

At the top of this particular hillside, however, the sense of ambient antiquity was compromised somewhat by cyclone fencing around a sheepfold dotted with cotton-swab lambs. A microwave broadcasting tower, which we now saw for the first time, hummed and sizzled.

"Did you say something earlier about Druids and electromagnetic fields?" Alison asked with wicked satisfaction. Our roles had been reversed. She was playing the skeptic. "Maybe you're trying too hard to find enlightenment. Relax. . . ."

"Seek and thou shalt find," I said, wounded. As we neared our hotel back in Rully, I stopped short and read the name of a crossroads. Rue Saint Jacques? Saint James, at last! In the garden of number 9 rue Saint Jacques stood a fortified farmhouse with a chapel attached to it. "A former pilgrim's hostel," I said. "You see, we're on the right road."

Alison crossed her arms and sighed. "So far this is the most unusual pilgrimage route I've ever heard of. It has everything on it but pilgrims."

"Maybe we're the pilgrims, and didn't know it until now."

Alison regarded me with what I couldn't help thinking was the gimlet eye of a disbeliever.

MOROCCO MEETS NEW ZEALAND

We were starving, for a change. But the dining room of Le Vendangerot was full to bursting, with too many mouths to feed all at once. Some of the same members of the luncheon crowd were back at their tables, faces beaded with sweat from the effort of feasting.

Expansive and enthusiastic, the proprietor told us her name was Marie-Laurence Lollini. It came out in her thundering voice sounding like *Lolita* run through a bread-slicer. Where most women have a neck, Marie-Laurence appeared to have replaced that extension with a pearl necklace. Her Italo-French husband Armand, the chef, was holed up in the kitchen, defending himself from her with saucepans. The dining room felt like another operetta set, this time *La Vie Parisienne* by Offenbach. Waiters in black-and-white outfits danced by us, singing out orders, raising their trays over the heads of clients and the vertical elements of the eclectic, fell-off-a-truck décor.

At around 9 P.M., the lamb filet finally arrived. It was wrapped in a pastry shell, and Marie-Laurence Lollini said it was dressed with a chorizo sausage-based sauce. Using chorizo with lamb seemed downright daring by Burgundian standards, and it certainly was not particularly Italian. I wondered aloud where Armand Lollini got the idea. Luckily the dish wasn't complicated or fussy, just tender and delicious.

"We don't do sophisticated, complicated food," Marie-Laurence said.

"Did the lamb come from that pasture above town?" Alison asked. "It's so flavorful."

Marie-Laurence looked startled, and I thought she might drop the tray she was carrying. "What pasture?" She disappeared into the kitchen. When she returned, her teeth and pearls were gleaming with embarrassment. "I hate to disappoint you, but my husband says the lamb comes from New Zealand. There isn't enough local lamb, and it costs too much." She seemed genuinely distressed. "What do you expect, with politics as they are? France can't compete, France has gone mad. It's not just lamb you can't find. We can't find anyone to work in the restaurant, not a single French person wants to do the heavy lifting. Everyone who works in this country comes from somewhere else—Eastern Europe, Latin America, Africa. We have Moroccans in the kitchen, not Frenchmen. We French don't want to work, the young prefer welfare, and everyone wants to be a college graduate and get rich without breaking a sweat. That's the reality. But I'm glad you enjoyed your dinner, and I hope you sleep well."

We said we'd be down for breakfast early. We were hiking to Mercurey and Aluze and back to Mercurey the next day. It was indeed an unusual itinerary for pilgrims and Marie was right to say so, but it was certainly not a pointless meander.

WINGED HEELS AND A FACE

The alarm clock went off but neither of us heard it. The sun was high in the cloudless sky by the time we hiked south out of Rully and crested a ridge amid the usual sloping grapevines. I turned back to admire the surprisingly arid landscape of the Côte Chalonnaise, which I'd always thought of as lush and green. "Apollo's chariot must've swung too low," I said; "either that, or the vineyards have just been sprayed with herbicides. Aren't you glad they're so careful and respectful of the soil?"

The scenery was strikingly beautiful in an ecologically unfriendly way—a stark mineral landscape of cement posts and weed-free vines, of the kind we'd seen on the Côte de Beaune. Here, too, the scent of pesticides and herbicides made me sneeze. "Not many snails this morning," Alison reported. "Do you see what I see?" She stopped walking and pointed. I squinted and strained but did not see what she saw. "It's a hiker, possibly a pilgrim."

"A hiker? Where? How dare he? The cheek! On our trail!" I was joking, of course, but also felt proprietorial. Why, suddenly, did we need to be surrounded by pilgrims? Minutes later, as we crept uphill, the lone trekker came into range. He closed on us. We crossed one vineyard and took a wrong turn into another. The hiker caught up and strode by before we could rejoin the trail.

"He's cutting us off at the pass," I said. At the top of the ridge that separates the wide Saône River Valley from the pocket concealing the village of Mercurey, the hiker pulled to the side and sat on the base of a tall stone cross. A scallop shell was tied to his pack. He mopped at sweat with an India cotton bandanna and rattled a string of prayer beads. An otherworldly look glazed his eyes. They were veined in red, and half-hidden by bushy eyebrows. He looked as if he'd stepped off the tympanum of Autun and found the Godhead while holding hands with Shiva. I knew the type from the Bay Area and Mendocino County. They'd driven me into the arms of the militant atheist materialists.

"Want to bet he's from California?" I asked Alison as we neared. She jabbed me with her elbow, shushing me, and strode ahead.

"Going to Santiago?" she asked the man, her irresistible smile blinding in the sunshine. "We haven't seen many other pilgrims."

"That's right," said the pilgrim, sitting up. "On the Way of Saint James." I cupped my ears, trying to understand him. His accent certainly was not American. "First to Taizé and Cluny I shall go."

I repeated the stilted syntax in my head as I studied him. Definitely not from California. He was about our age, thoroughly sun-bronzed, and gamey enough to smell at ten feet. "Have you hiked here from Germany or Switzerland?" I asked.

"Dublin," he blurted. "From Dublin I've come." He pulled out a pack of cigarettes, lit up, and blew smoke over his shoulder. "Off I go, then," he announced pleasantly. Before we could exchange another word, he leaped to his feet, slung his pack and scallop shell across his sweaty torso, trilled something like "ta-rah," and rushed uphill, swinging his beads and humming loudly.

Now I understood why, in Italian, the word for pilgrim—*pellegrino*—also designates an oddball. Is that why so many locals had fled at our approach? What would it be like to hike to Santiago de Compostela on a pilgrim's route filled with such questers from Dublin? I winced at the prospect and began to plot out a route that would avoid Taizé—the famous ecumenical-spiritual community about ten miles north of Cluny, created soon after World War Two by a monk who called himself Brother Roger. Taizé may once have been a place of inspiration, but in recent decades it had been overrun by tens of thousands of earnest young seekers who wore their faith like a scallop-shell badge, strummed acoustic guitars, and carried well-thumbed breviaries which were usually written in Romanian or Polish. Religion was fine, but religiosity got on my nerves, especially the holier-than-thou variety. Made curious by his fame and the tales we'd heard about Taizé, we'd been there and done that, years ago, when Brother Roger was alive and preaching. I for one would not do it again. Reportedly, the scene at Taizé had become even more ritualistic and less enlightening since Roger's dramatic death. But there was no time to think of Brother Roger now. The sun was high, and Mercurey awaited us over the ridge.

At the trail's highest point on a bluff above the vineyards stood the ruins of a windmill. I waved. But the Irishman bounded off the crumbling walls and scampered away as we neared. "He's even stranger than I am," I said. "Get thee to Taizé and Cluny, shall thee, ta-rah," I cried, watching his jostling backpack disappear down the trail ahead of us in a cloud of dust. Clearly he had even less interest in getting to know us than we did in him.

By noon we were sipping coffee in the shady back garden of the Val d'Or hotel on Mercurey's main street. There'd been no sign of the elusive, nicotine-scented Irishman anywhere in the village. "Let him get ahead," I said. "He certainly won't be hiking to Aluze with us on the Via Agrippa."

The hotel's yard was pleasant, the coffee delicious, and I couldn't help staring at part of the garden wall. It incorporated what looked like a neolithic mortar, the kind sometimes re-used in the Middle Ages as a holy-water font. The building the hotel occupied was modern—only two hundred years old, said the owner, a mild-mannered gentleman about our age named Dominique Jayet. "Nothing Roman in the hotel or restaurant, I'm afraid, not upstairs anyway," he said. "But the property does straddle a creek that runs through the cellar in a culvert, alongside ruins of what was the ancient Via Agrippa." He smiled around unsettling teeth and stated the obvious. "Mercurey is named for Mercury, the ancient Gauls' favorite god."

"Nothing to do with Romans, then?"

"Oh, the Romans also worshipped Mercury, but the temple has yet to be found." Jayot smiled again and eclipsed himself like Jeeves.

The Val d'Or had an excellent reputation, particularly as a restaurant, and I'd long wanted to eat here in my unregenerate, gluttonous heyday. Our upstairs bedroom was attractive but had been conceived for dolls, and I wondered how a standard-issue American or a descendant of the Teutons would turn around in it. There was no number on the door, bur rather a name, La Lévrière, "The hare's warren." Game, as in gamey? Fair enough, I said to myself, taking the hint, and thinking again of the gamey Irishman. I showered quickly, filled our water bottles, donned my pack, and caught up with Alison in the lobby. We'd picnic on the way to Aluze, which was about three miles away.

Outside the hotel, the noon sun beat down on the Via Agrippa, conjuring visions of chariots and centurions. Once upon a time, the ancient highway ran from Rome across Gaul via Lyon to the Atlantic, terminating at what's now Boulogne-sur-Mer, which was probably the source of the oysters that those oyster-relay runners carried to Roman oligarchs in a mere four days. The original roadbed passed through Mercurey but is now buried underneath an asphalt highway. Part way through the village, the ancient road resurfaces and veers south, climbs a hill, runs by a high school, and then disappears again underneath the vineyards.

We followed the Via Agrippa slowly, dragging ourselves uphill in the heat. Amid the dusty grapevines, sitting on upturned Roman paving stones, we pulled out a bag of apples, cheese, and crackers, and splayed ourselves in the shade of a pine tree. "I believe a Roman pebble is stuck in my boot," I said. Before tossing it away, I made sure the pebble wasn't a votive offering or tiny, precious sculpture.

After lunch, we headed off again under a scorching sun, the heat unheard of for early May. Our goal was the hilltop village two valleys over. Our reasons for going to Aluze were several. We knew it to be of remarkable antiquity. Second, we'd driven past it in a car years earlier, found the scenery to be particularly appealing, and swore we'd return one day for a closer look.

The trail ran through meadows, pine forests, and rolling vine-yards. At the bottom of a gully we crossed a stream and began the climb to the village on what felt like a section of the Roman road. I had Agrippa on the brain, and as usual couldn't keep my eyes off the ground, confident that fortune would smile upon me. This time it did. Lying on the shoulder of the dusty, unpaved road, a smiling stone face stared at me. I stopped and smiled back. The face was dirty and green from algae and moss, triangular in shape, and about an inch and a half thick.

"A face," I exclaimed. "I've found a face!"

Alison had heard this before. She'd seen stones and bones. Done stones and bones. Stones and bones were not funny anymore. She took the face from my hands, disbelief writ large in her eyes. "You really think it's a face?" She turned it over. "You know, you may be right. It is a face. I thought you were joking."

"My god," I stuttered. "Seek and thou shalt find. Picasso was wrong. It's just like those faces stuck on houses or churches to scare away evil spirits." Despite the ache in my back, I did a jig, unable to believe my luck.

How had the face found its way to a dusty roadside at the bottom of a ravine? Simple: even I with my bad eyes could see the collapsed walls of a building rising among boxwood and wild plum trees nearby. An abandoned house had fallen down. The face had come off the façade and tumbled downhill. It had sat here, run over by tractors and carts and stepped on by horses and goats and sheep and men for decades, centuries, millennia perhaps. And then I'd come along, seeking. Was it just another metaphor for our quest, or a real, bona fide stone face?

Alison turned it over one more time. "Even if it isn't an authentic anthropomorphic carved head, it looks kind of like one."

I felt the air rush out of me. "You skeptic," I said. "Anthropomorphic or not, I'm going to keep it. I'll show it to an expert. You'll see."

"Like the bone? I suppose you're going to carry it with you across France?"

"No worries, I'll carry it. I haven't asked you to carry anything, have I? I carry the water, the picnic, the clothes, the first-aid kit, the bone, and the face, okay?"

Alison sighed. "I think you should give it to someone at the mayor's office. For one thing, if it is authentic and if you don't hand it over, you'll be locked up for looting antiquities."

"Nonsense, it's just one of those faces on old buildings, and it's getting run over by tractors all the time. I'm saving it from destruction." Alison relented, I nestled the face into the bottom of my pack, and we marched on.

At the top of the hill, a trio of farmers were talking and smoking on a stoop that looked like the entrance to a neolithic cavern. We waved at them, walked slowly over, making sure not to spook them, and reassuringly admired the village and surroundings to soften them up. Alison remarked how wonderfully ancient everything seemed.

"Ancient? You don't know what ancient is," said one of the men, swelling with pride. His looks reminded me of Astérix and Dumnorix-Dean back in the Morvan. "Aluze is older than Mercurey, older than Bibracte," he added. "You've been to Bibracte?"

We explained where we'd been and where we were going, using a grapevine cutting to trace our path in the dusty front yard. They peered down at us suspiciously. One of them said he'd never seen pilgrims around here. Another of the men said that he and fellow winemakers and farmers like him often turned up Roman, Gallic, and pre-Gallic artifacts. "Some people around here have rooms full of things," he boasted, glancing around. "There's been a big find recently—it's going to make Solutré look like nothing. This is as important as Tautavel Man."

The village of Solutré was due south on our route, about one week away, and we were familiar with the Flintstone-era Solutrian Phase of the Upper Paleolithic. Once upon a time, everyone read about Solutré in history books, even in California, I said. Who could forget the image of horses being herded off cliffs by club-wielding prehistoric hunters? But the archeological site of Tautavel was less familiar to us. Alison said so, and we both grinned like the foreign ignoramuses the farmers took us for. They seemed delighted: nothing worse than a smart-alec foreigner, especially an American.

Tautavel is a place in the Pyrenees, they said, taking turns to tell us where and what the Pyrenees Mountains were, way down on the edge of Spain, a country south of France, you know, or possibly you don't know, seeing that you're foreigners. The skull of a Homo erectus from 450,000 years ago was found there, at Tautavel, in the Caune de l'Arago. "And what we have here is just as important," said the most talkative of the three men, spreading his arms. "But I can't give you details, because the research and excavations are still going on." He waved vaguely at the vineyards due north of the village.

The men seemed torn. They were clearly eager to tell us more, but it looked as if they felt they'd already said too much. "So," I asked, "are you by chance descended from Agrippa, or possibly Vercingétorix?"

The trio of farmers crossed their arms one after the other and chuckled. "Certainly not Agrippa," grumbled the talkative one. "Dumnorix," he said. "Vercingétorix wasn't from here, and don't even mention Bibracte or Alésia. We only talk about Gergovia. You know what happened in Gergovia?"

"Naturally," I said. "Your armies resisted Caesar there and almost wiped out our legions."

"Correct," Dumnorix said, clearly disappointed. I wasn't quite as ignorant as he'd hoped. "We would've defeated you in Alésia if only our reinforcements had come through, if only those German mercenaries hadn't sided with Caesar."

"Such a shame," I remarked. "We might've avoided the World Wars."

"America wouldn't exist, my friend," he quipped. "We would've taken Rome."

I nodded. "I'm sure you're right," I said amiably. "But just think, you wouldn't be speaking French, and you wouldn't be making wine—or have forks, for that matter."

Half an hour later, we ran out of banter and said our good-byes, wishing them many a happy Gergovia in resisting globalization and fast food. I could feel my stone face smiling in my backpack as we hiked up to the village church.

The church was shut, as expected. That was only right in such an ancient place where Christianity was still a novelty. I considered giving the face to someone at the mayor's office, but the building was locked up tight. On a billboard outside I spotted a notice about upcoming village events. A documentary film would soon be shown, titled *From Roman Bridges to the Bridge of Millau*. Star architect Norman Foster had designed Millau's spectacular new suspension bridge. But the town was also where anti-globalization protestors led by José Bové had dismantled a McDonald's restaurant. Well, I'll be, I said to myself. Was there a Roman road in Millau, I wondered? But I knew the answer. Of course there was.

Reading on, I discovered that the local mid-July extravaganza to celebrate France's day of independence on July 14th would include live music, a barbecue, and a movie projected on an outdoor screen.

"What movie?" Alison asked.

"Guess," I teased. She shook her head. "Astérix and the Vikings."

HARES AND WHITE RABBITS

We were late for a very important date. How had we forgotten the time? The truth is, I could barely remember what day it was. How many weeks had we been walking? My feet had become clay, welded to the earth. My breath was one with the air. Every step felt like a meditation, a prayer alloyed by the minor martyrdom I'd known since adolescence: my knees. Compounding the usual pain in my knees and lower back, I also had sunstroke and was beginning to wonder whether I might require hospitalization.

A handsome, elegantly dressed man in his late fifties was waiting for us in the lobby of the Val d'Or hotel as we clomped in. "Here they are!" said Dominique Jayot, rocking onto the toes of his polished black shoes. "The pilgrims."

Before we could beat the dust off, Jayot introduced us to Bertrand Devillard, owner of Château de Chamirey winery. I was momentarily confused, but then remembered. When reserving our room, I'd asked about visiting the château and talking to the winemaker. Apparently, our wish was someone's command.

"Take your time, please," said Devillard in a velvet voice. "Shall I come back later?"

For us? There must be some mistake. Devillard was rich, and he was also famous among winemakers. Blue blood coursed through the vein visible on his lean, muscular neck. His sports coat and slacks were perfectly cut. He had the features of a French Robert Redford, the quintessential gentleman. We tramped upstairs to the hare's warren, freshened up, and rushed back down full of apologies and slightly less musty.

Our room's name proved prophetic. Devillard whisked us away in a sporty convertible to visit his vineyards south of the Via Agrippa. At a panoramic point we got out and looked down just as three hares appeared from nowhere and chased each other through the vines, driven by spring fever.

Over the next several hours, the soft-spoken Devillard drove and walked us through the kind of sloping vineyards winemakers dream of possessing, and led us into the vaulted cellars of his magnificent Rococo château. On the way, he distilled for us the essence of a thousand years of Burgundian winemaking, from the monks of Cluny Abbey to the present day.

As everyone knows, in their heyday the Romans didn't make wine in Burgundy—they shipped it up in amphorae from easier to cultivate, flatter, hotter Mediterranean growing areas. But with the collapse of the Empire, the Mediterranean source dried up. Monks began experimenting with grapevines and vinification techniques. Who knows how long it took—centuries, certainly— before they discovered the right combination of climate, soil, and grape. Pinot Noir was the red grape variety that thrived best in cool, damp northern Burgundy, where the soil was a mix of limestone, iron oxide, and decomposed clay. Gamay thrived on the granite of the hotter south. Chardonnay was not always the prime white variety, but gradually it took over, performing well almost everywhere.

The secret? The geology of the Saône River Valley, an inland sea 150 million years ago. It retreated 120 million years later, meaning 30 million years ago. The escarpments along the former seabed marked the limits of Burgundy's best vineyards and were called *côtes*, so "coastline" was appropriate after all.

There were currently about 4,600 wineries in Burgundy, most of them small, all of them spun off from the great monastic properties taken away from the church during the Revolution of 1789.

I'd always wondered how the classifications of Burgundy wines had come about. Devillard smiled. "Complicated," was the single-word answer. Historically, the test was "did a vineyard consistently produce good wine-grapes over time?" From the time-and-quality test came the traditional classification of *grands crus* and *premiers crus*, and within them the various *climats* or parcels—the best of the best. "Local, loyal, and constant," Devillard said. "The standards were local, meaning site-specific, loyal to tradition and history, and constant over time."

It took generations for villages to develop a reputation. Nowadays the main test is geology. With scientific soil analysis, anyone can determine a vineyard's soil potential. "But soil is only part of the equation," Devillard explained. "There's also exposure. In Mercurey, southwest exposure is ideal. In other places there are variations, but south-southwest is usually the best. The trinity of elements," Devillard concluded, as we stood in a *premier cru* vineyard and watched the sun disappear over the western hills, "is microclimate, subsoil, and topsoil." Subsoil is the real key, he added. Burgundy's vineyards are old and tired, and most of their good topsoil eroded away long ago. "The roots of the grapevines must delve deep," he said, spreading his fingers and thrusting them downwards. "They're like us, feeding off a buried, ancient civilization."

That struck me as particularly profound.

Later Devillard told us he was recently widowed, which explained his soulful, endearing demeanor. From a terrace, we surveyed the château's handsome formal garden. His wife had planted the yew trees and lawns and flowerbeds, he said. He maintained them in her memory, a living shrine where order apparently reigned. Beyond the garden wall grew rows of gnarled vines. Again they seemed to me to be hanging on crosses.

UNNECESSARY BUT VITAL

Did millions the world round rave about milk or apple juice? Did learned connoisseurs write encyclopedic volumes about mineral water? Did peoples sell each other into slavery over the juice of cranberries? What was it about grapes and wine that had made them not only a multi-billion-dollar industry, but an obsession of mankind for the last five thousand years?

A possible one-word answer came to me as I opened my backpack before leaving the Val d'Or in Mercurey and realized I'd forgotten to throw out the picnic leftovers from the day before. The word was "fermentation." Cheese was fermented milk, and much more interesting and edifying than milk. Calvados, cider, and applejack were fermented apple juice. Eau de vie, the "water of life," was fermented and distilled anything—potato skins, dregs, cranberries. The decomposing, bubbling, frothing genie in the bottle had given us both gin and sauerkraut, or perhaps the other way around, since it was neolithic man who first made sauerkraut, from turnips and wild kale. The minute anything edible rose from an unexciting natural state to its fermented, distilled essence, it became worthy of attention, at times of reverence. The alcohol genie somehow appeared to release the bonds of the body, allowing the mind to experience altered states of being. That's what Dionysian rites and Bacchanalia were about, like today's ecstasy rave parties. That's why it was wine and not water or milk or apple and cranberry juice that featured in the transubstantiation, the divine metamorphosis of Christ's blood.

Such were a few of the meandering thoughts that accompanied me uphill among the vineyards on the morning of May 3, on Grande Randonnée trail GR-76 from Mercurey to Givry, where we'd be spending the night. The red-and-white GR stripes flanked by yellow European Union scallop shells on a blue background lifted us as far as a village called Touches. There, a squat Romanesque-Gothic church and its belfry marked the center of the hamlet. This was Devillard's family church, I remembered him saying, and as I gazed at the solid old buttresses and lifesized tombstones I couldn't help wondering if his beloved wife were buried nearby.

Solidity and antiquity emanated from the site. It was heavy baggage for a man to carry, but also something to lean on.

Beyond the hamlet, GR-76's colorful flags and the scallopshell signs of the Way of Saint James parted ways. We were torn about which way to go. Our map showed the ruined Château de

Montaigu ahead in woodlands on GR-76, however, so the choice was quickly made.

If a jury had to nominate castles for the Atmospheric Crumbled Ruin Award, Château de Montaigu would certainly be short-listed. A tower with gaping eyes for windows, arm-thick creepers dangling from it, shrubs sprouting at unlikely angles from moat and dungeon, hewn stone walls rising high above scented robinia trees, and fallen arches more dramatic than my own—such was the scene awaiting at Montaigu. We'd cheated and read about the monument before leaving Mercurey.

In the late 1500s, during the Wars of Religion, King Henri IV had ordered his soldiers to demolish the Protestant stronghold. As we poked around, admiring the moody anarchy, we were surprised to notice that fresh mortar had been poured, and the robinia trees trimmed. Someone apparently maintained the grounds, after all. Would the castle be restored and made into a tourist attraction, or merely kept from falling further into ruin? Maybe somewhere, underneath the massive foundations, lay the lost temple of Mercury, the god beloved by Romans and Gauls alike. And maybe it would be better not to know. I thought of the stone face grinning in my backpack, Roland's bone next to it, wrapped in a blister pack, and Philippe's words about the primal sea, and was glad to live with tantalizing uncertainty. Admitting to myself, for a start, that I didn't know everything, and would never know everything, felt like another one of the small enlightenments, the unexpected rewards, of our journey.

A mile south at the village of Saint-Martin-sous-Montaigu we strolled past a house where Methuselah might have lived. Hook-shaped carved stones sprouted from uneven walls, the same kind of hooked stones the builders of Bibracte had used in their *murus gallicus*—or so it appeared. Another venerable hovel nearby stopped me short. I raised a finger and waited for Alison to finish taking her 478th digital photo of the morning.

"What now?" she asked. I wiggled my finger. Three stone faces stared down at us, two grimacing, one smiling, and very much like the face in my pack. "Maybe it really is a face," she said brightly. "Let's take it out and compare. . . ."

"Never," I said, marching on, triumphant. "First, I prefer not to know and, more importantly, the face is at the bottom of my pack."

Many miles and hours later, atop a boxwood-tangled plateau called Chaume des Champs Bouton, we came upon the usual stone crucifix rising high above a crossroads. Carved on its base were the words, "Happy is he who rests in the shade of the cross."

The shadow was too slim to provide shade, but we picnicked nearby and gazed back at the cross, happy indeed. Afterwards, Alison inspected the cross closely and reported that it had been erected on May 3, 1810 in those difficult days of rekindled Catholic faith following the French Revolution. I was glad we hadn't experienced them.

"Today is May 3rd," Alison observed with a starry look in her wide, blue eyes.

The penny dropped. "Destiny," I said. "Are you suggesting that on May 3, 1810 the builders of this monument knew that exactly 196 years later a freethinker and an agnostic fallen Catholic would show up and be united to the faith? I may be more tolerant and open-minded than before, but tolerance doesn't equal credulity and superstition, and I think you need a coffee as much as I do."

"Tolerance hasn't stifled your sarcasm," Alison said.

"Touché, though it's irony, not sarcasm." I tried to think of the many wonderful and miserable things that had happened in the world in the last 196 years, but soon ran out of memory. "How about this, instead?" I asked. "Happy is he who recognizes the smiling face staring up at him from the well-worn path." I patted my backpack before slipping it on. "Or, happy is he who recognizes unpredictability and the delight of pondering nothingness as he hikes the final miles toward Givry."

OF VIRGINS AND WATER-TREATMENT PLANTS

The perfumed tunnels of clustering viburnum and wild plum echoed with birdsong and the buzzing of bees as we approached Givry en route to our B&B for the night, after which we would return by another path and pick up the Way. We would be bedding down at a place called Moulin Madame. Our trail was clearly another Roman road, though our map didn't say so. The road ran into the backside of a large iron Madonna perched on a cliff. Beyond her, the *premier cru* escarpment fell away, revealing vineyards and a fairytale town with slanting tile roofs, cupolas, and towers. I preferred not to notice the cluttered floodplain of the Saône River, crisscrossed by railroad tracks and a freeway. They were so far away, I could barely make them out. "Another Virgin of the vines," I sighed, thinking of the tenacious phylloxera. On the Madonna's plinth we discovered that, as pilgrims, we were entitled to three hundred days of full indulgence—*indulgentia plenaria*—in exchange for three Ave Marias, but only sixty days if Mary was hailed at a distance. Like her sisters, this Madonna wept tears of rust. Through her white mantle the corrosion puckered, welling up from the oxidized core of an outwardly indestructible structure.

To get into Givry from the towering Virgin, we slid and scrambled down the rocky Roman road, past thick, knotted grapevines, lopsided stone shelters, and a ruined windmill. Givry did not look like Mercurey or Rully or Santenay or any other winemaking village we'd seen. It was an authentic miniature town planned by a rationalist architect, with city gates topped by sculpted onions and a striking main square with a round stone building in its center. The rotunda turned out to be the former grain hall, now a wine information and tourist office, with a dizzying spiral staircase. Nearby it, a fountain splashed, its cockleshell moist and mossy. On the terrace of the first café we saw, we ordered espressos. The service reminded me of slow-cooked beef stew: a question of hours. Judging by their dress, manner of speech, and stiletto-heeled swagger, the ladies in charge of the café appeared to have less in common with the Madonna on the hill than with Mary Magdalene in her first profession.

"The oldest profession, I've heard said. Now all we have to do is get a coffee out of them, and find Moulin Madame." I tried but failed to get navigational assistance from the waitresses. No one recognized the B&B's address, and neither did the butcher's wife or the baker across the square. A phone call confirmed that Moulin Madame still lay several miles away, out of town, along the main highway to Chalon-sur-Saône. It wasn't in charming Givry after all.

"Panic" would be too dramatic to describe our reaction. I could hardly understand the woman at the B&B on the other end of the telephone line—she seemed to have a clothes clip on her tongue. A close reading of our map showed a roundabout way to get to Moulin Madame via the Roman road—clearly identified now. It followed a creek past the municipal pumping plant. "No pointless meandering," I said; "we're heading straight to the hotel."

We began smelling the type of pumping plant it was about half a mile before reaching it, and recognized the creek as an open sewer. Tractors trundled by, raining clods of mud. "Happy is he who recognizes that the Roman road runs by the sewage treatment plant," Alison muttered.

"Don't be sarcastic," I quipped, stripping off my T-shirt and revealing flesh the color of uncooked poultry. The air temperature was about 90 degrees Fahrenheit, a little hotter than we'd expected for early May.

Serendipity struck. Beyond the treatment plant, the road led to a fortified farmhouse surrounded by a moat. Though it looked like trespass, we persevered. Our path did a dogleg around the property. On the far side of it, low and unspectacular, a Roman footbridge spanned the clear, rushing creek. How many soldiers and pilgrims had marched this way, I wondered, marveling. Somewhere in the distance, across fields and a modern highway, lay our B&B.

PARKER BARRELS AND THE BLISS OF IGNORANCE

The industrial sheds, colza fields, and rusting railroad tracks along the highway didn't bode well. But hiding down a driveway amid mature sycamores with mottled trunks, and tender-leafed horse chestnut trees, stood a hulking, fortified millhouse ringed by stone walls. The façade was tangled with purple wisteria, the roof topped by terracotta tiles clotted with lichen and moss. A pair of Geisha eyes peered down at us from a bull's-eye window. "Bonjour," piped the voice associated with the eyes, speaking English. "I'm coming down."

The woman who introduced herself as Miki Manabe did not actually have a clothes clip on her tongue. With shy, balletic motions and delicate peeps, the lithe young Japanese hostess led us into the millhouse, plied us with cool drinks and hot coffee, and told us of her transformation from computer scientist in Tokyo to budding winemaker in Givry. Wine was about tradition and ritual, she whispered, shyly answering our questions about how she had wound up here. Japan had tea, she added. France had three-star restaurants and peerless estate wines.

Miki eclipsed herself with bows and blushes when the B&B's manager strode in. He was named Romain, he said, and indeed he looked like Julius Caesar or Agrippa, a strapping fellow with a Mediterranean cast. Before we could climb to our room, Romain led us back outside, along the millrace and through a shady grove. Moulin Madame was built circa 1380, he said, delivering the short history of the property. A reclusive biotech billionaire exploring the ethanol potential of colza had bought the estate and saved the millhouse from ruin, turning it into a luxury B&B.

I joked that Miki wasn't in Burgundy to make ethanol. "Miki is allergic to colza," Romain explained, "which is one reason she's moving on as soon as she can." Were there others like her who had come to study wine but were thwarted by this new development, Alison wondered? "She's going to make wine," Romain remarked, "and frankly she's a little too timid to be a hostess, so it is probably for the best. We thought it would be good to have someone who spoke English and Japanese, but it turns out what foreign visitors want is a French host, even if he speaks bad English and no Japanese. The feeling is what counts, the appearance of authenticity."

The ceiling timbers of our room were too far up for me to distinguish details, and the carved stone fireplace was of the type we'd seen before—apparently designed for spit-roasting sides of beef. Behind a movable screen lurked an oval bathtub. We took turns sinking into it, and emerged around sunset lightened of dust. By then, Romain had uncorked samples of local wine, donned an apron, and cooked something resembling a curry. Whether or not the spices exalted the wine seemed unimportant. Romain's passion for ladybugs and hand-picked, organic grapes won us over, and his descriptions of how some clever local winemakers keep a special "Parker Barrel" of fruit-forward wine to hoodwink the supposedly omniscient American critic Robert Parker, came as an entertaining surprise. As big as a barrel, and overflowing with self confidence, Parker roamed the vineyards of the world, judging wines and making or breaking wineries.

According to Romain, "Parker Barrel" wines are made for export to countries where they will please the infallible Parker and the palates that share his florid tastes. Essentially, they go to America, England, and Germany. The same château's same vintages sold in France might be different, more nuanced and less oaky. "People drink Givry wines here and love them," Romain said good-naturedly. "They go home, they buy what they think are the same wines, and they say 'Hmmm, why are they always better when you drink them on the spot?'" He paused for effect. "Is it because wine doesn't travel? No! It's not just travel or even psychology, it's actually a different wine. Winemakers here have learned how to please Monsieur Parker. Consumers want to believe Parker. Parker has his criteria. He gets what he wants. We get to keep what we want. Everyone's happy."

DAILY FLOPPY DOLL

Early the next morning, Miki set out our breakfast with the skill of a computer scientist executing a tea ceremony, except that we were drinking coffee—mugs of it. After the usual polite banalities about rain and sunshine, I couldn't help asking her whether she was glad to be "moving on," as Romain had put it. Miki turned the color of her homemade raspberry jam. She agreed that a change was for the best. She would soon be making wine, not serving guests at a B&B. Transitions were difficult.

By Japanese standards, Miki was a rebel. She'd given up a career and a family and left the country. "Now, may I please ask you a question?" We prepared ourselves for the usual queries about pilgrimage and religious belief—or lack thereof. Miki surprised us. "What is the exercise regime you do in the morning?"

Alison grinned with relief. So did I. Our morning stretching and muscle-building was based on yoga and Okinawan Daruma Taiso. We'd learned the Daruma Taiso from a Japanese master of Shorei-Kan karate. After about twelve years of it, Alison had reached the level of brown belt with three stripes—one exam away from a black belt. I'd managed to make it into the black-belt category, but after being struck by optic neuritis I had to quit. I was proud to have been among the world's worst first-*dan* black belts, permanently scarred by bruising, cracked ribs, and loose teeth. "But we both keep up the Daruma Taiso," I finished explaining.

Miki tittered, covering her mouth. "I am so sorry, but I do not know this term. Daruma Taiso?"

"Isn't it Japanese?"

"Oh, yes," Miki said. "But it makes no sense. It means 'daily floppy doll.'" She tittered uncontrollably, and pantomimed a floppy Raggedy Ann.

Daruma Taiso wasn't about building muscle. The goal was to become agile, quick, and loose-jointed, to be able to turn an opponent's strength against him, as in Aikido. Metamorphosing into a floppy doll or Raggedy Ann made sense. Miki nodded. "Yes," she said, shaking our hands and bowing. "That is a powerful philosophy."

As we climbed back up through Givry's budding vineyards I felt stiff, not floppy, and couldn't help thinking about the paradoxes of Japanese and French society. Success in Japan was about combining flexibility with wiry tensile strength and solidity. Metaphorically, this took the form of traditions, ceremonies, and belief systems anchored to Buddhism and Shinto. It might also explain why the Japanese share with the French a great respect for rituals and traditions, such as the rigorousness of training and education, the professionalism of engineers, waiters, chefs, and the physical solidity of stone houses, châteaux, vineyards, and wineries. Certainly, the Japanese admired the apparent flexibility of America, and the dynamic potential of floppy rootlessness. But they were in awe of France. They understood that, like the Japanese themselves, what the French feared most was the loss of their traditions, a model of society fashioned centuries ago, based on patterns thousands of years old. I couldn't help wondering if the Japanese had their own equivalent to Janus, the god of thresholds and paradoxes, and if he were straining his neck nowadays keeping an eye on China and India.

HEARTY BURGUNDY

It may have been exhaustion. It may have been elation. Or maybe it was the intoxicating spring blossoms. Whatever the reason, as we hiked through the ridgetop hamlets of Russilly, Jambles and Moroges, with vineyards splayed below, I felt something akin to runner's high. Gone was the pain in my knees and back. Was this the long-awaited epiphany, an intimation of spiritual awakening? The succession of Romanesque churches, thick-limbed old trees, barking dogs, and reclusive natives swam in my head, mixing with the airborne white cows and tilting rooftops in a seamless, bright panorama. It was gorgeous, beautiful, stunning, magical. Then somewhere between Moroges and Buxy, just after the trail split, I tripped and fell into a hedgerow. Before standing up, I stared at my boots and realized that I had stumbled on a fossil the size of a football. It was cracked open and revealed a cockleshell within, a shell left behind when the Mediterranean retreated millions of years ago. I couldn't help laughing. I laughed hysterically, slapping my thighs as I rolled to my stomach and did a push-up to get back on my feet. First a bone, then a face, and now a cockleshell. Hello, Saint James! I bent over again and picked up the fossil, feeling my vertebrae click, and a spasm about to come on. The petrified symbol of Saint James must've weighed about thirty pounds. Alison caught up with me in time to see me hefting the fossil and wiping tears from my cheeks. Her eyes swept from the fossil to my backpack. "You're not?"

"No," I said, bending my knees carefully and putting the fossil down where I'd found it. "I'll come back for it one day. But it's some kind of message." She waited long enough to decide whether

I was joking. "The proverbial message from a flounder," I said, and laughed again.

I was still chuckling when we hiked downhill through the grapevines, past a pair of mossy manors and a clutch of pictur-esque hovels, and then around the perimeter of freshly built tract housing development. We wound up on the semicircular road marking the former moat of medieval Buxy. Sycamores unfurled fresh leaves on either side of the road. Under the trees were grocery stores and gift shops, a newsstand, bakery, butcher shop, restaurant, and cafés. "That one," Alison said, pointing to a cluster of outdoor tables where locals were drinking and chatting. While I stocked up on food, water, and Buxy's sweet specialty— nougatine with hazelnuts or pistachios or chocolate—she headed for the towering village church and met me back at the café on the boulevard.

It was blissful. The heat had calmed. The scenery was pleasant. We had cool water and hot coffee and a table under spreading old trees. The only minor drawback was the company at the next table. A shrieking toddler sat in a dirty stroller surrounded by three teenage girls, all of them smoking and drinking beer. Two of them were in advanced pregnancy. One of the pregnant ones was the baby's mother. His name was Jimmy. The girls pronounced it "gee-me" and took turns swearing at the toddler and describing to each other the unpleasantness of pregnancy, childbirth, and housekeeping.

Jimmy's mother had a tattoo on her arm. I couldn't make out what it said. Alison tilted her head and read it. She wrote the words out for me, using my notebook. *l'Amour c'est comme la mort, ça fait mal.* Love is like death, it's painful. It sounded like the lyrics of a soupy song, something by the ageing French rock idol Johnny Hallyday, for instance.

Alison picked up the café's copy of *Le Journal de Saône et Loire,* the regional newspaper. Splashed across the front page, headlines

DAVID DOWNIE

screamed. The article below recounted the tale of Aimée and Edmond, an aged couple who'd been attacked in their home by an unknown assailant in the sleepy village of Saint-Yan in southern Burgundy. It was a modern-day *Crime and Punishment*, though the perpetrators had little in common with the philosophical, tormented Raskolnikov, and the reporter wasn't exactly a Dostoevsky. By the time Alison had finished reading me the grim tale, I'd realized why so many people along our path had shuttered up their houses or fled. It wasn't because we were pilgrims and they didn't want to give us water or food. They feared something darker, perhaps rightfully so.

"They thought we were murderers, posing as pilgrims." I couldn't hear Alison's rebuttal, because just as she opened her mouth, three teenage boys roared up to the café on dirt bikes that spluttered and buzzed and spat out blue smoke. The boys settled in next to Jimmy and the girls, lit up, fiddled with gold chains and lighters and cellphones, ordered beers and hard liquor, and went through the broad, hormonal gestures of acting out a 21st-century French version of *American Graffiti*. It was as if global warming from greenhouse gases and lung cancer from cigarettes had yet to be discovered. We're young and invincible, the boys' scripted machismo screamed, *vive* Vercingétorix.

On the way to our hotel, we paused to peer into the window of a gift shop, where fossils and minerals propped up a fading Kodak sign. I thought of Eva Fage and Miki Manabe. Change was difficult, yet sometimes it was for the better. To each his own version of change.

Buxy's claim to fame as a Protestant stronghold in the Wars of Religion was that of being ransacked and destroyed by Henri IV himself, aided by his valiant men. It was a strange tale, for Henri had begun life a Protestant and had only embraced the Vatican's religion for political reasons. In any case, by the time the king rode out of Buxy, carrying the good

248

wine with him, all that remained of the 10th-century walled town was a moat filled with rubble, a city gate, and parts of a few wrecked towers.

In the dusk, after a nap at the grand-sounding but blessedly simple Château Fontaine de Baranges, we trawled the town's alleys and then poked around the church, another sturdy edifice rebuilt in the 1800s. A single taper burned inside, near a finely carved 16th-century sculpture of Saint Anne. We had the church to ourselves. "Do you want to light a candle?" I asked. "You certainly could do with some help from the tooth fairy."

"My molar is okay," Alison sighed. "Go ahead. I'll catch up with you." She waited until I'd stepped through the door. Creeping back inside, I watched her drop a one-euro coin into a trunk. She lit a taper. Something was going on. In two weeks, she'd invested at least five euros on votive candles.

DEAD RELIGIONS AND FORGOTTEN BORDERS

Château Fontaine de Baranges is wrapped in a pocketsize park on Buxy's southeastern edge. When we first arrived and staggered in, the overeager, overly educated desk manager had poured the history of the place—and of Buxy—into us. His words, delivered with a rubbing of his dry hands, came back to me now, over breakfast the following morning. From its origins as a private villa dating to the late 18th century, the château had done service in a variety of incarnations, from Catholic seminary and girls' school during the post-revolutionary religious revival of the early 1800s, to a hotel in the 1990s. The cricket-like manager, who'd formerly rubbed his hands together in a bookstore, had casually added that, to his mind, it had taken France two hundred years to kill off state-sponsored religion, and that the hotel had followed the fall and rise and fall again of Catholicism with uncanny parallelism.

"And you think Catholicism is dead in France?" I'd asked.

"Oh, certainly. Without a doubt," he'd answered, smiling like Jiminy Cricket. "However, Islam is on the rise; Islam, materialism, Nihilism, and Buddhism. Some say there are five million Frenchmen who embrace the way of the Buddha without even realizing it. But there are also five or six million Muslims, and it's our atavistic fear of the Moors that's getting the better of us."

"Saint James the Moorslayer, to the rescue."

"Indeed, you're right to recall the saint's *nom de guerre*, and you might wish to ask yourself why the Saint James pilgrimage has become so popular again."

I shrugged before responding. "It isn't popular around here, that's for sure."

"No, not here in Burgundy, not yet, but we already have Buddhism and Mary Magdalene and Brother Roger in Taizé. Elsewhere in France and Europe, the pilgrimage certainly is a success. You'll see, if you make it to Le Puy en Velay and Roncesvalles. You'll find thousands, tens of thousands of pilgrims on your route, the closer you get to Santiago de Compostela."

I gulped, visibly uncomfortable. "Most of them are on a lark, recharging batteries, having a good time, I'll bet. Either that, or how can Catholicism be dead?"

"Yes, of course, you're surely right to ask, but I suspect you may be surprised by what you find, digging down into the subconscious of your fellow pilgrims. In any case, take my word for it, Catholicism is dead and buried in France, and who knows what will replace it, now that globalization is inevitable. Scientific racism, perhaps, or some kind of muddled-up blend of religion, a dash of the evangelical, a pinch of Buddhism, a drop of neo-Paganism. It will be amusing to see."

"Have you ever been to northern California?" Alison asked. "It's always ahead of the curve."

TOP: Detail of shrine, Notre Dame de Muret, Bearn.
MIDDLE LEFT: David's footprints, Lot.
MIDDLE RIGHT: My staff, Midi Pyrenees.
BOTTOM RIGHT: Our boots caked in mud, Midi Pyrenees.

Walking the Way
TOP: Road in rain,
Auvergne.
MIDDLE: Woodland road,
Lot.
BOTTOM: Cliff road,
Valley of Célé, Lot.

TOP: *Quercy Blanc*, Lot.
MIDDLE: Dirt road, Aveyron.
BOTTOM: Road through
fields to Condom, Gers.

TOP LEFT: Notre Dame d'Esclaux calvary, Gers. TOP RIGHT: Stone cross near Conques, Aveyron. MIDDLE LEFT: Stone cross near Golinhac, Aveyron. MIDDLE RIGHT: Stone cross near Marsolane, Gers. BOTTOM: Stone cross near Faycelles, Lot.

TOP: Cross on bridge over river Bès, Aubrac.

MIDDLE: STONE Cross near Nogaro, Gers.

BOTTOM: Memorial cross for a pilgrim, Pyrenees forest below Roland's pass.

ALL IMAGES BOTH PAGES: Crossing the Pyrenees into Spain.

Arrival in Roncevaux/
Roncesvalles.
TOP: Fallen tree on road
descending towards
Roncesvalles.
MIDDLE: Pilgrims' crosses
at Roncesvalles.
BOTTOM: Roncesvalles
Abbey cloister.

BLURRED LINES

Given the bloodletting of the Wars of Religion, I suppose it shouldn't have come as a surprise to us that Buxy was still thoroughly secular and devoted to the cult of the French Republic. There was no hint of a California-like fusion of religiosity and spirituallty. Proof of this came at the bakery and tourist office, where no one seemed to know anything about the Way of Saint James, and had never before seen a pilgrim. We were the first in years, they said, in centuries, perhaps. When I pointed out that an outlying district of Buxy was marked on our map with the name "Saint-Jacques," the unflappable tourist office manager seemed perplexed but not embarrassed. "It must be an error," she said. "I'll have to find out."

After breakfast, we walked a few blocks east from our hotel to rue Saint-Jacques, which proved to be a narrow road that apparently once linked Buxy to Chalon-sur-Saône, a major pilgrimage site, as we knew.

"There are a lot of old stones around here," said an elderly woman I buttonholed in the front yard of a house. She was referring to the ruins, she said, up and down the road. "I've never seen a pilgrim come by," she confirmed, adjusting the thick frame of her glasses. "Good luck to you."

I sensed from her expression and the way she thrust her hands into her housecoat that she was keeping something back. "Did anything unpleasant happen on this road a long time ago?" I questioned. "Something during the Wars of Religion, perhaps?" She hesitated and then fluttered her large, rough hands.

"I was only a girl and don't really recall," she said. "The *ligne de démarcation* ran by here, and there was some unpleasant incident."

"The *what* ran by here?"

"The border between Occupied and Free France. During the war." She paused. "But you'd never know it, would you? There's not a trace of it left."

An hour later, as we huffed and puffed southwest up a steep grade, I couldn't help thinking of the woman's remark, and the phantom, Nazi-era borderline. During the war, the imaginary safety of "free" France lay to the south of us, the overt oppression of the Occupied Zone to the north. But as recent revelations had made plain, the free area ostensibly controlled by the puppet government in Vichy had been none too free. Vichy had not only collaborated with the Nazis; Vichy was itself zealously racist, anti-Résistance, and anti-semitic. Vichy simply wanted to exist in its own right as a nationalist entity, safe from war damage that might be caused by either side in the conflict. Perhaps that was less surprising than it might've been, given the traumas of the time and the fresh memory of World War One. What did give me pause for thought, however, was how thoroughly the line of demarcation had been obliterated. The ancient Roman road was still clearly visible on maps, and, in some places, across the landscape. The Vichy line, a scarlet letter drawn in relatively fresh ink, was invisible.

As we hiked along in silence, a thought nagged me, nipping from behind. Back in Buxy, the hotel manager—clearly of Protestant stock—had pronounced Catholicism dead in France. Was there a link between Rome, Catholicism, and Vichy and, similarly, between Protestantism, the cult of the Republic, the Résistance, and the ancient Gauls? The Romans had killed the Druids and their religion, and imposed the Emperor and then Catholicism. The Protestants had demanded a direct relationship with God, rebelling against the church hierarchy, and fighting bloody wars to win religious freedom. The Revolutionaries and founders of the secular French state had tried to destroy the church outright. Did the many dots join up, or was I reading too much into the landscape and the oft-changing aspirations of the French nation?

RUTTED ROADS AND SAINTED CUCKOLDS

Back up on the ridge, far above the Saône River Valley, a seemingly endless rank of high-tension power pylons marched along the rutted, ancient bed of the neolithic-Celtic-Roman-Saint-James road now known as GR-7. The trail followed the sizzling power lines south, and we made a noble effort to view the galvanized iron pylons and thick black cables with the same admiration we might show for Roman aqueducts, bridges, roads, and other ancient infrastructure. Why not? The pylons were beautiful in a way—tall, sleek, and symmetrical. They were merely the latest addition to a trail that for tens of thousands of years had been the path of least resistance, meaning it was already there whenever a new conqueror arrived to oppress the natives, from Megalithic Missionaries to Nazis. Rutted roads were not always bad. They saved time and energy. Why beat a new path if the old one did the job? So it was with infrastructure, technology, people, and religion.

Beyond a field where horses gorged themselves on daisies, the silhouette of a blue-caped Madonna seemed ready to leap off a cliff—or into the sky. A lightning rod ran down her back and into a pile of boulders that looked suspiciously like reclaimed prehistoric dolmens. Below them stretched the vineyards and rooftops of Saint-Vallerin. What effect did the Madonna and the neolithic dolmens have on the townspeople living at their feet, I couldn't help wondering? Were the ancient objects *memento mori* or *vanitas* that whispered mortality? Or were they a comforting reminder of the antiquity and tenacious perseverance of civilization, drawing lightning into the ground? Did anyone down there remember the *ligne de démarcation* that also ran near the site?

Above the toy villages of Chenoves and Saules we strode, with turreted little châteaux below, amid pastures and woods and vineyards, and a range of low green hills curling southeast to cup the still-distant town of Cluny. Uncluttered, unjunked up, uncrowded, and unsung—the scenery kept us shuffling along happily despite cumulative fatigue, and a growing host of ghosts.

Approaching the nested village of Culles, we picked wild strawberries and waded through rock roses and irises and lilac, our eyes on the Romanesque steeple ahead. "Watch out for pilgrims," I said. "I have a feeling we'll see another, one of these days." The words had barely escaped my lips when on the door of the first village house, we spotted a carved wooden cockleshell, clearly a recent, varnished addition to the property. Gentrification was under way. Pilgrims would soon follow.

The rutted road plowed through forests and fields, and as we neared Saint-Gengoux-le-National we heard the tinkling of wind chimes. A sign on what had once been a farmhouse, but was now an artist's workshop, advertised handmade marbled paper. Oriental incense perfumed the spring air. You had to wonder. Out here, they were sure to get walk-by customers.

Below the sloping woods, pastures, and vineyards, in the narrow alleys of Saint-Gengoux-le-National, fallen stucco revealed Gothic arches and Romanesque columns in the walls of tumbledown houses. Pencil-tipped church towers poked up in a jumble that oozed atmosphere, like Buxy on the cusp of gentrification.

"Roman or medieval?" I asked. "Place your bets."

We followed the crooked rue Cesarée and rue Jouvance, surprised by the bustle and tempted by the bakery scents. At the local tourist office, an efficient young female volunteer confirmed that Saint-Gengoux-le-National had been a late-imperial or Merovingian town and pilgrimage stopover. She knew nothing of the Résistance or *ligne de démarcation*, however. "The town used to be named Saint-Gengoux-le-Royal," she said. "Then it became Jouvence during the Revolution—Jouvence was the original Merovingian name," she said, getting fuddled. "Then it became Saint-Gengoux-le-Royal again with the Restoration of the monarchy. The 'national' was added after the Franco-Prussian war of 1870, when the Third Republic was created." She handed us a stack of brochures. "Now you'll want to know who the saint was, won't you?"

We nodded. It proved to be a convoluted tale. As usual.

Unhappy Gengulphus of Burgundy was a devout knight and courtier, said the volunteer. He had the misfortune to marry a noble lady of insatiable sexual desires who was unfaithful to him countless times while he was off slaying dragons and infidels. Too kind-hearted to seek revenge by the usual means, and mortified by embarrassment, Gengulphus became a hermit in his castle at Avallon, in northern Burgundy. But one of his lustful wife's lovers decided to take no chances. He murdered Gengulphus in the Year of Our Lord 760, thereby aiding Gengoux to become one of the few martyred saints whose task it is to protect and soothe stilted lovers, cuckolds, separated spouses, and those trapped in "difficult" marriages.

"This would be a great place to spend a honeymoon," I said, thanking the girl as we left, and taking Alison by the hand with proprietorial interest.

A wooden sign pointed to the ramparts, though we were hard pressed to miss them. On the outskirts of town was our B&B, a massive 1800s house backed by a shady garden. It had been a good day during which we'd crossed three survey maps. We'd walked as many miles as Madame Gengulphus reputedly had lovers between dawn and dusk on a busy day. She truly was diabolically insatiable.

FOUNTAINS OF JUVENILITY

Tall, distinguished yet not stand-offish, Jean-Luc Reumaux removed the pipe from his lips and greeted us as we entered the B&B's garden gate. He wasn't exactly "from" Saint-Gengoux, he said, though part of his family had been, generations ago. He'd spent boyhood summers in the vast old country house, he added, leading us up a gravel drive and onto the porch. Jean-Luc's love for the place was contagious.

Our room had overstuffed armchairs, an armoir and desk, and was as cozy and old-fashioned as a Victorian inn. We washed up in a porcelain pedestal-sink down the hall, but decided to skip a nap and explore the house and garden instead. Jean-Luc and his soft-spoken wife Marie-Claude gentled us along, tiptoeing as they spoke. They'd "retired" here, Marie-Claude said, though Jean-Luc still commuted to Paris by TGV to work part-time in H.R. In reality, that meant almost fulltime, but who was counting? They'd reinvented themselves in retirement as innkeepers, after careers as professionals, only to discover that innkeeping was a lot of work. "I suppose we wouldn't have been happy to be idle," she mused. "It's ironic. Jean-Luc was a personnel manager who had to fire hundreds of employees, and now he negotiates on behalf of workers facing layoffs."

"It's a booming business," he remarked, "what with globalization and the Internet." Marie-Claude smiled and sighed. Bad news was always good news for someone.

The house exuded sturdiness and simple good looks, from the patterned tiles and polished plank floors to the wide oak staircase and the fireplaces with stone surrounds. Knick-knacks perched on every flat surface. Jean-Luc's aunt had been a painter and novelist, we learned, and had lived here to a ripe age. Her watercolors and drawings hung from every wall, showing scenes of medieval Saint-Gengoux—its towers and twisting alleys and splashing fountains—and the woods, vineyards, and farms sprinkled nearby. As dusk approached, Alison pulled a book from a shelf and directed me to a lounge chair under a shade tree, facing a ruined tower. The book was titled *L'Écho du Prieuré* and had been written by Madeleine Du Charme, the pseudonym used by Jean-Luc's late aunt, he'd explained. The novel told the story of monks from the Cluny Abbey and their life at the Priory of Nollanges near Saint-Gengoux. Though well written, it wasn't gripping enough to keep me awake. I dozed, listening to birds, bees, and the buzz of a distant sawmill, trying but failing to follow what Alison was reading. It seemed to hold some important truth about the village and life.

Jouvance, Alison said, meant "youth." The name was given to the town over a thousand years ago because a miraculous fountain of youth gushed here in the days of yore, before unlucky Gengulphus came along. It wasn't just any fountain of youth. Plunge the hand of your fiancée or wife into it and if she'd been unfaithful, the skin would peel off "like a glove." Naturally every enlightened, trusting man for miles around herded his beloved to the fountain for, as everyone knows, that was indeed a Golden Age for women.

"Isn't the Pope's summer residence in Castel Gandolfo near Rome?" Alison asked. "And isn't there a famous spring there that fills Lake Albano?" I shrugged in answer. She flipped another page, her voice rising. "Guess what: this is the same Gandolfo. Gengulphus is the Latin name."

"Cuckoldry has never gone out of fashion," I said. "Have you ever wondered if youth and infidelity are mirror images? You know, as in philandering keeps you young? Look at Henri IV, *le Vert Galant*. The Evergreen Galavanter is what they called him. Henri ate raw garlic and drank white wine from dawn to dusk, sired fifty-four bastards, would have lived to be old had he not been assassinated, and is beloved to this day. Not to mention that paragon of morality, François Maurice Adrien Marie Mitterrand, our much-lamented late president. The case studies are infinite in number. Philandering is the national sport in France. It must be good for the health."

Alison turned her patented gimlet eye on me. "That's not what the fountain of youth is at all," she said. "This is the fountain of youth." She spread her arms, puckered, and scooted nearer to finish the sentence: "A loving relationship and peace and quiet."

As if demons were listening, several cars rolled up the gravel lane to the house and disgorged a dozen occupants, including five children. The kids tore into the garden, shouting, scrambling, and tumbling. I shared Alison's wry look and kissed our rejuvenating, quiet evening good-bye.

QUAIL EGGS AND AN EGYPTIAN CRANE

Our hostess Marie-Claude's quiet enthusiasm shone through in her cooking. The lentil-and-quail-egg salad, roast pork, and homemade apple pie were generously served and delicious. Despite the sixteen mouths to feed, there was plenty to go around and dizzying conversation on tap. Our dozen fellow guests were in Saint-Gengoux for a wedding party, they explained. I wondered aloud if they would be stopping by the fountain of youthful infidelity for a premarital checkup. Alison stomped on my foot when I began to tell them about Gengulphus and the peeling of women's skin. The rest of the evening was a blur.

To say that we awoke would suggest we'd slept. The wedding party's comings and goings into the early hours made for serialized napping, not real sleep. I felt like an omelette being flipped in a frying pan as I turned over and over and over again in our bed. At dawn we awoke for the final time, to the plaintive cry of a mysterious bird. It sounded like a peacock blowing a trumpet, and in our punch-drunk state we thought it might be Gengulphus announcing the second coming, or the arrival of the primordial Buddha. Over a ropey breakfast we learned that the trumpet-bird belonged to a neighboring farmer and was none other than a very large, very venerable Egyptian crane, resident in Saint-Gengoux for the last thirty-five years. The unusual pet had slowly won the affection of its lonely owner, replacing several dearly departed members of the owner's family. "It shares its master's table," said Marie-Claude, the teabags large under her bloodshot eyes. I imagined the crane with a napkin around its neck, supping and conversing with the farmer, and hoped the old bird would live as long as an elephant. "Did you two sleep at all?" Marie-Claude asked. "We're terribly sorry for the disturbance. That's the problem with wedding parties."

"We slept like babies," Alison lied.

I wrinkled my face into something resembling a smile, and spread homemade raspberry jam on Marie-Claude's buttery croissants. "Oh, yes," I murmured, yawning until my own bags pushed my eyeballs backwards. "We feel like little children this morning, completely rejuvenated."

ON THE RIGHT TRACK

Passenger and freight service on the Sâone Valley trunk line was suspended in the 1970s, driven out of business by trucks and private cars. The last train from Mâcon to Cluny, Cormatin, Saint-Gengoux, Buxy, and Chalon-sur-Sâone had, nonetheless, left its tracks and railbed behind. The tracks rusted and the beds grew weeds until someone had the bright idea in the late 1990s of turning the former right-of-way into a linear park, dubbed *la Voie Verte*. The Green Way somehow sounded better in French.

The straightness of the *Voie Verte* reminded me more of the Canal du Centre than the Way of Saint James, and so did the occasional rusting, tumbledown factory by the wayside, flanked by tract housing projects. Unlike the canal, however, the former railway bed wasn't shady or cool. After leaving Saint-Gengoux, we walked swiftly along it for the first few hours, until the asphalt softened underfoot, and the sun was high in the sky, illuminating the strange, seemingly endless yet narrowing perspective ahead and behind. Like the boulevards of Paris, or the avenues of New

York City, the straightaway appeared to the eye to close down on itself. You could only see so far before the sides converged. It was an optical illusion, a phenomenon familiar in cities to photographers, architects, and urban planners. I'd never experienced it before in the countryside. The disquieting sensation of finite infinity took hold of me and would not let go. How different were the meandering, leafy paths and twisting roads of other ages, the ones we'd walked on so far. Paradoxically, the *Voie Verte* felt like the offspring of Rome, of rectilinear logic, industrialization, standardization, and commerce. But it had done its time, and was now given over to quiet cyclists, rollerskaters, and the rare pilgrim on a seemingly pointless meander.

Despite the straightness and full sunlight, Alison disappeared from view. I assumed she was behind me. Digital photography was turning out to be dangerous. It transformed analog white rabbits and hares into trigger-happy tortoises, which was fine in most circumstances, but not when it meant roasting under a merciless sun. I marched on alone, confident she would show up sooner or, more likely, later. We'd agreed to stop for lunch in Cormatin, and visit the château, before continuing on to Salornay-sur-Guye to spend the night. In the meantime, an offramp led me from the *Voie Verte* to the nearby hamlet of Malay. A little further on, I stopped at neighboring Ougy, where the peaky campanile of the Romanesque church was roofed in stone. Though obtuse, I'd noticed how each Romanesque church in Burgundy is subtly different. The earliest types, from before the year 1000 AD, have herringbone brick patterns, the later ones Lombard-style bands and arches of stone and brick. It also helps to read up on the subject, which I had, at the B&B in Saint-Gengoux.

All of Burgundy's Romanesque churches were affiliated with the abbey at Cluny. The mothership church, the biggest outside Rome, had spawned thousands of franchises. Each reflected the organization of medieval society. The tall, fortified belltowers were paid for by the local lords and erected by stonemasons. They were still generally in good repair after a thousand years of service. The clergy had paid for the rounded, equally sturdy apses, and they, too, were in fine shape. Peasants had built the barnlike naves, working overtime after milking the goats and plowing the fields and cutting the woods and giving most of what they'd eked out to the lords and the clergy. That explained not only the French Revolution, but also why the naves are often in less good repair than the apses and belltowers.

In search of shade and enlightenment, I took off my pack and sat on a pew under the barrel-vaulted nave at Ougy's church, resting my aching eyeballs and back. Staring out at me was a crusty 12th-century fresco of Saint Philippe, and a naïf, contemporary, handwritten plea scrawled on a piece of cardboard. I got up close enough to read the curlicue script. It stated that the *commune* of Ougy-and-Malay, with 219 inhabitants, has two landmark churches it can't afford to maintain. "Give," was the message. "Open your wallets." To locals, whether pious or *républicain*, the historic "patrimony" of heritage sites is both a blessing and a curse. I dropped a euro into the collection box, put my billed cap back on, and hiked back into the sunlight, expecting to see Alison at any moment.

She was nowhere ahead or behind. Another mile south, and still on the *Voie Verte*, a noisy frog pond and grassgrown passenger platforms marked the former location of the railroad station of Cormatin. Seeing an exit, I got off the railway line again and headed into the village.

Cormatin is the kind of place that would be easy to get used to, I said to myself, as I bought an apple turnover at the bakery and ate it lustily while limping under shade trees to a pleasant café. A pharmacy, a grocery, butcher's shop and bakery, and one of the country's great châteaux, not to mention antique shops and other sellers of useless but amusing paraphernalia, all housed in handsome landmark buildings with trees out front and yards out back—such was the village of Cormatin. I sipped my espresso and felt at peace. There was no way for Alison to get past me without being seen. She couldn't have gotten lost on the straightest hiking trail in France, a feat requiring genuine talent and cardinal-point dyslexia. Had she been run over by a speeding skater?

I drank my second coffee, drummed my fingers, and eventually decided to take a tour of the château on my own.

CHÂTEAU OF A DOUBT

The grounds of Cormatin Château seemed considerably dreamier than any dream I'd had in recent decades. Out of nowhere appeared the meandering Grosne River, pronounced "groan," but in no way indicative of the site's character. Conveniently the river embraced the site, providing a natural moat, doubled with a man-made one about eight hundred years ago by the Du Blé d'Huxelles family. They and their forebears were the original military governors of the district, and later climbed socially to the height of royal courtiers in Versailles.

The three-story, L-shaped residence rose ahead of me down a leafy alley of hedges and trees, past a clump of fortified outbuildings and a tidy kitchen garden the size of several tennis courts. On the north side of the property, the side I was expecting to see Alison appear on at any moment, spread geometrical parterres of lawn, lavender, and boxwood. Punctuating them were wispy beeches or pyramidal, clipped yews. The boxwood labyrinth exuded intoxicating scents. Overlooking the maze of its foliage was an elevated view-point built atop a birdhouse, which had been made to look like a neoclassical temple. Several large, lively parrots fluttered around as I walked by them on a spiral staircase, and stopped to gaze over the landscape. Around the garden looped another ring of the Grosne River. Beyond the river ran the *Voie Verte*. It was empty.

In a reflecting pool the castle's golden stones shimmered. They were dressed up with white stucco on the garden-side façades. The effect was stunning, so much so that I collapsed into a garden chair under a beech tree and decided to wait again for Alison.

An hour later, and increasingly worried, I entered the château and found myself surrounded by a tour group. Built in the early 1600s on 12th-century foundations, this was, said the tour guide, the archetype of the Henri IV-Louis XIII style, a tasteful blend of late Renaissance Italianate and Dutch, with slate-covered mansards, gables, and turrets. A dozen of us stood shoulder to shoulder in an airy, vaulted stone staircase of impressive proportions, and then tramped through a succession of dazzling salons, *cabinets*, bedrooms, and madame's celebrated boudoir. Alison was still nowhere to be seen. To say that I was worried would be understatement. However, after over two decades of waiting for Alison—a true female Godot—I had learned to master my anxiety.

Many of the château's rooms were what might be termed a floor-to-ceiling feast of 1620s décor. The grotesques, allegories, and painted landscapes sparkled with gold leaf and liquefied lapis lazuli, reportedly the most extensive and best-preserved wall decorations of their kind in the country, according to the tour guide. She was a serious young woman, an art historian, and I could tell she would not go in for the usual folksy, dumbed-down promulgation of information. This was high culture and as rare as an authentic native Burgundian snail or frog's leg.

Nearly as fascinating as the many-limbed genealogical trees, and the accomplishments of the châteaux's illustrious owners, was the story of the property's restoration. It was an object lesson in the political power of culture, and the paradoxically forward-looking variety of *passéisme* once prevalent in France. In 1980, a trio of art historian-librarians with modest means bought the château, which had seen no upkeep since 1914. They paid a mere one million francs, about $150,000 at the time, suspecting that beneath the grime lay treasures. They were right, and earned themselves the privilege of spending the next twenty-odd years and about $2.3 million fixing things up. Luckily, matching funds came from the government, thanks largely to friends in high places, one of whom had François Mitterrand's imperial ear. Once the trio of new owners had removed over-painting and driven out the woodworms, they turned to digging and shifted twelve thousand square meters of soil from the moats. The number meant nothing to me, but it sounded impressive. They also rebuilt 360 linear meters of bastions, which by my reckoning came out to nearly four hundred yards, or four football fields in length, and then recreated the gardens, reclaiming swamps and fields, basing their work on original plans drawn up by Louis XIII's royal gardener. His name escaped me.

In reality, said the guide, Mitterrand-style largesse was a thing of the past. Subsidies for heritage sites such as Cormatin had dried up, and the government now spent more propping up a single soccer club in Lyon than it did on the entirety of its four thousand landmark buildings. "Art is something humanity invented in order to turn the mind toward eternity," she said, quoting André Malraux, France's first culture minister, appointed by De Gaulle in the early 1960s. Perhaps, to some, soccer was too. Luckily that wasn't my table.

Except for kitchen appliances too heavy to steal, the original furniture had been auctioned by previous owners, most of them penurious heirs of the Du Blé d'Huxelles. An inventory dated 1643 helped the trio of restorers to refurnish accurately. They opted to maintain a layered reality, with the best of each century. Upwards of sixty thousand paying visitors tour the château yearly, and the owners have the additional privilege of telling their tale in great detail to each and every one of them.

Thrilled by the visit, but worn from the heat and an overdose of history, I eased myself into another garden chair under what must be one of the world's largest oak trees, and lounged there, thinking of eternity and Alison, until a gaggle of geese chased me away. The time for action had come. I plodded to the gatehouse, wondering where I would find a gendarme to report that my wife was missing; but lo and behold, there she stood, maddeningly insouciant and—luckily—wholly undamaged. "I stopped to take a picture and," she said blithely, "I guess I walked across a field and took the wrong road and. . . ."

BROTHERLY LOVE

Knowing that Cluny was too far to reach in a single day from Saint-Gengoux, we'd reserved a room at a B&B in the still-distant village of Salornay-sur-Guye. Once Alison had shown up at Cormatin, only slightly bedraggled by her three-mile detour, we set off together, veering west. According to our maps, Salornay was almost as far away as Cluny, and turned out to be even farther. But there was a big advantage in going there, and both of us knew it. By detouring, we would avoid passing through Taizé, headquarters of Brother Roger's spiritual community, where the lone pilgrim at Mercurey, the wild-eyed Irishman, was headed. He and god only knew how many others. Questers like him, and tens of thousands of teenage Eastern Europeans, have turned the district around Taizé into a sprawling Boy and Girl Scout encampment, nowadays run by the ageing acolytes of the late charismatic friar. We'd been to Taizé more than once and had even met Roger Schutz, the monk's real name. To his followers, Frère Roger is a martyr. A madwoman from Romania murdered him, leaping up during one of his evening prayer sessions in August 2005 and driving a knife three times into his back. The monk was ninety years old. More than 2,500 of his followers had watched in horror.

Brother Roger's effigy is everywhere in southern Burgundy, not that he'd encouraged followers to worship him. His organization had taken over several semi-abandoned villages and hamlets, unwittingly driving up real estate prices and antagonizing longtime residents, who resented the crowds of newcomers. The manner in which many visitors to Taizé revered the monk, the way cult members I'd known in California had revered their gurus, had always troubled me, and zealous crowds of any kind make me itch.

I couldn't help wondering what it was that had made California and Burgundy centers for legitimate and loony questers, monks, gurus, neo-Pagans, and Buddhists, from the Druids to the present day. California and Burgundy could not be more different physically, topographically, and historically, the one sun-baked, dry, hot, and bereft of antiquity, the other a moody, damp, green place, a place of emptyness, of layered history and apparent timelessness, the timelessness so dear to the world's *passéistes*.

Happily, before I could get lost in meandering thoughts, the sunwashed Roman road appeared again, as if by magic, and marched us from Cormatin across the valley to a ford in the clear, rushing Guye River. With joyous shouts we crossed it on glistening stones, the same stones Caesar had laid his jackboots on, or so I liked to think. As we reached the river's western bank and spotted the ruined church of Saint-Hippolyte, a TGV high-speed train flashed by, heading north to Paris. Cattle grazing near the railroad munched stolidly on, apparently unmoved by the geyserlike swoosh and deafening roar. The train topped 200 mph on this stretch, I knew from the experience of riding it many times. Had the locals, too, grown used to it? We'd often read of NIMBYs fighting the bullet train, but the government had prevailed, as governments do in France, and the sizzling, electrified scar had steadily transformed southern Burgundy into Paris's back yard. It was our back yard. Mea maxima culpa, I muttered. We were typical TGV riders.

Somehow we made it uphill several more miles and hiked through the stonebuilt village of Bonnay, reaching Besanceuil shortly afterwards, where nary a Frenchman appeared to live. Dutch, Swiss-German, and English rang in our ears, and Dutch, Swiss, and English flags flapped over a castle and several tidy kitchen gardens. A contemporary art gallery had taken over a farmstead. The fields were scattered with hard-to-classify artworks, many the size of tractors, and dinosaur-shaped cutouts, studies in rust. They reminded me of two things—Richard Serra's octagon of steel in Chagny, and the long shadow of Paris's art establishment. In a rare moment of disgust, Alison wondered aloud whether the exhibition was titled "Tetanus Galore." I held my tongue. She'd said it all.

After the unpronounceable Besanceuil, the trail mounted steeply and tunneled through deep forests to the west, forests few humans had entered in recent years, or so we thought we understood a stag to say in his own non-verbal language. He stopped his barking and roaring and stared at us, pawing the forest floor and wagging his magnificent seven-pointed antlers. How had we strayed this far off the wheel-worn road?

A cloudburst opened while we were under the canopy of trees, and it was dark and cold, and we were soaking wet by the time we found Salornay-sur-Guye, tramping around it in mounting frustration for half an hour before at long last finding our B&B. It was in the village château, but the château was cleverly hidden by trees and high walls, and someone had removed the signs pointing to it.

FOR WHOM SALORNAY'S BELL TOLLS

Exhaustion is no guarantor of sound sleep. If dinner at the Auberge de la Guye and the evening at Château de Salornay are but a vague memory, experienced like a dream, I put it down to the meticulously organized sleep deprivation we experienced. A wedding party, another one, occupied the rest of the rooms in the B&B, a charming and handsome property lovingly restored by a retiring, pious family. Less a château than a cozy, small manor, it was, we saw in morning light, wrapped in a park crowded with mature trees, all of them budding. Our room occupied the upper floor of a stubby tower, which had been built in the 1400s, according to the owners. The nuptial party's comings and goings through the night would've delighted monks bent on mortification of the flesh, I told myself, trying to pull my thoughts together and drive myself from bed. It added another set of purses to our dark, badger eyes.

Before dawn I found my fingers in the dark and counted them backwards and forwards. We had another ten miles to cover before reaching Cluny, where we planned to rest for several days and see a dentist and physiotherapist. Alison could no longer chew without discomfort, because of the breach in her molar. My stride had slowly metamorphosed into a limp. Over breakfast, the B&B's owners must have thought me an ape as I fumbled with the homemade jams and almost broke a fine porcelain plate. Somehow I could not wrap my mind around the conversation, starting with the fact that the mild-mannered owner, who still worked fulltime in Paris, was in charge of the European Union scheme to dismantle mothballed Soviet nuclear submarines. I shook my head and asked if he could repeat that. Rocket science was a piece of cake compared to cleaning up the radioactive, toxic Russian mess, he explained. How had the couple wound up in Salornay-sur-Guye, far from any ocean?

"Family roots and affection," said the nuclear scientist. "We love Salornay."

Salornay. Salornay? Why did I know that name? The penny eventually dropped when, after our breakfast, we explored the village church, kittycorner from the château. A hulking sanctuary of Romanesque origin, many times rebuilt, and in excellent condition, it brimmed with fresh flowers. Dong, dong, dong, rang the soulful bell, reminding me quite suddenly of gluttony, waywardness, and a vow I'd made. I stuck my head out of the church and glanced down the road. There it was, the doctor's office where, several years earlier, I'd been diagnosed with steatosis and hepatitis, and declared a walking foie gras. Like Bibracte, where I'd had visions before collapsing, Salornay was my private pilgrimage site. I'd come full circle, but by all accounts still had a long way to go.

CHEESE THIEVES AND A DUD MADONNA

Salornay seemed remarkable not only for its butcher shop and deli, and its pair of multiple-arched medieval bridges. It also appeared to be bracketed by the largest concentration we'd seen so far of modern tract homes. As we headed toward a place marked "Roche" on the monk's trail to Cluny, the old song about San Francisco wormed its way into my ear. *Little houses on a hillside, little houses made of ticky-tacky. . . .*

In comparison to these semi-detached banalities, the ticky-tacky developments of my distant hometown looked downright attractive. The reasons why Salornay and villages like it across France have suffered an outbreak of semi-detached ticky-tacky are complicated. The standard explanation is that wealthy Parisians, Lyonnais, and foreigners have snapped up and restored *les vieilles pierres*, driving prices for vintage properties beyond the range of locals, especially the young, and so ticky-tacky, cheap residences spring up to meet demand. This was true, but left unanswered one small question. Why had the countryfolk of France let so many of their historic houses fall into ruin in the first place, and why had they sold them to outsiders?

Vineyards spread their budding vines above Salornay, and the monk's road ran between them. It became a magical time-tunnel through forested hills, easily as mossy and Druidic as any we'd seen in the Morvan. Along the flanks of a hollow cupping the hamlet of Sirot, the pastures were swirled with buttercups and milkweed, and daisies as white as the lambs nibbling them. Thick forests shouldered along the ridges. Giant trees hundreds of years old shaded a broad, drumlike round tower and the fortified manor flanking it. Across the dirt road, what had obviously been a winery was now being used as a barn. Hay bales spilled out of it. A tractor sat out front.

"Phylloxera," I said. "Sirot was where the monks of Cluny made wine."

As in Chastellux-sur-Cure, trout swam in a bathtub-like pool, the hamlet's former washhouse. Up the road from it, a woman of mature years gazed down at us, her arms folded over a cotton apron. A dog barked in the yard below. She was framed by the porch of what had once been a winegrower's house. "It used to be nothing but vineyards around here," she said pleasantly, in answer to my question about the winery. She said her name was Henriette Touzot and she waved at the woods and pastures. "They put up crosses at the crossroads, and a Virgin of the Vines, up there." She pointed again, but we could not see the Madonna. "I guess it didn't work."

Near her porch hung a large cage made of wood and wire. It wasn't full of birds. "Goat cheese," she confirmed with a winning smile. "I still air-dry it. You're not supposed to anymore, not safe, they say, but nobody died eating goat's milk cheese dried this way, not in a thousand years."

Henriette got her dog to calm down enough so that we could lean on the stone wall of her yard and hear her better. In a singsong Burgundian accent, she took the opportunity to tell us the history of the hamlet, not since time immemorial, but circa 1934, when her husband's family bought the stone house she lived in. Not many people were left, she remarked, glad to exercise her rusty voice. Only a handful. The youngsters decamped to the city decades ago, she added, and no one had moved back. A truck loaded with bread passed three times a week, and the baker who drove it also sold other things. Foreigners had been buying up the hamlet down the valley, a place called Flagy, full of artists and fancy folks, she said, all nice enough but not from here. Now that her husband was gone, she and the farmers with the trout in the old washhouse were about the only ones left. Sirot was pretty quiet.

Henriette sighed and adjusted her apron, scolding her tired old dog. "You've got to wonder who'd come all the way out here to steal my cheeses," she said, shaking her head. Twice she and the hound had caught malefactors in the act, but they'd run away.

"Your cheeses must be especially good," said Alison, brandishing her camera. "May I?"

Henriette watched, bemused, as the city folks with funny accents immortalized her goat's-milk cheeses, some fresh and fluffy and white, others yellow or blue with age and mold.

We bought one, a nice, fresh, creamy one, to supplement our picnic. It had a good goaty flavor, the flavor and nose of hay, we discovered. We ate it at the top of the hill, on a mound of rocks, the kind the monks piled up when clearing fields and making vineyards a thousand years ago.

Between us and Cluny stretched another five miles of achingly beautiful countryside, a tuck-'n'-roll patchwork. We crossed them without encountering a single living human. Cattle, birds, and the dead seemed present in a reassuring way—the ghosts of monks and Caesar, for instance, flitting along the road, leading us off the beaten trail to a chapel in a hamlet called Collonges. That wasn't its original name. Try Colonica instead. It had been founded in the year 898 by two monks from Mâcon, as a refuge for pilgrims and itinerant artisans, the cathedral-building stonemasons of the Middle Ages. The chapel was only seven hundred years old, stated a notice inside, and recently restored by the kind of neo-rural types who'd fixed the village houses, raised foreign flags, and displayed photographs of Brother Roger of Taizé.

I sat resting in the chapel, listening to Alison read out the historical report card. The complicated process of colonization, decline, restoration, and gentrification, repeated again and again over the centuries, felt like a continuum, a wheel turning slowly overhead. The primeval forests had become pastures and then vineyards and were now pastures and forests again. I closed my eyes and forgot my back and knee. We were into our fourth week of walking, a week when the spirit was supposedly no longer shackled by the body or mind. I felt the wheel turning inside me and wondered what lessons I'd learned so far, if I'd walked and thought enough. Enough for what? The answer was, I still didn't know. The phrase *assailed by doubt* welled up and I held it in my mind, meditating in a pleasant daze, repeating it like a magic formula.

"If you can't find it within yourself to answer Him," I heard Alison reading aloud from a book left open on the altar, "He will respect your silence." She paused, letting the words sink in. "Doubt, at times, is none other than the flip side of faith."

She turned the page, closing the book, and lit another candle.

ABBEY ROAD

A prosperous town of about five thousand inhabitants, Cluny spills its stone buildings from a rise to the bottom of the Grosne Valley, named for the same small, sinuous river we'd seen at Cormatin. The goddess of abundance has sprinkled the bowl of hillocks and vales around Cluny with a cornucopia of ticky-tacky tract homes, but I kept my eyes on the monk's road as we marched in from a suburb portentously named Clos Saint-Hugues.

What used to be a main road a thousand years ago is now a narrow back street, rue de la Chanaise, and is still lined by medieval houses, though the city gate is no longer. A sculpted stone salamander clinging to a wrinkled façade watched us pass. We rattled our bones on the cobbles, and once deep into the medieval center of town looked up to see the abbey's 900-year-old towers looming beyond a weathered, monumental double-arched doorway. Once upon a time the door had opened into the narthex of the church, but the narthex was no longer, like most of the abbey, destroyed by Revolutionaries and real estate speculators. We paused by the eastern arch, which picturesquely frames the right transept of the church, about a quarter-mile down and away. The arch, tower, and a wine cellar, a pilgrim's hostel, granary, and cloister are all that remain of what was the largest monastic complex in Christendom, girded by walls and watchtowers, and peopled by tens of thousands of workers, hard-driven by the Abbot of Cluny. My mind's eye fogged at the thought of how many lives over how many years had revolved around this small plot of land and its constellation of monasteries and churches.

We knew the history in some detail, thanks to a zealous medievalist friend, and also because we'd read half a dozen books on the subject over the years. It was hard to credit today, especially on a hot, sleepy Sunday afternoon, but Cluny had for centuries been one of the richest, most powerful ecclesiastical strongholds in Europe. The abbey, founded in 910, was the right arm of the Vatican, managed by a succession of abbots, the most enterprising of them later made saints. Saint Mayeul ran the abbey early on, from 948 to 994. Saint Odilon took over in 994 and reigned for fifty-five years—until 1049. That's when the abbey's real hero, Saint Hugues, stepped on stage, outdoing his predecessors by maintaining control for sixty years, from 1049 to 1109.

At its zenith in 1109, Cluny had control over 1,100 dependent monasteries. Some sources put the number at two thousand. *Partout ou le vent vente, l'Abbé a rente.* The expression entered French jargon a thousand years ago and, loosely translated, means "Wherever the wind blows, the Abbot of Cluny rakes in revenues." The magnificent Musée de Cluny in Paris, once an Imperial Roman bathhouse and now home to the *Lady and the Unicorn* tapestry series, was the abbot's big-city mansion. It sits, as anyone who has been there knows, near rue Saint-Jacques, which for the last thousand years was the main pilgrimage route from Paris to Santiago de Compostela, itself built atop a Roman road, with a Gallic roadbed underneath. For years, Alison and I had marched on sections of that road in Paris. Now we'd crossed Burgundy on it, though of course the original road had often been buried under fields, forests, and asphalt.

Cluny's other possessions were scattered across the Continent and England. They operated like feudal fiefs, with allegiance not to a local lord, but to the Abbot. So powerful was he that his wealth and influence sometimes troubled Rome. Cardinals and popes were dispatched regularly to consult with the abbot, and many a robe was quietly stained by the blood of those who strayed off the Clunysian path. In other words, if you weren't with Cluny, you were against Cluny, and you might wind up in a ditch before your appointed hour.

It was Cluny that built, staffed, and bankrolled many of the important stopover monasteries on the Ways of Saint James not only in France, but also in northern Italy and England. The abbey's empire declined over the centuries, as all empires do, and was rolled up by Revolutionaries and then quarried from 1811 to 1823. The pilgrims stopped coming, and Cluny lapsed into a long, fitful slumber, which was precisely what I, too, now craved.

Unable to believe we'd made it this far, we dragged ourselves through the ruins of the narthex and nave, now the epicenter of town, thinking of Rome's Forum. Around us lay broken columns, parts of walls, and battered flooring. Most of the watchtowers along the perimeter wall appeared to be standing, and reused architectural elements from the abbey jutted out of townhouses and the Hôtel de Bourgogne, where we'd reserved a room.

A raven hopped and flew out of the roofless nave. We followed it, staggering into the hotel, signing the register, and climbing the creaking wooden stairs to our second-floor room. It perched above what would have been the western aisle of the main church, and from it we stared up at the transept and down into the National Stud Farm, which has occupied much of the abbey compound for the last century. A stallion stared back, neighed and frisked. Moments later it galloped into our dinner-less dreams. When we awoke the following morning, rain pattering and magpies caw-caw-cawing, the first thing we did was drink an entire pot of coffee, eat two breakfasts each, and then head for the abbey.

MY CLUNYSIAN CUP FLOWS OVER

The Ochier Museum is a stonework-encrusted Renaissance townhouse also known as the Palais Jean de Bourbon. It stands directly behind the hotel where we were staying, which was convenient, given the wet, muggy weather. Though I could've spent another hour peering at the 3-D scale replica of Cluny, circa 1100 AD, we were encouraged by sharp elbows and sopping, braying toddlers to move on and view the abbey's salvaged treasures, kept elsewhere in the palace. So down a spiral staircase we went into a cellar, where displays ranged from capitals delicately carved with infernal monsters, to sculpted windowsills and inlaid pavements. It was hard to imagine anyone taking a pickaxe to them. Then again, it was hard to imagine how rapacious, arrogant, and cruel the Abbé de Cluny and his followers must have been. Revolutions don't come from nowhere.

The heavy rain and unusual heat suggested that we'd eased from May into an August thunderstorm. We were glad to get into the ruins of the abbey, a moody, dank grotto with pitted dirt floors and moldy stones, more conducive to Druidic magic than Catholic prayer. The dust stuck in my throat. Pigeons winged across the transept into the tower topping it. The sheer size of the place when whole must've been daunting. A video with special effects, and several scale models set up near the cloister, helped us along, but I had to strain my mind's eye to imagine that, when it was completed in 1130, the main church was over four hundred feet long. Its width was such that it accommodated processional floats and thousands of faithful side-by-side, under a lofty cupola. Not only cardinals and popes but kings had paid their respects here.

Discipline and Draconian law were what made Cluny thrive. Admixed with greed and power-lust, they also brought down the abbey. Eschewing manual labor, hundreds of resident upper-echelon monks did little else than attend holy offices, seven per day, praying and meditating, shuffling paperwork, and imbibing their daily ration of a "single beaker of wine." A Clunysian beaker held one liter, we learned, meaning a modern 750 centiliter bottle's worth and another third of a bottle too. It was less than an amphora, but more than what doctors recommend, and the thought of wine at breakfast, lunch, and dinner made my liver ache. Not everyone lolled around getting drunk, however. Thousands of lesser lay brothers and peasants toiled to supply the monks' worldly wants.

Ahead, the compound's medieval mill tower and granary rose over the rooftops. They were spared the Revolutionary axe and wrecker's ball because experts had judged them to be useful civic buildings. The granary's upstairs hall held several remarkable vestiges of the abbey, including a set of 11th-century capitals salvaged from the nave and rearranged in a semicircle. Reportedly, they're the earliest surviving Romanesque sculptures in Burgundy, gracefully sculpted with garlands and curls and monsters. But it was the granary's ribbed wooden ceiling that gave me a neck ache. I couldn't help gazing up astonished, like Jonas in the belly of the whale, or, more precisely, as if we'd had a large wooden ship turned over on us. That was how such ceilings and roofs had originally been devised by Norman invaders: build walls and flip a boat over on them.

We joined other visitors atop the Tour des Fromages, one of the abbey's original watchtowers, to take in the view. Having studied the museum's scale map of medieval Cluny, I was pleased to see a familiar pattern in the streets. Russ Schleipmann's visual memorization technique took hold of me. "Look at the view, close your eyes, and try to reconstruct it," I heard him whispering into my mind's ear. I blinked. The nave appeared, its broken columns reminiscent of the Roman Forum, and there was the cobbled, winding street we'd hiked into town on yesterday, lined by gaily painted leaners—one antique house leaning on and propping up the next. And there were the dreamy-eyed kids and the crazed Irishman from Dublin via Taizé, and the silly-looking pilgrims in their black capes and three-cornered hats, two of them, a couple, with staffs and cockleshells and a leather canteen. I shook my head and opened my eyes.

"Did you see what I saw in my mind's eye?"

Alison joined me on the west side of the tower and peered down. "Is it Carnival?"

"Pilgrims!" exclaimed a fellow tourist as she leaned from the crenellated gap next to me. "Look! Real pilgrims!" The young woman rushed for the staircase. I couldn't help wincing, and feeling unregenerate.

"That's what awaits us on GR-65," Alison said, "once we make it to Le Puy-en-Velay."

"Pilgrims in silly outfits?" Oh, dear. The prospect of hiking five hundred miles with "spiritual" people in fancy dress filled me with dread. "We're not wearing pilgrims' gear," I said, "nor am I displaying my cockleshell from Utah Beach or other spiritual paraphernalia, so we don't look like pilgrims, we're not playing the pilgrim game, and no one will mistake us for pilgrims, no matter what we have in our hearts and souls." I paused long enough for Alison to take several dozen more digital pictures. "Was that quote you read me back in the chapel at Collonges written by Brother Roger of Taizé?"

She smiled, her cheeks pinking. "You may not have a lot in common with his followers," Alison said, "but don't throw out the monk with the holy water."

This was the second pun she'd made in less than a week, and it rattled me. The more I became like her, the more she became like me. That was not necessarily good news.

Loudspeakers mounted on the façades along Cluny's shopping streets played the kind of dentist-office music French provincials appear to enjoy. The window-shoppers and gentrifiers were out, spending to the beat. Where had the quiet meditation, the spirituality, disappeared to? Could anyone ascend the ladder of enlightenment in this now thoroughly materialistic town? I twitched uncomfortably at the thought of what might happen to Cluny once it celebrated the thousandth anniversary of the abbey's founding. The specter of Beaune appeared before my inner eye.

At an old-fashioned tobacco shop off the main drag, we bought several copies of an egregious postcard showing the cliffs of Solutré with an effigy of François Mitterrand floating in the sky above like the Holy Ghost. Apparently the former president not only imagined himself to be Vercingétorix reincarnate, he was also symbolic of the Trinity, and the primordial Frenchman, the hunter-gatherer of the Solutrian Phase of the Upper Paleolithic.

The time had come for us to leave Cluny. I wasn't confident I could make it much further: it was the revenge of the Gorges de la Canche where I'd wrecked both knees and back. But I said nothing to Alison, took an extra-strong dose of Ibuprofen, and gritted my teeth, realizing that we'd failed to find a dentist or a physiotherapist. No one was available in Cluny at the drop of a hat, not even a pilgrim's tricornered one. Perhaps a practitioner would turn up down the road, in a bigger city such as Mâcon.

A SKULL AND CROSSED BONES

Humpbacked and not intended for vehicular traffic, the medieval Pont de la Levée conveyed us out of Cluny and over the Grosne River, which was swollen by spring rain. The temperature had dropped again, even faster than the dollar. It was glove weather, but we had no gloves. I turned to say farewell to the abbey, catching lovely, reassuring glimpses of steeples and round-tiled roofs, the roofs of Rome in southern Burgundy.

The Abbot of Cluny was not one to mortify the flesh. In the heat of summer, he and his ecclesiastical court retreated from their stuffy, fortified compound in the Grosne Valley to an airy country house on hills at Berzé-la-Ville, which is where we were headed that morning. One of the Roman roads from Cluny to Mâcon, upgraded by monks, ran from Pont de la Levée to Berzé, branching to other historic, protohistoric, and prehistoric sites including Azé, Blanot, and Igé, renowned for their grottoes and châteaux. As we climbed out of the valley, we discovered that the ancient road was now little more than a rutted dirt farm track. It led into deep, dripping forests of mature firs, their tips tender and pale green. I'd looked at our maps closely, and knew that the Buddhist community at Sancé was just over the hill, but the road felt like a slice of the Morvan, and I expected to see a pile of Druid rocks at any moment.

Amid the trees, a muddy spot on the north side of the trail stopped our snail-like progress. It was marked not with one or two, but with dozens, perhaps hundreds, of improvised crosses. Twigs, feathers, branches, and straws were tied together with twine, shoelaces, twist-ties, yarn, or electrical wire. Each cross was different. Many had fallen over. Some stuck out of the mud, or dangled from branches. I checked our map again, and found the water-drop symbol and the words "Fontaine des Croix."

Fountainhead of the Crosses was apt indeed. The wind blew and rain fell. I put away the map, shivering. With the tip of my boot I cleared a patch of stinging nettles near the spring. Beneath them were more crosses, and the source of the spring. Water welled up. I used a fallen fir branch to push thick ferns aside. Hidden in a niche above the spring was a candle in the shape of the Virgin Mary. Something white, jagged, and hard lay nearby. "We may have found the relics of Mary Magdalene," I remarked, clearing away more nettles. A pile of bones and a broken skull emerged. "Satanic rites again?"

"It's probably the Grail of Saint Nazaire stolen from Autun," Alison said. "Remember Canon Grivot's story?"

"Or the bishop from Marseille, the one they thought was Nazaire." We stared at each other. "I know," I said, "it gives you the creeps. It gives *me* the creeps."

"What'll we do?"

"Take pictures, and show them to the authorities. Don't touch the bones." I backed off, thinking again of the stolen relics of Autun and Vézelay, and the murdered couple back in the village of Saint-Yan. "On second thought, let's get out of here before some Romanian cross-builders from Taizé show up, knives drawn. Or neo-Druids. Or whatever—militant Buddhists from Sancé."

"Just a second," Alison blurted, fiddling with her camera. "Buddhists don't revere bones and make crosses, and they're not dangerous."

"All fanatics are dangerous, especially those whose job it is to persecute fanatics."

"I've got to take some pictures before we leave. Put your boot by the skull for scale."

Wincing at the prospect, I shuffled back to the muddy nettle patch. Ten minutes later, Alison was still clicking away. My boots were wet, my hands numb. Rain ran down the back of my neck. "Do you think that might be enough? Doesn't the place give you the creeps?"

"Not when I'm photographing. Only before, and after."

We practically ran uphill, out of the forest, and, once over the ridge, stopped to gaze down at a medieval castle. No one had followed us, dead or alive. The high-rise housing developments of Mâcon were a distant backdrop to the east, the hogback silhouettes of Vergisson and Solutré, the most famous mountains of southern Burgundy, lay due south of us. As panoramas go, you couldn't get much better. Even the east-west expressway, the Route Centre Europe Atlantique N79, appeared elegant, a concrete span on 200-foot pylons, bridging the valley. A TGV raced alongside the expressway, glinting. The wind blew south toward Solutré. We heard nothing but the patter of rain on our ponchos.

Nearing the celebrated castle of Berzé-le-Chatel on a steep, narrow road, Alison began counting out loud. "Thirteen towers and turrets," she said, running out of fingers. "Wasn't this the place we read about, where they walled up a man and a bull? What an awful story. Why are men such beasts?"

"What was the story?" I asked, trying to recall. "The lord of Berzé-le-Chatel wagered a fellow nobleman that a peasant locked in a dungeon could outlive a bull locked in the same dungeon and both left to starve or die of thirst?"

"One on each floor," Alison said. I asked her if she remembered who'd won. "Neither. Can you imagine the agony, the suffering?"

As we got to within a hundred yards of the castle, I wondered which of the towers or turrets had been used to starve the peasant and bull. There were too many to choose from. I re-counted them as we passed. Alison was right: thirteen, and three rings of walls. Certainly, Berzé-le-Chatel wasn't the Disney type of fairytale castle, but rather a gloomy, forbidding fortress at least a thousand years old, astride the Roman road. It still belonged to a single family. Were they descended from the sadistic lord?

Around the château spread steep vineyards. Reportedly they were the fountainhead of the Mâcon area's Chardonnay grape variety, and they'd been planted here long before loved-to-death Chardonnay took over California, Australia, New Zealand, and the rest of the winegrowing planet, giving rise to the reverse snobbery of ABC: *Anything But Chardonnay.* That was nonsense. The finest white wines of Burgundy and Champagne were made with Chardonnay. "We are a strange species," I couldn't help remarking. "We unwittingly send the French phylloxera, and then 150 years later turn their Chardonnay into soda pop wine."

For the last two hundred years, the Abbot of Cluny's former residence at the next village, Berzé-la-Ville, has been in private hands. Tall stone walls keep the curious out. Abutting the mansion, the so-called "Monk's Chapel" is also privately owned, but open to paying visitors. It's decorated with landmark Romanesque frescoes from the 11th century, painted about the time the peasant and bull were starving to death up the road at the château. I bought us tickets, slid out from under my pack, and found a seat in the pews. It felt like we were back in Beaune. The fresco-painter's flair for halos, expressive hands, and meaningful, mournful glances was moving, and the art-historical value of the site inestimable. But the clinical quality of the experience, the amalgamation of religion and commerce, overwhelmed the deeper feelings the frescoes were intended to inspire.

We hiked out feeling we'd been cheated, and walked thoughtfully downhill into the Val Lamartinien. Apparently it wasn't just the Abbot of Cluny who favored the area, to escape monkish intrigue and cultivate spirituality. Evidently this was also home to the famous Romantic poet, politician, and serial philanderer Alphonse Marie Louis Prat de Lamartine, still a local hero almost a century and a half after penning his last lines. Lamartine is required reading for French high schoolers. He wrote the kind of florid verse punctuated with *Oh!* and *Alas!*, and though his following has diminished, he certainly had a good run of it.

At the bottom of the Val Lamartinien, we crossed the *Voie Verte* and spotted a cryptic, hand-painted sign in someone's front yard. *Lamartine did* NOT *sleep here*, it said, presumably because he slept everywhere else—with the consorts of many, many other men. Sleep was what we both needed, not to mention a meal, and while we were at it, I could use a new body too. I wasn't going to make it any farther today, and, with a feeling of regret and foreboding, I said so to Alison.

Luckily, minutes later we arrived at our hotel, le Relais du Mâconnais, an old-style roadhouse next to the *Voie Verte* on what used to be the main highway—until the N79 Expressway replaced it, running along the south side of the valley. Gone were the trucks and cars and trains of old. A creek curled lazily through the hotel's backyard. We barely had time to listen to its sing-song chant. I opened our windows, stretched out, and snored so loudly that the neighbors knocked on our door to complain.

IT'S A LONG WAY TO SOLUTRÉ

Dawn broke resplendent the following morning. As we hiked toward the expressway in tenuous, pinkish light, I shook my head in admiration and disbelief, remembering our dinner. The hotel may have been old-country simplicity itself, but our meal at le Relais du Mâconnais had been sumptuous and eclectic, served in designer surroundings seemingly imported whole from Sydney or San Francisco. It confirmed long-held suspicions that the French really are the heirs of Imperial Rome and the Baroque. With soothing music lifting our forks, and a hostess in an elegant tailleur serving us, we'd worked our way through half a dozen bite-sized courses, our legs twitching under the table from exhaustion, our wrinkled clothes impossibly inappropriate to the swank setting. First came tuna and eggplant "carpaccio," followed by a snail lightly battered and fried tempura-style, surrounded by dabs of spring turnip purée. As if they'd known we were heading to Spain, they'd trotted out a Pyrenees lamb with stuffed, fried artichokes, and finished us off with suckling pig and mushrooms—Japanese mushrooms, braised and served in a tall crystal glass.

"You must try the local chèvre," said the smiling proprietor, Monsieur Lannuel, a stout, pale-skinned man who said he was of Norman extraction. But as it transpired, more than mere goat's-milk cheese awaited on the platter. Before we could rise and climb back to our room, out came a savory-sweet "pre-dessert" conjured from salted butter and chocolate cream, forced into a cigar-shaped cookie and poised atop a dollop of chocolate mousse. Unbidden, the strawberry *millefeuille* floated across the dining room toward us, as ethereal as the warbling pseudo-Celtic music on the sound system.

"We'll burn off that chocolate mousse in no time," I said now, guiltily, as we reached the expressway on the south side of the valley and walked through an underpass.

But Alison patently wasn't worried about maintaining or losing weight, nor was she listening to me. She could eat a whole spit-roasted mammoth and an iceberg of chocolate and not gain an ounce. "Just a second," she commanded, in the familiar, authoritative tone she used when working. She stopped halfway into the underpass to take a photo of graffiti sprayed on the walls.

"Génération Mitterrand 45 millions de nouveaux pauvres."

The "Mitterrand Generation" had been the former president's last campaign slogan, way back in what, 1988? Forty-five million "new poor?" I puzzled over the cryptic graffiti. Did it suggest that François Mitterrand had bankrupted the country? What really interested me wasn't the message itself, but the fact that more than a decade after his death, and two decades after the slogan had been invented, Frenchmen were still talking about François Mitterrand. You couldn't escape him, any more than you could escape his arch rival Charles de Gaulle.

Sologny was the name of the handsome village part way up the south side of Val Lamartinien. From the Romanesque church, dedicated to Saint Vincent, protector of winemakers, the view of the vineyards, expressway, and TGV line was remarkable. The traffic and trains of old were no longer in the bottom of the valley on the east side. It was the south's turn to live with blight and noise for a century or two.

Over the next ridge, we entered the land of fossils—1970s cars driven by octogenarians, antique American tractors rusting in millennial vineyards, and houses built of fossil rock, the kind of rock I'd seen and tripped over a few days earlier near Buxy. "Saint James would love it here," I remarked, laying my hand on a giant scallop shell encased in a fossil-rock threshold. The contrast with the tract homes nearby could not have been more complete.

We pulled into Pierreclos in time to resupply and have coffee in what might have been the smokiest café in France. Luckily the sun was out, the temperature back to summertime levels, and we sipped our espressos outdoors. The café was called Auberge du Poète, which seemed a good name, since Pierreclos was Alphonse Marie Louis Prat de Lamartine's second home.

On the way up to Pierreclos château, an address Lamartine knew well, we passed a variety store. There was François Mitterrand again. He stared out at us from a rack of postcards, his head floating above the Roche de Solutré. "Popular image, that," I said. "Do you have a feeling François Maurice Adrien Marie Mitterrand has been following us?"

"Like Caesar and Vercingétorix?"

"Exactly. And Buddha. Funny, you haven't mentioned Saint James."

Before reaching the château we stopped for a snack on a panoramic bench near an alley of mossy, carefully clipped linden trees. I paused before sinking my teeth into a pear, removing the sticker that said "Chile." The baker had told us that the crust of the quiche we'd bought was made with Canadian flour, and that the bacon inside was from Hungary. The mineral water was Italian, the chocolate Swiss. I thought of the vaguely Japanese-Australian meal we'd enjoyed at the neo-Druidic-Buddhist Relais du Mâconnais, and wondered just how notional was the Frenchness of French food and "French identity."

Rising high over the end of the linden-tree–lined alley was a hulking medieval castle with a colorful patterned roof of glazed tiles and an impressive array of turrets and towers. Trying not to slip back into my old habit of feeling jaded and world-weary, I forced myself to admire the château and pronounce it exceptionally attractive. It was not "run down," but rather atmospherically down at the heel. The gates stood open, so we wandered into a rock-paved courtyard. Clearly, Pierreclos was now a winery. Potential customers were welcome to visit the premises and taste the wines, provided they took a tour. A sign encouraged us to ring a large bell mounted high on a wall in the courtyard. This required a vigorous yank of an iron handle attached to a long, hand-forged iron chain. I pulled once, twice, three times but the bell would not ring. So I yanked a fourth time, throwing my body and soul into it. As the bell clanged, my back screamed in pain. I stood frozen, my arm raised, unable to move. "Now I've done it," I whispered in terror, knowing that I'd revived the damage I'd done when I fell weeks earlier in the Gorges de la Canche. "Please come over and do something about my back or I'll look like the Statue of Liberty forever."

As I stood in the courtyard, clearly paralyzed and in pain, a young woman's head popped out of a window far above. The head peered down at us, and, understandably, expressed surprise at seeing two raggedy backpackers wrestling, trying to unlock my lower vertebrae. "Coming," she barked. She reappeared and stood at the threshold to the kitchen, watching us with undisguised bafflement.

"That's quite a bell-pull," I said, as the woman beckoned us indoors. She tore two tickets off a stack and raised her index finger, untroubled by my irony.

"Start out there, in the garden, come back in, go down there, go straight, left, back to the staircase, up to the second floor and into the room on the left and then into the one on the right." She paused long enough to draw breath. "Enjoy your visit. If you'd like to see the medieval vaulted cellar and taste the wine, shout when you're ready." Her smile was wooden. It made me think of Saint Joan of Arc and the sculptures we'd seen of other fierce French women with hard features. We backed out of the room carefully.

"Care" was the operative word. Alison ran her eyes over me. "You've really done in your back."

"Nonsense," I protested, crabbing across the garden to the ruined chapel, then admiring the apse and tower—they always seemed to survive. Ever since the village of Ougy near Cormatin I understood why: wealth had built them. There was no nave left. The peasants had done a rush-job. Alison caught up with me and frowned.

"Can you walk the rest of the way to our B&B?" she asked.

"Oh, sure," I said. "No worries." The B&B was in a village called La Grange du Bois, still about three or four miles away, at the top of a ridge. "Let's just finish visiting the château, and maybe my back will sort itself out."

In my fulsome imagination, the castle of Pierreclos seemed of the type inhabited by Bela Lugosi and Lon Chaney, cast as Dracula and The Mummy. Our footfalls echoed. Bats and birds took to wing. "Remind you of anything?" I asked. "The peeling wallpaper and dust?"

"Rully wasn't nearly this sinister," Alison remarked.

The kitchen of the château seemed to be the size of several tract homes. The fireplace looked big enough to park an SUV in, and was equipped with what may be the world's largest and most complicated mechanical rotisserie, a contraption of strange beauty made of cast iron, with cables and weights and clockwork gears in varying sizes. "No doubt devised for spit-roasting a whole Charolais beef," I observed.

"For a whole wild boar," said Alison, pointing at a dead one on the kitchen table. We both gasped, recoiling. Then Alison giggled, which proved contagious.

Laughter is supposed to be spiritually nourishing, but it made my back ache. "I'd like to know who the taxidermist was," I managed to say, propelling myself forward as if handcuffed from behind in an attempt to straighten up my back.

Alison studied the photocopied page which the humorless caretaker had hurriedly handed us with our tickets. Of all the properties in and near Val Lamartinien, Alison said, giving me an edited version, Pierreclos was the favorite of Alphonse such-and-such de Lamartine. A dust-blackened plaster bust of him greeted us in an otherwise empty salon. As we shuffled by, I realized that Lamartine's effigy had been made to look not like Vercingétorix but Caesar. He was wearing Imperial Roman clothes, and was modeled on a bust from the Capitoline Museum in Rome. I couldn't help wondering for the first time in my life what had become of the head of Caesar I'd made years ago, in Miss Nelson's dreaded Latin class. At least I wasn't having that recurrent dream anymore, a sign, perhaps, that I'd gotten Caesar out of my system?

Pierreclos was Lamartine's favorite castle, we learned, though he had his own château, which still stands, over the hill to the east, near the expressway we'd passed. He also owned yet another château to the west, near the lake of Saint-Point. But we had reason to wonder how much time he'd spent in any single residence.

Alison said she'd go ahead and see if it was worth it for me to climb upstairs. She blazed a trail through the dust, up a wide spiraling staircase, which had been conceived for horses. I followed, slowly, and caught up with her in the poet's study on the second floor. Through a hole in one of the walls, a pair of birds hopped back and forth, then flew around the room, panicked to see us. We batted at the dust motes the birds stirred up, and I gasped again, this time at a grinning, lifesized waxwork of Lamartine sitting behind a desk. He was wearing mid-19th-century clothing, the kind seen in costume dramas. A black bow tie wound around his neck, and a long housecoat hung low. Its color had faded to Confederate gray. Lamartine held a quill pen between his wax fingers and seemed pleased with himself.

Perhaps I would be too, I reflected, had I managed to thrill the French nation with the kind of verse he'd quilled. But I suspected there were other, saltier reasons for his grin. Lamartine had conquered the hearts of innumerable demoiselles and ladies, which might also explain his longevity as a poet. Among his lovers was the wife of Pierreclos's impotent lord. With madame, the poet produced an heir, which may have been the object of the gallant exercise. The lady of Pierreclos, previously thought to be barren, was pleased, because it proved her fecundity, and the cuckolded lord acquiesced, because he now had a son. Lamartine had done his duty again, in the best Romantic style. Nowadays the unhappy couple would have visited a sperm bank, picked out a genetic profile, and deprived generations of a fine, salacious story that had the great merit of a happy ending.

SUNSET OF THE IDOLS AT SOLUTRÉ

How we managed to climb the steep, switchback roads and trails from Pierreclos to the ridge and then hike south to La Grange du Bois, past ancient chestnut trees and prehistoric rock piles, is a Druidic mystery. Perhaps it was the beneficial effect of the imported Chilean pear I'd eaten for lunch, the second dose of Ibuprofen I took before leaving the castle, or the inner chant *I think I know I can I think I know I can*. Somehow, driven by mis-remembered metaphors from childhood and primordial urges, we pushed and dragged ourselves to the gate of the B&B, talked our way past the horse-sized guard dog, and sank into a pair of plastic chairs for a long, thoughtful meditation upon our contingency plans.

Due east and far below us rose the Roche de Solutré. From this angle its cliff face looked vaguely like the prow of a steam-ship ploughing into waves of russet, white, and green. The soil was russet in places, white in others, and the unfurling leaves of the grapevines footing the rock were a fresh, almost acid green. Overhead, a hang-glider circled the cliff, swooshing silently on alternating layers of hot and cold air. Mesmerized, we watched it go around and around as our hostess, Karin, plied us with nuts and thimble-sized goat's cheeses, and poured glasses of cold water and beer. "Veni, vidi, vici," I said, feeling at once victorious and on the verge of defeat. The Saint Bernard gnawed on a bone and watched us with drooping eyes. "What's his name," I asked, "Caesar or Vercingétorix?"

"He looks fierce," Alison joked.

"He is," said Karin. "That's what's left of last night's guests. Yukka didn't like them." Karin laughed from the heart, a sincere, unself-conscious laughter that exposed her gums and small, white teeth. "What part of the country am I from?" she asked in response to the question I'd slipped in. "You mean, which country? I'm Swedish, you know."

No, I didn't know. Her French was perfect, and maddeningly unaccented. But genetics explained her physique and Nordic coloration, and perhaps her cheerful temperament too. We'd met many a chummy Dutchman on our walk across Burgundy, and a handful of English, but Karin was the only Swede. How a recently retired former IKEA manager had wound up here I couldn't imagine. "Widowhood and reinvention," she remarked. "I started all over again."

"So it wasn't because of Mary Magdalene, or the Druids, or François Mitterrand, or Brother Roger, or the primordial Buddha, or Caesar and Matisco?"

Karin shook her head and laughed. "I'm afraid not."

Her partner, a blue-eyed, gray-haired man named Guy, turned out to be the maker of the goat's-milk cheeses we were snacking on. We'd glimpsed him earlier. He was of local stock, Karin said. Guy's family had owned the farmstead across from the B&B for the last two hundred years.

There was something about this place, I couldn't help feeling, trying to avoid the word "magical" that seemed shopworn and not quite right. Something about the isolation of the hamlet atop a ridge inhabited since antiquity, and the view. Across the two-lane country road, the steeple of a Romanesque church poked into the air, a church no longer consecrated, said Karin. Near it flowed a spring, a sacred spring, she added, used since time immemorial. Around here, that meant a very long time. Guy lived in front of the church, a few hundred yards from the spring. The water welled up in the pasture where the grass was a brighter shade of green, like the buds of the grapevines below. The goats and cattle ate the grass nourished by the spring. The cheeses were made from the milk of the she-goats that nibbled the grass and drank the water. I had to wonder, was that why the cheese was so good? Was this the proverbial pasture where the grass grows greener? Maybe there was no need to seek elsewhere, and we'd come to the end of our pilgrimage?

South of the Roche de Solutré, in the Sâone River Valley, trucks beetled by on the *autoroute*. A TGV train flashed along its inclined track. Low-income housing projects, occupied primarily by immigrants from North Africa, hedged Caesar's Matisco—modern-day Mâcon. The real world was down there, far enough away to be unthreatening, but I knew it awaited us.

As the cliffs of Solutré turned from yellow to orange and the sky colored itself indigo, I had the same kind of inkling I'd had in Bibracte of what "spirit of place" might mean. La Grange du Bois radiated sympathetic magic, the friendly, life-giving magic of quiet, green, uncontaminated places. It seemed to me that spirit of place wasn't the same thing at all as spirituality, which suggested an ability to transcend earthly realities and ascend into a presumptive world of the spirit. Spirit of place had nothing to do with crucifixes, the effigy of a guru or a revered monk, or the words and gestures of a neo-Druid. My body was tired, and I knew deep down that I had to stop walking, but my spirits were as lively and receptive as they'd ever been. It struck me as ironic that now, on the threshold of some kind of revelation—I wasn't sure what kind—I would not be able to walk much further. The body would fail, not the spirit.

"Would you like to visit the farm?" Karin asked. Alison agreed before I could say that I was too tired, my back and knees were shot, my mind full of disquieting thoughts.

I leaned on Alison's arm and crossed the road. Like Karin, Guy's cheerfulness was contagious. "Two hundred years?" he snorted, goats bleating and goat-bells tinkling around us. "That's when my family moved into the farm. But we've been in the area much longer than that." Used to this refrain by now, I asked if he thought he might be descended from the ancient Gauls. Like Astérix, Dumnorix-Dean, and others we'd met, the diminutive Guy swelled with pride and in stature. But he added that he felt no animosity toward Caesar. Guy professed himself an unabashed lover of Graeco-Roman culture, like his ancestors. What he meant was the cultivation of grapevines. He filled and quickly refilled glasses with a local white wine, and swore that he wasn't a neo-Druid. "I know a few," he admitted. "They're more interested in what you'd probably call animism or nature-worship than human sacrifice, and they also like wine, and speak French."

"I know the type," I said, thinking of Mendocino County, California.

Back at the B&B, I propped myself at a table and examined the wrinkled contents of a sweaty envelope. "You have a postcard view," I said, flourishing the card I'd picked up in Cluny, the one with François Mitterrand's head floating above the Roche de Solutré. "Have you ever seen this?"

Karin said yes, she'd seen the postcard many times. "Mitterrand came here often," she said, handing Alison the bowl of tiny goat's cheeses. "He may even have lived in your room for a time."

Alison glanced at me. I looked at her and felt my backbone tingle. "We're supposed to be walking on the Way of Saint James and feeling spiritual," she said, "and we keep running into Caesar's ghost and François Mitterrand. Did Mitterrand stay here when he hiked up the Roche de Solutré each year for that phony photo-op pilgrimage?"

I recalled the images, broadcast each year on French TV and published in the papers, of Mitterrand looking presidential, the great Résistance hero, the heir of Vercingétorix, marching to the cliff and gazing meaningfully out across France.

Karin laughed. "This place isn't fancy enough for that. He came here during the war. The owners were his . . . friends. How to put it? The owner himself was his friend. Susanne, the wife of the owner, was his mistress." She paused. "Mitterrand was an admirer of Lamartine. People used to follow in the footsteps of the poet. Now they come to see where President Mitterrand slept." She added that she'd been told by parties involved, parties now deceased, that Mitterrand hid out here, in our room, in 1943, after escaping several times from Nazi POW camps. How he went from POW to Vichy bureaucrat and back to POW again, and how he finally escaped, if he did escape, as opposed to being sent out as a spy or double agent, was unclear. "The French Résistance was supposedly born here," she said, "in this building, possibly in your bedroom."

"An eleventh-hour birth," commented Guy wryly.

So, I reflected, patting the Saint Bernard on his head, Mitterrand and his PR flaks were thinking not only of primeval Solutrean man when they organized the yearly pilgrimage up the outcrop; they were also beating the drum of the Résistance, the great foundation myth of postwar France.

RETREAT OR DEFEAT?

It wasn't a question of our feet. With twenty toes between us, we hadn't grown a single blister in something like two hundred miles. Caesar had risked defeat at Gergovia and beaten a tactical retreat. Critognatus the wily Gaul, more realistic than heroic Vercingétorix, had tried to convince his besieged brethren at Alésia to do as their ancestors had and "keep themselves alive by eating the flesh of those who were too old or too young to fight." Napoléon had retreated after claiming Moscow before a superior enemy: winter's deadly cold. Mitterrand had collaborated with the Occupier until the time was ripe to join the Résistance and fight back. Or so he'd claimed. Live to fight another day—that was the message. Live to fight, learn to compromise, or wind up dead and possibly crucified.

The answer to the question in my case was less dramatic. It came to me at dawn as I carried my pack down the ladder-like staircase of the B&B. Clearly, the Gorges de la Canche and Pierreclos were taking their revenge. The damage to my knees and back wrought by my fall in the gorge had rung my number at Pierreclos, when I pulled the bell-pull, reviving structural weaknesses that had dogged me since adolescence. It felt like someone was slipping a greased lightning rod down my back. How would I break the news to Alison? Solutré was the end of the line for me.

We said farewell to Guy, Yukka, and the Swede, and as I hobbled down the steep trail, my eyes automatically searching for bones and arrowheads, I wondered if François Mitterrand had enjoyed the view as much as I had. From our bedroom window we'd watched the cool pink sunrise behind the outcrop, and felt the dawn wind rising, stirring the goats and roosters and cattle below, moments more magical even than the twilight of the night before.

Gravel and rocks, polished by fifteen thousand years of scuffing feet, now slipped under my boots. I picked my way down on the ancient path, my mind drugged from pain and lack of sleep. How could I sleep in that room, looking from the same window that Mitterrand had looked through, watching the Nazis trundle up and down the valley, past Matisco, where Caesar's armies had camped, where the amphorae of wine had entered Gaul on Roman ships? How could anyone sleep with just one night to look upon the black silhouette of the Roche de Solutré, the lair of migratory hunters, the mysterious stalkers of wild horses those many millennia ago? Where had they come from? Where did they go? Did they worship the Earth Mother and keep the eternal flame burning, camped among dolmens and menhirs? My ignorance of history and religion was vast. I could spend my next lifetime exploring layer after layer. If only I could believe in a second or third lifetime, or a reincarnation.

Following behind Alison, I limped through the prehistory museum at the foot of Solutré, unsure whether I was dreaming or really seeing laurel-leaf spearheads and arrowheads fashioned from flint, and ingenious weaponry made of stone, bone, or antler. The hunters of Solutré hadn't herded their prey off the top of the cliff, from the spot where Mitterrand always had his picture taken. The truth, we learned, was less exciting. The hunters had simply lain in wait at the bottom of the rock, surprising horses and elks that trotted by. The paleolithic wanderers never set down roots here, or so our current state of ignorance suggests. They'd been forever on the move, following the herds, in tune with the four seasons. Climate change had slowly altered their habitat, until the herds had disappeared, and the men of Solutré could no longer eke out an existence. If that wasn't a lesson to be learned, quickly, then what was learning for?

Alison waved her arms and looked down at me from the top of the cliff, egging me on. A Mirage fighter jet darted over her head, its engines spewing flames. On his pilgrimages, Mitterrand and his entourage had used helicopters, walking only the last hundred yards or so, preceded by journalists and camera operators. Alison had walked all the way to the top, all the way from Vézelay, in fact, but I would not be able to join her.

By the time I stopped climbing, I'd hauled myself almost halfway up the hogback. There my legs refused to obey me. I thought of Donkey Hotey and the windmills of my mind, but could not summon laughter. Judging from my own unscientific, non-representative sample of life experiences, two things seemed clear. First, I could go no further and would probably have to be removed by helicopter. Second, reason was in control of only one small part of my brain. Reason was one of the many gods clamoring within. Related to that revelation, it struck me that the great migrations of man were more complex than I'd imagined. Whether stone-age, proto-historic, Graeco-Roman, medieval, or contemporary, treks and pilgrimages such as our own were not just about survival, greener grass, or fatter elks with thicker hides for teepees. Likewise, my own motivations, the urges that had driven me to attempt crossing France, were more complex than I'd realized.

As I tried to communicate with Alison using hand signals, an ancient Latin motto floated to mind. *Navigare necessit. It is necessary to navigate.* What that poor literal translation really meant was, man must sail, humans must explore, travel, move on, and on. Mystery, adventure, a quest for understanding—each was fundamental to the human condition, the unknown equation. I began to inch back down the cliff, shocked by the lightning rod of my spine. The sails of a Quixotic windmill—a windmill I'd been tilting at metaphorically all my adult life—turned now before my eyes. I blinked and thought hard, because I would soon be gone from here, and the revelations were coming fast. The rituals of prehistoric man and the church alike, the magic of the Druids and of every religion in every country in the world, were there to egg questers onward, to keep our fears of death under control as we moved forward, to propitiate the fertility of the soil or of men and women, at least in our minds. They were there to ward off evil spirits, get men to toe the line of civilization and respect order and law. Rituals, magic, and religion were part of the big equation. But what was the equation? I still didn't know and, having whetted my appetite for knowledge, I felt the irrepressible need to know, with greater urgency than ever.

I looked down at the hamlets scattered between Solutré and Mâcon, and wiped the sweat out of my eyes. There were no menhirs or dolmens in view—nor were there Quixotic windmills, for that matter—but I did see several crosses, half a dozen steeples, and one Virgin in the vineyards. Had these lichen-frosted symbols of Christianity lost their power, I wondered, like the buried fertility goddesses of earlier times? If so, what did we have to replace them? Ideology was dead. Even the cult of the republic and the belief in democracy were dead or dying.

"I can't make it," I shouted up to Alison. The pain in my back was now unbearable.

What did we have to replace the old religions and ideologies? Simple: we had science. Science, technology, and medicine. The new Trinity. Science would unlock the secrets of the universe, and technology would fix the things we'd wrecked, from the environment to the economy. Medicine would slim our waist-lines, fill barren wombs, enlarge our breasts, and provide penile enhancement to the under-endowed, restore fertility more efficiently than an idol or a Madonna, stave off death better than a fountain of youth, and take us to other planets where we could start over again.

I watched a pair of hang-gliders pass above. A TGV train flashed by below in the valley. Another one pulled into Mâcon-Loché station. It was only five miles from the cliffs of Solutré, and I had to find a way to get there, and from there to a doctor. Science, technology, and medicine were the new Trinity, all right. But they were too cold for some, too distant or expensive for others, and they'd often let us down, as trinities in the past had done before them. Unable to move forward confidently with them, we were turning back to the fertility goddesses and Druids, the crosses and Virgins, the moorslayer Saint James or the prophets of jihad. My encounter with the two Philippes, the first one in Pierre Perthuis, the second in Marigny, came back to me now, to the tune of *What's it all about, Alfie?* Would science explain the chemicals bubbling in the primal sea, the big bangs and black holes? Would we figure out one day how something came from nothing, and if it did, could we find the words to define nothing? While we were waiting, how long could it possibly take for a helicopter to arrive with a stretcher, and get me out of here? As if in a dream, I felt myself sliding back down the steep, dusty path I'd climbed. How would I ever reach the mighty Pyrenees? My mind soared like the hang-gliders above. I closed my eyes and, though I failed to understand why, felt no pain.

BACKWARD AND FORWARD

We had a fine view of the cliffs of Solutré from a second-class car on the TGV, sitting backward as we rode home to Paris the next morning. A pair of crutches leaned on my seat. I gritted my teeth. It was a strategic retreat. Unlike Vercingétorix, I would fight to walk another day. We had the rest of France to cross. *I know I think I can I think I know I can* played in my head. But the smooth, silent locomotive of the TGV made no such comforting sound.

Within minutes, the sleek blue-and-gray bullet train reached 200 mph, shuddering as it spun together the Val Lamartinien, Cluny, Cormatin, and a hundred other places we'd walked through over the past month. I thought of Nietzsche's eternal return, and Alphonse Karr's quip about changelessness, of twin-faced Janus, the quintessence of France. I felt great kinship toward Janus. For thousands of years he had been advancing backward into the future, and forward into the past. Right now, for me, backward was the only way forward.

EPILOGUE

⬦

THE LONG AND WINDING ROAD

BASKING IN UNIQUENESS

The Pyrenees Mountain hamlet of Huntto at 1,700 feet above sea level is aptly named. Hunters' blinds surround it. Hunting had been a leitmotif for the last month. It was the main reason we were now equipped with tuneful brass bells dangling from our packs. During our zigzag approach to Huntto, several dozen acolytes of Elmer Fudd had roared up and down the winding panoramic roads in four-wheel drive vehicles bristling with gun barrels. Not a one of the dark-eyed, beetling Basque occupants had waved at or spoken to us, not even the pair who grazed us with their side-view mirror. Could they have guessed we preferred our wildlife alive?

We checked in for the night at Ferme Ithuburia, a pilgrims' hostel perched a third of the way up the mountainside. This was our last stop in France—or so we expected. Actually we'd already left France when we entered Basque Country a week earlier on October 10, four months after our train ride back to Paris from Mâcon way back in May. We'd restarted our trek in the town of Le Puy-en-Velay and had been hiking again for nearly two months. Now we were on the homestretch of our little saunter: another twenty miles or so and we'd made it.

By now, we had realized the exactitude of certain clichés. The Frenchmen we'd met on our way to the Pyrenees were right: the Basques *are* different. Everything about them is different, from the pizza-sized berets they wear and the wild *Pottök* ponies they eat to their region's topography, art, architecture, spicy cooking, and especially their language.

Village names had gone from being merely difficult in the Béarnaise Region to becoming unpronounceable in Basque Country. Bouhaben, a hamlet, led to Aroue-Ithorots-Olhaïby. The scenery also morphed: wonderful became actively sublime as we crept south from the hot, dry, delicious southwest of France, crossed the pleasing Béarn and reached the land of mountains, myth, and magic. Dreamy broadleaf forests waved rainbow leaves as fall advanced before our kaleidoscope eyes. Sheep ranged in meadows too green to be real. Here was the emerald we travel writers are forever searching to find. Outsized whitewashed, half-timbered houses with red shutters stood shoulder to shoulder in sturdy, neat-freak villages where nary a crumb of gravel was out of place.

Nearing the town of Aroue we'd caught first sight of the Pyrenees, a formidable barrier between us and Roncesvalles Abbey, our goal in Spain. We'd devoured Caesar's *Conquest of Gaul* in Burgundy in the spring; *The Song of Roland* had been our bedtime reading for the last few weeks. By now we knew a thing or three about these man-eating mountains. True, Hannibal had made it over them. But defended by Basque insurgents, the 5,000-foot-high Col de Bentarte—the pass we needed to traverse—had defeated Charlemagne's rearguard in 778 AD. It has claimed many an army and pilgrim since. I'd gulped at this realization, and wondered more than once if we would make it over. The saw-tooth peaks ahead were the real deal, nothing like anything we'd scaled in the past 750 miles since we started walking in Vézelay.

Sparsely populated and windswept, the Pyrenees notionally separate France from Spain. Basque County straddles the mountain chain, enjoying enough political autonomy on both sides to keep most Basques from advocating separatism—or being actively unpleasant to outsiders. The Basque language is not Indo-European and resembles neither Spanish nor French—nor anything else, including ancient Gallic. Happily, the Gauls didn't take this route or take root here: the last we'd seen of Vercingétorix was a portrait of his surrender to Caesar hanging in a museum in the Auvergne Region. There was no blessed Gallic or French heritage to tussle over. Hardy Basque locals staked their claims before newcomer Romans showed up speaking Latin—and failed to subdue the wily natives, who may have arrived about the time the prehistoric caves were painted. Luckily, most Basques we met weren't overly fierce and most also spoke several tongues, some-times simultaneously.

One of the owners of the pilgrim's hostel shuffled up to us and identified himself in three languages as Frère Ourtiague, a retired priest. Ruddy-faced and unsteady on his pins, he seemed pleased to be able to stamp our pilgrims' passports, documents issued to us by the Catholic Church, which by now were covered page after page with scores of colorful seals, stamps, signatures, and a variety of other marks evoking the locales where we'd lodged since starting our journey again in Le Puy-en-Velay in late August. Yes, we had resigned ourselves to carrying the passports on this second leg of our journey: we needed them to gain access to pil-grims' hostels along the way. I was also feeling less antagonistic about the church, having profited from the shelter of several hundred sanctuaries as we walked. If for no other reason, the institution needed to survive simply to maintain the architectural heritage of the centuries. And if people of faith also found comfort under the Catholic umbrella, so be it. As long as they respected the religions or lack of religion of others, and didn't brainwash their children, that was fine by me.

Brother Ourtiague's cough brought me back to reality. He glanced at the calendar, licked his plump index finger, and paused before finishing the job of stamping our passports. His pink cheeks paled.

"Today is October 17 . . . the 18th is Saint Luke's Day. *Jour de Saint Luc, jour du Grand Truc!*" he exclaimed cryptically. "You're planning to cross the Col de Bentarte into Spain tomorrow?"

We nodded, cheerful if somewhat tired: we'd covered nearly twenty roller-coaster miles starting at dawn, climbing the picture-postcard foothills in frisky, high winds, then tackling the first slippery slopes of the Pyrenees.

"Snow is expected the day after tomorrow," I remarked, feeling the wind-burn on my own unusually lean, unusually pink cheeks. "The pass might be closed. So either we climb through the wind-storm tomorrow or we don't get to Spain until spring, unless you have skis to loan us."

The priest did not laugh. Huntto and the hostel looked pretty swell, I added. But the attractions might be somewhat limited. Six months of waiting up here wasn't on the cards, despite our new and improved relationship with time.

Brother Ourtiague's eyes rolled heavenward, a sincere, unscripted expression of concern. "The Lord Protect you," he uttered.

"Thank you," Alison said.

"What kind of festival is Saint Luke's Day?" I asked.

Brother Ourtiague shook his jowly head at my ignorance. "Saint Luke's is not a festival; it's the biggest pigeon-hunting day in Basque Country. *Le jour du grand truc*. That's what it means: the big deal with shotguns." He raised his arm and pulled a pretend trigger. "Hundreds of hunters will be out there. They do not like it when pilgrims appear."

MEMORY LANE

On the way to our see-forever bunk on an upstairs floor, I borrowed a pair of camouflage hunting binoculars from a coat rack in the dining area. We might very well be eating our last supper here tonight, I reflected, suddenly nostalgic for life and sorry to have dragged my wife into peril among the migratory pigeons. The woeful feeling didn't last. The tranquility I'd discovered in recent weeks stifled it and calmed any panic. Gazing from the windows of Ferme Ithuburia was something I could get used to, I thought, putting aside images of the trigger-happy Basques preparing the battlefield outside. On a clear afternoon like this, the views swept north into France for tens, perhaps hundreds, of miles. If only I had access to Google. I'd be able to find out just how far the eye can see at 1,700 feet above sea level with no impediments.

Perhaps, after all, god was an algorithm. Google would come up with the equation that not only demystified life on Earth, but also unraveled the secrets of the universe, black holes, and the heretofore unanswerable. That probably would not put out of business a skillful pope and other adaptable spiritual leaders: the algorithm came from somewhere. I sighed with pleasure. The most important and enjoyable revelation of all I'd had so far was: pilgrimages weren't really about finding an answer. More vitally, they were about asking questions—an infinity of questions. Paradoxically, the quest itself was both the question and the answer. And it had to continue, it would continue, but only after a nap.

Showered and rested, I awoke to find Alison studying the landscape through the binoculars. Her pilgrim's passport and a map were spread open nearby. "I need reading glasses," she said. "I can't see close up anymore."

"I'm useful at last," I chortled. As long as something is squarely before my good eye, at a range of a foot or less, I can focus on it better than Alison. "Can you see back to Le Puy-en-Velay?"

"Why not ask me to look for the Eiffel Tower?"

"Good idea. Raise your aim," I encouraged her. "Look just below the cloud line. We're up pretty high here. Maybe you can see the cathedral of Le Puy where they issued us these passports?"

Alison sighed and ranged widely with the binoculars while I focused on the *Crédenciel*—the origin of our word "credentials," I suddenly realized, a word itself derived from credo. I had to admit that "credo" had not been part of the pilgrimage algorithm, not for me, anyway. In three months of trekking, we'd had plenty of micro-epiphanies about ourselves and the world, past, present, and potential. But no great revelation had driven us into the arms of the Mother Church, or united us invisibly to the often garrulous, self-styled spiritual seekers we'd usually wound up trying to avoid on the trail. Utterly unlike our solitary trek across Burgundy, we'd seen thousands of other pilgrims since Le Puy-en-Velay, and all they seemed to want to do was yak, gab, chat, eat, drink, sleep, compare blisters, race each other, and plan their next vacation.

After a couple of months of physiotherapy and rest, we'd left Paris by train for Le Puy-en-Velay, where we pig-headedly picked up the trail again, determined to make it to the Pyrenees. An unusual town, Le Puy lies about two hundred miles south of our stopping point at the Roche de Solutré near Cluny and Mâcon. Why leave from Le Puy? For the simple reason that this spectacular site clinging to the southern edge of the inhospitable, volcanic Massif Central is France's main pilgrimage trailhead on the so-called Via Podiensis. The modern-day GR-65 hiking trail retraces the original, ancient route. From Le Puy's airborne cathedral, it's 800 kilometers or 500 miles to Roncesvalles Abbey, and 1,600 kilometers or 1,000 miles to Santiago de Compostela. We'd opted for the closer destination. The reasons were many.

Like Vézelay, Le Puy-en-Velay is a pilgrimage site in its own right, famed for a Black Virgin and a medieval chapel poised atop a volcanic spur. Current estimates are thirty-five thousand walkers set out from the Black Virgin's shrine each year, though no more than ten percent make it to Santiago.

Luckily, that meant nine in ten of our fellow travelers would not be zealots, and, as it turned out, few were walking for more than a week or two at a time. You could easily pick out the remaining one-in-ten heading for Saint Jacques's putative resting place in Compostela. It was clear from the look in their eyes, the purpose in their stride and, usually, their remarkable lack of mirth. Most were French, earnest and young—in their twenties. They were also distinctive in appearance, likely to be covered with scallop shells, draped with crucifixes, dressed in pre-modern garb, and, like most French, highly competitive. This meant that they often elbowed others—people they referred to as "tourists"—out of the way on what was in places a narrow and dangerous trail.

But France was only a foretaste, we knew from first-hand reports, and from having driven along sections of the pilgrim's route in Spain ourselves in years past. The mainstream of tourists and hardcore believers flowed on the south side of the Pyrenees, 200,000 of them per year on the Camino de Santiago, where the jamboree has become as institutionalized as the running of the bulls in Pamplona, and about as inspiring or enticing.

"Can you see that forested spot on top of the Massif Central?" I asked Alison while studying the passport. "That chapel where we met the wild-eyed nut with worn shoes and a broken pack? Remember, he'd walked three thousand miles from Switzerland to Spain, then to Jerusalem and back to wherever we were."

Alison lowered the binoculars to inspect me. "I thought his story was moving," she said, "and inspiring. What incredible hardship, and he had a great spirit."

"Ummm," I agreed, wondering whether he'd made it home to a numbered bank account in Geneva. "Can you see Aubrac?"

Soon after meeting the wild-eyed pilgrim, we'd been herded along by the local long-horned cattle. They'd nudged us across the boulder-strewn plateaus and peaks to the medieval town of Aubrac. Once it had been the sole pilgrim's refuge in a windswept wilderness. Now it was a quaint mountain resort. Thinking back to it, a tinkling came to my mind's ears. We'd awakened in Aubrac before dawn to a symphony of a thousand cowbells, as shepherds moved their herds to high pastures.

I closed my eyes and clicked back to mid-September and the Southwest—a place of ducks, drakes, and dangerous quantities of foie gras: eating it made me feel like a cannibal. After perched Golignac on the serpentine Lot River, the steep, rough descent to Conques had turned my knees into rubber, and I'd been forced to stop at the nearest sports emporium to buy telescopic walking sticks. Without them, I wouldn't have made it another step.

But Conques had meant much more to me than being humbled by wobbly knees. Behind the apse of Sainte-Foy Abbey, a semi-circle of Merovingian-era stone caskets had seemed to be gazing up at our windows night and day. We'd spent two nights in Conques, sleeping in a Spartan hostel run by the Premontrian Brotherhood in charge of the thousand-year-old site. The golden mask of Sainte-Foy, displayed in the abbey museum, proved as haunting as the huge, sonorous abbey bells rung by the head priest, Brother Jean-Regis, or the organ music played by the abbey's four other Premontrian monks.

"You wouldn't be able to see Conques, would you," I asked Alison.

"It was in a valley," she replied, lowering the binoculars again and sitting next to me on the bed. "It was so beautiful when they climbed the belfry and turned to listen for that other little bell in the ruined chapel. It rang out from across the ravine. . . ."

I felt a shiver. The monk had thrown his weight onto the rope with childlike glee, and the abbey's ponderous bells had replied to the little bell, thundering farewell to the pilgrims who'd made it up the hill across the way, en route to Compostela.

"They ring when they reach the chapel," Jean-Regis had explained to us in a singsong tenor. "They ring when returning, and we try to ring back."

The monk had also said something that had made great sense to me, and lodged in my brain's leathery convolutions. "The only thing all pilgrims have in common is an interior necessity—*I must go, I don't know why.* . . ."

Perhaps I still didn't know why. But finally it no longer mattered.

It seemed to me that of all the things we'd seen, perhaps the one that had marked me most was also the most unexpected: a timeless treasure in a grotto near the riverside village of Cabrerets on the intoxicatingly gorgeous Célé River. That's where, in the stalactite-encrusted caverns of Pech Merle, we filtered out the presence of other visitors and were paralyzed by the magic of the 25,000-year-old cave drawings. An outline of a young man's hand, a hand exactly like mine or Alison's, forced me to rethink everything I'd ever thought about art, history, and superstition.

Another brand of timeless magic emanated from the Romanesque sculptures of the 11th-century abbey at Moissac. Further south, the Gers Region turned out to be a patchwork of farmlands studded with storybook hilltop villages such as Miradoux and Lectoure. There we'd dined at a B&B with a cloistered nun who, after a life of adventure, had taken a vow of silence. She was out on medical leave, and was anything but silent. But she seemed happy, genuinely glad in her unlikely choice of what might appear to be imprisonment. Most surprising of all, I felt I understood her and had no desire to judge or ridicule her for her seemingly retrograde choice of lifestyle. Perhaps I had changed a little, after all.

Images from our trek were flashing by thick and fast in my head now, stimulated by the stamps on the passport. Rising up like the Emerald City among the orchards and woods of the Gers, La Romieu startled us. A megalomaniac pope had built the gloomy sanctuary seven hundred years ago to celebrate his own glory, and diverted the Way of Saint James to reach it.

Until we wandered into Navarrenx, we'd never heard of it. This walled fortress-city served as a prototype for others erected by my favorite military engineer, the heroic Vauban, he whose castle we'd visited in Burgundy back at the start of our trek. Nor did we expect to meet the town's ninety-year-old Second World War death-camp survivor, a man still full of inspirational vitality and curiosity. He said he felt no bitterness. He was not angry. He was glad to be alive and talking. And talking.

For weeks now the divine views of Pyrenees peaks had enticed us further south into emerald Basque Country and, on our penultimate day, this very morning, we'd almost been undone by the attractions of Vauban's masterpiece, the walled citadel of Saint-Jean-Pied-de-Port. It turned out to be the Basque Beaune, complete with elephant train for tired tourists with or without scallop shells. I could have stayed, lounging at a café by the roaring Nave River or marching along the ramparts, waiting for Vauban or Louis XIV to show up. They didn't, so we bought supplies and girded our loins.

"Snow," said a butcher in a tidy shop where we assembled our picnic of Basque ham and cheese.

"Wind and rain," rebutted a customer. He was wearing camouflage hunting gear and winked at us.

We feasted and watched a few dozen of the twenty-five thousand pilgrims who each year rashly begin their pilgrimage to

Santiago from Saint-Jean-Pied-de-Port—with a killer, mile-high climb that decimates their ranks. Later, a red-faced pilgrim clutching scallop shells retreated past us in a taxi. Several others followed. Luckily, we'd long ago metamorphosed into mountain goats. We even had our bells.

We'd nearly reached the end of our tramp, a little wiser and not too much worse for wear. It was as if all the months of walking, talking, thinking, reflecting, opening ourselves up to each other and welcoming the outside world into our heads and hearts had been in preparation for this last stretch, the final push up the Pyrenees.

"I've come to the end," I said to Alison, who'd put away the binoculars.

"The end of what?"

"Memory Lane."

After a frugal repast at Brother Ourtiague's table and now back in our wind-buffeted upstairs room, our current panoramic setting and leap-of-faith situation reminded me of our last night in Burgundy, staring out at the primal Roche de Solutré from President Mitterrand's Résistance-era hideout. I hadn't slept much that night, and wasn't expecting to tonight, either, despite the accumulated fatigue. I stretched out and floated on runner's high. The main difference was, I felt no pain as I had when a cross-country runner, no anxiety, and the high was constant. Elation seemed the best word. I hoped Alison was feeling it too. Judging by the deep stillness of her breathing, Morpheus, as usual, was coddling her. She heard no wind rattling the panes. The mounting gale had picked up force, if that were still possible. The farm already felt as if it were spinning into the Kansas sky.

I watched my wife with something akin to awe. Neither sleeplessness nor noise nor time itself had ever troubled her. The troika had yapped at me, keeping me running for years. Now time felt different. It slipped and slid like a Möbius strip, an odd-shaped continuum. Days, weekends, weeks, months, years, millennia no longer meant what they had. Fossils were yesterday. I'd developed an affinity for infinity, a fondness for finitude. It probably wasn't finitude at all, just a twist in the strip, a reshuffling of sub-atomic particles. My unspoken fears of the unknown and my anger at so many things had dropped by the wayside, like that talking pedometer. Serenely savoring the sequences, the unexpected segues of life, was what the rest of mine was going to be about. And sound sleep, too, despite the driving gale. With that gentle promise in mind, my eyes popped open. The gloaming had magically merged with a spectacular dawn. I roused Alison and we saddled up.

LOOKING BACK, LEANING FORWARD

Fifteen vertical miles separate Huntto from Roncesvalles. We tanked up on coffee, consumed as many calories as the good Brother would give us, and left before dawn's light had fully revealed the number of heavily armed hunters stationed nearby. Without Google or even a vintage transistor radio, there was no way to be sure, but I estimated the gusting winds at 80 to 100 mph. Speech was problematic. We communicated with signals, and wound up holding hands, then alternately pushing and pulling each other forward. Despite having visited about 959 churches en route without much effect, I thought of the Holy Ghost depicted as a dove, and hoped we and the squabs would survive the crossing. Hunters to the left and right began raising their guns, only to topple over in the wind without firing a shot, the pigeons swirling overhead. It was miraculous.

Near the Virgin of Biakorri, a shrine amid boulders with see-forever views back to France, a nun stumbled past, clutching her winged hat. I swear she leaped and flew—a yard or so at a time—singing and laughing and crying. Alison tried to get a photo of her but was blown over by the wind.

"A breeze," I shouted, cupping my hands. "No sign of snow."

Approaching Col de Bentarte, GR-65 reverts to a proto-historical dirt trail, climbs between pinnacles, and snakes through the celebrated pass where the knight Roland blew his horn, calling for Charlemagne to save him. Unfortunately for Roland, Charlemagne arrived too late. Even if he'd been by my side, I wouldn't have heard Roland's hoots: the roar of the wind was deafening. We were beginning to wonder if we, too, would leave our mortal coils behind at the pass. Buffeted by the gale, we had our last, achingly scenic view of the country we'd crossed. It didn't reach to Le Puy-en-Velay, but almost.

I stared for a long while and held Alison tight: our windbreakers had become sails. Quiet triumph and joy filled me. We'd talked the walk, and walked the walk, and talked, talked, talked for months until our thoughts and feelings and irrational urges had become as round and familiar as long-sucked candies. I knew that for me many of the most intense moments on our journey had come in Burgundy, where I'd been dogged by doubt, fear, fatigue, and the need to find answers. In comparison, the rest of the trek had been a lark—or perhaps a pigeon. Exhilaration had always outstripped exhaustion, and it kept us going now when we found ourselves temporarily unable to move forward, hardly able to breathe because of the force of the gusts.

Beyond the pass, another five miles of thick beech forests and drifts of fallen leaves awaited. Treeless chasms, the graves of fallen pilgrims, and 1,300 vertical feet of switchbacks downhill followed. We staggered into the fog-wrapped Roncesvalles Abbey. In the medieval, candlelit interior, cloaked monks chanted in Latin around the altar. Hundreds of faithful murmured back. They took no notice of us.

"Where to next?" Alison whispered. "The Spanish Camino de Santiago starts here." Another five hundred miles? My eyes closed, but, mind still in motion, I lost count of the small epiphanies we'd had, knew the pilgrimage into the rest of our lives had just begun, and suggested we save Compostela for another twist in the Möbius strip.

ABOUT THE AUTHOR

DAVID DOWNIE is a San Franciscan who moved to Paris in the mid-1980s and now divides his time between France and Italy. His travel, food, and arts features have appeared in over fifty leading print publications worldwide. He is currently a European contributor to the Internet's popular literary travel Web site Gadling.com, and co-owner and operator (with Alison Harris) of Paris, Paris Tours (custom walking tours of Paris, Burgundy, Rome, and the Italian Riviera).

Downie is the author of ten nonfiction books and two thrillers, most recently *Paris City of Night*. His nonfiction books include *Enchanted Liguria: A Celebration of the Culture, Lifestyle and Food of the Italian Riviera* (Rizzoli International); *Cooking the Roman Way: Authentic Recipes from the Home Cooks and Trattorias of Rome* (HarperCollins); and *Paris, Paris: Journey into the City of Light*, a critically acclaimed collection of travel essays (Broadway Books/

Random House). Downie's latest food-and-wine-related books are *Food Wine The Italian Riviera & Genoa*, *Food Wine Rome*, and *Food Wine Burgundy*, all in the Terroir Guides series published by The Little Bookroom. Also published in 2011 is *Quiet Corners of Rome*, a loving exploration of the Eternal City, with striking photos by Alison Harris. In 2013 Downie launched his first app, featuring the history of Paris: the Paris Timeline.

Downie's Web sites and blogs: www.davidddownie.com; http://blog.davidddownie.com; www.parisparistours.com; http://wanderingliguria.com; http://wanderingfrance.com/blog/paris; www.cookingtheromanway.com. He was graduated in Political Science and Italian from UC Berkeley and received an M.A. from Brown University, where he was a University Scholar and Kenyon Fellow in Italian literature.

ABOUT THE PHOTOGRAPHER

❧

ALISON HARRIS is a professional photographer based in Paris. Her work has been published by HarperCollins, The Little Book-room, Rizzoli, Chronicle Books, Stewart Tabori & Chang, and Random House, among others. Her latest book *Paris in Love* is published by Parisgramme. She graduated with a degree in Art History from Mount Holyoke College. Harris exhibits regularly in Europe and the United States. A selection of her Paris photographs is in the Musée Carnavalet (Paris Historical Museum) and the Paris Historical Library. Harris is an inveterate walker. The photographs made while walking across France with her husband, David Downie, are part of an ongoing photo essay about France. A selection of these photographs is published for the first time in *Paris to the Pyrenees: A Skeptic walks the Way of Saint James*. www.alisonharris.com